Indians
in Transition

Curriculum Resource Books Series

GENERAL EDITOR
Mollie E. Cottingham, M.A.
Faculty of Education
University of British Columbia

1. Today's World
Selected Sources—
from 1688 to Modern Times
J. Arthur Lower

2. The New World
Selected Sources – Canada,
the United States and
Latin America to 1914
Patricia M. Johnson

3. The First Million Years
Selected Sources – from
Prehistory to the Christian Era
Mollie E. Cottingham

4. East and West
Selected Sources – from the
Fall of Rome to 1700
Mollie E. Cottingham

5. British Columbia
An Introduction to
Geographic Studies
J. V. Horwood

6. The Landscape of Europe
Four Geographic Studies
James Popple

7. Canada's Pacific Province
Selected Sources – British
Columbia from Early Times
Patricia M. Johnson

8. Self-Government
Selected Sources in the History
of the Commonwealth
J. Arthur Lower

9. Renaissance to Revolution
Selected Historical Sources
Mollie E. Cottingham and
J. Arthur Lower

10. Canada Since 1867
Selected Historical Sources
Patricia M. Johnson

11. The Northland
Studies of the Yukon and the
Northwest Territories
John Wolforth

12. Confederation 1867
Selected Sources – from
Durham's Report to the
British North America Act
Thomas F. Bredin

13. Adolescents in Society
Selected Sources in Personal
and Social Relationships
Anne McCreary-Juhasz and
George Szasz

14. The Prairies
Selected Historical Sources
Kenneth Osborne

15. Careers Today
Selected Sources
Joan Morris

16. Nationalism to Internationalism
Selected Sources – from
1844 to Modern Times
J. Arthur Lower

17. Industrialization and Society
Selected Sources
Gerald Walsh

18. The Family
Selected Sources
Phyllis J. Meiklejohn

19. Black and White in North America
Selected Sources
Terence D. Tait

20. Communities in Canada
Selected Sources
Leonard Marsh

21. Patterns of Settlement in Southern Ontario
Three Studies
R. C. Langman

22. China in the Twentieth Century
Selected Sources
Jason Wong

23. Indians in Transition
An Inquiry Approach
Gerald Walsh

24. Life in Upper Canada 1781-1841
An Inquiry Approach
Dean Fink

25. Parliaments and Congress
Selected Sources
J. Arthur Lower

26. Four Cities
Studies in Urban and
Regional Planning
G. P. Nixon and M. Campbell

27. Saskatchewan
Sample Studies
J. Newton and L. Richards

Indians in Transition

An Inquiry Approach

GERALD WALSH
Faculty of Education
University of British Columbia

MCCLELLAND AND STEWART LIMITED

Contents

Preface

This is one of a series of resource books designed to encourage the student to think for himself. The young person living in Canada today has inherited a free society in a rapidly changing world. The way in which he will carry on and improve this world depends upon how he prepares himself to do so.

These books contain material that will enable the student to draw his own conclusions about man, his activities upon this earth and the manner in which he has described them. Some are books of geographical studies. By examining pictures, maps, charts, and descriptions of landscape the student will discover how man has been influenced both by culture and by natural setting, and how he has learned to use these to his advantage. Some books contain raw materials of history. Inscriptions, news accounts, official documents, and letters of people who lived in the past provide some of the evidence from which history has been written. In other books, materials have been selected and organized with the purpose of helping young people to think about the issues and problems which men and women encounter in their daily lives, both as individuals and as group members of society.

The material in each book has been used successfully with students of an age and maturity level suited to the content of the book. By design, the student is not asked to memorize the opinions of others, but rather to make his own analysis and draw his own conclusions, and then be prepared to defend or modify them in discussion with his teachers and his classmates.

Though this approach to learning may at first glance appear to be an innovation, it is in fact a return to one of the best traditions of education.

Every society has its own peculiar problems. These problems pose both a challenge and an opportunity. If the society fails to respond effectively to the challenge, the problems persist and often grow more serious. If the society deals effectively with the problems the quality of life in that society rises to a higher level.

Canada is no exception to this rule. Our peculiarly Canadian problems include such concerns as: the relations of English speaking and French-speaking people in Canada, the problem of poverty, the relations of Canada with the United States, the problems posed by rapid urbanization, and the problem of the role of Indians in Canadian society.

It is with the last of these that this book is concerned. Its purpose is to introduce you to the study of this important and complex problem, to present you with facts, ideas, and often conflicting points of view so that you will be able to develop your own well-informed opinion.

The book consists of three parts. Part One is a brief introductory section which contains data to illustrate the fact that there is a problem, and that it is becoming increasingly important to find a solution to it. Part Two examines the experiences of the Indians in their contact with white men from the arrival of the first Europeans to the present time, together with the effects upon the Indians as a result of these contacts. Part Three returns to the problem for a consideration of the various views as to what policies should be adopted to deal with it. In this part you will have the opportunity to analyze, compare and evaluate different viewpoints and to define your own position on the problem.

ONE

The Problem

During the period since the end of World War II the question of racial and inter-cultural relations have become an important focus of concern both at the international and the national level. The superiority of the white man, an idea long accepted without serious question, has been repeatedly and persistently challenged. The peoples of Asia and most of Africa have freed themselves from European colonial domination. Within nations racial minorities have asserted their rights to equality as never before. Recent events in the United States have shown that minority groups within a democratic society who have been classified as inferior by that society are no longer willing to accept that status. First the Negroes, then the Indians and the Mexicans and now the poor people, have taken action to improve their conditions. Their tactics have ranged from non-violent protest to the threat of militant action and the disruption of American society.

Canada has until now been more fortunate in the case of its principal racial minority, the Indians. This has not been because Canadians have been wiser or more just but because the Indians of Canada have been slower to become aroused and to demand improvements in their status. But there are unmistakeable signs that Indians in this country are rapidly becoming more conscious of the disadvantages under which they live and their demands for change are becoming increasingly militant. There is more than a faint possibility that if Indians fail to achieve improvements in their situation by peaceful means, some of them may resort to more violent methods. It is doubtful whether such methods would benefit the Indians; it is certain that they would not be beneficial to Canadian society. The problem for Canada today, then, is to find ways in which the aspirations of these first Canadians for a better life can be satisfied.

The following selections are introduced to show some of the realities of the social, economic and political conditions in which Indians live and to show how the problem is seen from a number of different viewpoints.

1.   Prejudice and Discrimination

And Indian-hating still exists; and, no doubt, will continue to exist, so long as Indians do.   Herman Melville, 1857.

How true is Melville's prophecy? Many Canadians today believe that we live in a society virtually free of prejudice.
   The following table was made by a team of social scientists who conducted a government-sponsored study of Indians and Métis in Manitoba in 1955.

1. What conclusions about prejudice could you arrive at on the basis of the information in this table?

2. Do you think that the attitudes of non-Indians in your community are similar to those expressed in the table?

3. Using the same topics either conduct a class opinion poll or take a sampling of the opinions of friends and acquaintances outside the school (or both).

Prejudice Concerning Certain Topics Compared by Occupational Class

Topic	Professionals, Managers, Craftsmen, Foremen	Farmers, Labourers, Operatives
I would not allow my children to play with children of Indian descent.	5.4	15.9
Children of Indian descent should not be educated with the White.	1.1	14.3
People of Indian descent disregard completely the common standards of decency.	10.9	23.8
All homes of people of Indian descent are dirty.	4.3	12.7

Jean H. Lagassé, *A Study of the Population of Indian Ancestry in Manitoba* (Manitoba: The Department of Agriculture and Immigration, 1955), p. 172.

Prejudice is invariably accompanied by discrimination. That is to say, that people against whom there is prejudice receive inferior treatment by being denied rights and privileges that others enjoy and which are often legally theirs. In the Manitoba study mentioned above a number of examples of discriminatory practices towards Indians and Métis are reported:

1. Are there any cases, in your opinion, in which the discriminating behaviour is justifiable?
2. Select two or three of the examples. In each case, try to imagine that you are Indian or Métis. How would you react?

Examples of Inferior Treatment

The few [examples] that are listed below were chosen because they represent the standard policies of groups of White people rather than the prejudiced behavior of individual persons. Each example was verified by the Social and Economic Research Office in the course of its study.

1. Three years ago an Indian family left its reserve and settled on the fringe of a White village. Adult members of the family sought and obtained employment with various White employers and managed to save some money. Last year they decided to move to the village site proper. A house was chosen for purchase and a small deposit made to guarantee the contract. When villagers heard of the sale, they urged the owner to refund the deposit. They feared that other Indians would also want to stay in the village. The money was refunded and the Indian family is still residing in the fringe settlement, fully aware of the efforts made to prevent them from integrating. The Secretary-Treasurer related this incident to one of the research assistants, concluding, "We do not have any Indian problems in town because we know how to deal with them."

2. One of the devices used in the study to arrive at an estimate of the population of Indian descent living in large villages and towns was to check each name on the provincial voters' list. As this was being done in one town, a municipal official, who had taken part in the enumeration advised, "That list will not help very much. We did not list Half-Breeds and Indians for fear they would believe they have earned residence in town and ask for relief."

3. News that Treaty and Non-Treaty Indians were moving in prompted the Municipal Council of one village to discuss this matter at its regular meeting. The council decided to have an inspection of their homes and surroundings made at once and if found unsuitable or their inhabitants liable to be on relief, to have their homes condemned and action taken to have them removed from the village.

4. Married couples applying to Welfare agencies to adopt children are queried about nationality preferences. They are asked whether they would accept Métis and Indian children. Approximately 75 per cent answer in the negative. Amongst those who would not object to Métis and Indian children are many parents who would accept them only if their Indian physical characteristics were not too pronounced.

5. Theatre usherettes in at least two Manitoba towns are instructed by theatre proprietors to make Indians sit in a special section of the building.

6. The House Committee of an urban church received a request from a group of Indians for the monthly use of a meeting room. After considerable discussion the Committee refused on the basis that the Indian group might include some undesirables who would not respect church property.

7. Ten of the 31 hotels located in the centre of Greater Winnipeg were asked, in the course of this study, if they would accept Indians and Half-Breeds as lodgers. One answered it would not and three said they would prefer not to.

8. Indians visiting a better class restaurant in a town located close to a reserve are refused service. This is not done overtly but waitresses are instructed not to wait on them. Indians have come to know that no one takes their order in that restaurant and they go elsewhere.

9. An Indian who had enlisted in the Armed Forces was transferred to Winnipeg. He located a semi-modern three room apartment which was advertised for rent and applied for it. The owner referred him to other less desirable apartments saying, "You would not want the apartment you have chosen. It is not suitable for your needs. I have two other suites in another part of the city which I am sure you would enjoy." These other two apartments were not as modern and were located in a less desirable section of the city. There is evidence that this is a standard practice amongst several real estate firms in the Greater Winnipeg Area.

Each of the examples listed above represent a refusal on the part of the White majority to grant to Indians and Métis certain rights or privileges which members of other ethnic groups enjoy in Manitoba.

Ibid., pp. 167-168.

In Canada Indians suffer from an image which is, to a large extent, stereotyped. Stereotypes have been described as "beliefs about a group which lead individuals to attribute to all members of that group certain exaggerated and distorted characteristics."

1. Briefly jot down the popular stereotype of one of these: a Scotsman; a Jew; a Negro; an American tourist.
2. In what ways is the following statement a stereotype:
". . . I guess I'm typical of your non-Indian. To me the Indian, well, he's got it made, and he knows it. They don't want to work, they get the social welfare money, you see 'em in town, a dirty bunch of drunken slobs. I got no time for any of 'em."[1]

Stereotypes

There are several stereotypes of Indian life co-existing in Canada. Most Canadians receive information about the Indians very early in their lives through a variety of channels such as legends, comics, textbooks, cinemas, radio and television. Four different stereotypes of Indian life are superimposed in the minds of Canadians from childhood to adulthood.

The first image that a young Canadian receives is that of a people with painted faces, feathered headdresses, bows and arrows and pinto horses. If he lives close to an Indian Reserve and his parents allow him to play with Indian youths, he will eventually come to realize that the people living next to him are also Indian, but this fact will not be self-evident until he is almost of school

[1] *The Way of the Indian* (Toronto: Canadian Broadcasting Corporation, 1963), p. 5.

age, as the following story illustrates: Two five-year olds were in a rural bakery shop when a salesman commented to one of them, "My, what a wonderful tan you have." The other replied, "That is not a tan, he used to be an Indian."

The second picture that Canadians receive is contained in history books where Indians are shown as a nation of trappers and canoemen, an angry people seeking white scalps, men at war with each other, and of faltering allegiances easily influenced by White men carrying firewater.

The third picture, this one taught by the press and other media of public information, is one of an impoverished people with large diseased families in overcrowded homes. It is a picture of people who are immoral, lazy, frequently inebriated, unambitious and unwanted.

The fourth picture of the people of Indian descent often co-exists with the third one. It is derived from the statements of well-meaning persons who wish to promote the welfare of Indians and Métis. It shows young people attending high schools and vocational training institutes. Adolescents who have abandoned the "shiftless ways of their people" and are living "decently" like the White man. They are Indians and Métis who are said to be "advanced" because they no longer "live like the Indians." The authors of this last picture attempt to establish a contrast between the new and the old generation when actually both are part of the same continuum.

> Lagassé, *op. cit.*, p. 170.

> It is not surprising that, in the face of prejudice and discrimination, Indians are suspicious of the motives of people who feel sorry for their plight and try to help through charitable acts. Harold Cardinal, a young Cree leader, has expressed these feelings forcefully:

Unfortunately, these do-gooders get involved in spheres of activity ranging from simple, charitable church projects to the political arena, where self-appointed spokesmen for the Indians do incalculable harm. Their view of the Indian almost always, even if subconsciously, is that native people are incapable of handling their own affairs. The assumption that they must become actively involved in order to protect the Indian from himself follows naturally. We don't for a minute question the sincerity of these people, but we have to be realistic. It is our lives they are playing with. We do have to examine their role in the light of its potential effectiveness. We must ask them to do the same. We must ask that a non-Indian who is sincere show a little more sense of judgement. What he does or attempts to do must nourish the initiative of the Indian people. What he attempts must not discourage or inhibit the growth of individual potential. He must not set himself up as a decision maker for the Indian.

Such people can't seem to get it through their heads that the simplest and most important thing they can do is simply to accept the Indian for what he is, another human being, and treat him with the same consideration they would show any other individual.

All too often the do-gooder carries the virus of bigotry where he goes. While the typical do-gooder would swear on a stack of oil stocks that he does not believe that Indians are in any way inferior, his actions and his statements suggest a subconscious philosophy that even he may not be aware he harbours. But it shows and, like being a little bit pregnant, being a little bit bigoted is too much.

Quite unintentionally, the average non-Indian can fall into the cycle of paternalism. Take a typical, charitable, well-meant do-gooder project. A member of a women's church auxiliary has read in the local press or seen an item on television that certain Indians are running around barefooted in the snow because they are destitute or can't send their kids to school because the seats are out of their pants.

"Terrible, terrible," she clucks. "Absolutely scandalous; we can send three men to the moon but we can't keep our own Indians in decent clothes." So the good ladies get together. Each one paws through her closets and comes up with some clothing that is perhaps outgrown but still usable, perhaps some that the family simply has grown tired of and, really to turn her conscience on, even an item or two of practically new clothing. Then she goes around in a do-gooder glow for days. What did she actually do to earn such a glow? Perhaps she rummaged through a few closets, maybe made a few phone calls; she might even have helped pack the stuff for shipping one morning. So, okay, the stuff was needed; it might even prove useful. But are such people entitled therefore to feel they have made a private peace with the Indians? They must somehow be made to realize they have a deeper responsibility as citizens. Indians do not enjoy scrounging; they don't want to continue having their clothing bundled in to them, secondhand. While native people may truly appreciate whatever assistance they receive, they would appreciate far more efforts which would enable them to provide for the needs of their own families.

We understand full well and are sorry that the good ladies are hurt and upset when we fail to kiss their hands in humble, grateful thanks. But we suggest that they and all the others like them, those who do less and those who do more, take a deeper look at the situation. They can avoid the frustration that comes with apparent rejection of their lofty motives if they will take the time and make the effort to understand more deeply the temperament of the native people and the issues involved. Too many times the interested non-Indian assumes the role of an overpossessive mother who feels she must go on overprotecting her only child, must go on making decisions the child should be allowed to make. We are big boys now; we don't want to be mothered. Even if we suffer because we make wrong decisions, we would rather have mother suffer a little with us (if she insists) than have her deny us the choice.

> H. Cardinal, *The Unjust Society: The Tragedy of Canada's Indians* (Edmonton: M. G. Hurtig Ltd., 1969), pp. 90-92.

1. In what way does Cardinal consider that the so-called "do-gooders" are prejudiced?
2. What is Cardinal's main objection to the "do-gooders"?
3. What kind of help for the Indians do you think Cardinal would welcome?

In a similar vein a much older man, Chief Dan George of the British Columbia Squamish Indians, has replied to those who have asked what they can do to help.

What can you do? You might buy textbooks for our children, that they can have books clean as their white brothers. The other day my wife was sad, because her daughter was washing blankets that were patched and repatched again, and you might buy her blankets, so that she might cover herself and her children. As I walked through the reserve the other day I saw houses, Indian houses, run down, and decrepid. You might buy and build houses for my people. And the white men driving by the reserve and seeing these new houses, would never know what they conceal, poverty and frustration. And so a man came with a sore, an ulcer on his leg, and a clean bandage was placed over his ulcer, so nobody knew that an ugly ulcer was there because nobody saw and nobody looked underneath.

You may buy textbooks for our children, you may cover them with blankets, you may hide them behind newly built houses, you may cover their sore with a clean bandage, so that no one may see that sore any longer, and you may go to bed at night with your social conscience free of feelings of guilt, because the evil your forefathers have done is covered only and out of sight. Perhaps there is not much that you can do in a positive way, for we must make our own bodies strong and healthy. But in a negative way, perhaps you can do much.

You can stop discriminating against my people.

You can stop patronizing them in your usual manner.

You can stop feeling awful good within yourself when you make a paltry offering in the form of some money.

You can stop feeling guiltless when you buy us textbooks and blankets and houses.

You can try to understand what cultural adjustments are demanded of our younger people, who are forced to think and to work and to accept the standards of your culture.

You can stop making us look ridiculous in your plays and on your television. Go and see how we have been degraded in your social study books.

The First Citizen, Edition #1, November, 1969, p. 8.

1. What does Chief Dan George seem to be saying about the most important needs of Indians?
2. Discuss his last comment. Have Indians been degraded in social studies books? Can you find any examples to justify the statement? If it is true, what should be done about it?
3. What do the statements of Harold Cardinal and Chief Dan George have in common?

2.   The Poverty of the Indians

TORONTO – "You have to go out and smell it and taste it and feel it. That's the only way you'll solve Indian poverty and all their problems in Ontario.

"When you see a little girl pick a mouse out of some drinking water or 14 persons living in a one-room shack then you've just got to know it isn't right."

These were the words of Joseph Dufour, 37, who shocked Queen's Park recently by announcing his resignation from the $16,000-a-year post as director of the Indian development branch of the department of social and family services.

Six of his nine community development officers supported him and resigned because they felt the branch was ineffective. . . .

Dufour says the greatest problem in understanding Indians is that people in government live in their own urban groups and do not really know what is happening in other parts of the province.

Dufour does not pass over threats of Red Power lightly. He knows of Negro organizers from the U.S. who have tried to infiltrate Indian organizations.

"If Red Power demands start anywhere, I think they would be in the Lakehead," he said.

"There has been trouble in Kenora but I don't think they are too well organized there. That is why we have to act now. We have to do something before we have some militancy."

Vancouver Province, May 26, 1969.

1. Why did Dufour resign?
2. What, in his opinion, is the main obstacle to effective action on Indian problems?
3. What does he see as a possible result of the failure to take effective action?
4. Is there a branch of the Red Power organization in your area? Find out what the goals and policies of NARP (National Association for Red Power) are.

Table A contains data on income and employment in a number of selected Indian bands across the country. The bands were selected to be representative of the overall Indian population. In fact they are a little better off than the average.

Study the data and make supportable generalizations about:

1. The average per capita income earned by Indians compared to that of the rest of the population ($1400 per annum).

2. The level of unemployment.

3. The kinds of work done by the majority of the Indians.

4. The degree to which Indians are engaged in "white collar" occupations (clerical and professional).

Table A. Per cent distribution of main sources of employment of bands by industry and/or occupational status

Bands Ranked a/c Average Per Capita Real Income from Gainful Employment	Per Capita Real Income	Average Months Employment Per Worker	Average Months Employment Per Job	Forestry	Fishing	Guiding	Handicrafts	Food Gathering	Farm Labour	Casual Unskilled	Skilled	Clerical	Professional	Farm Proprietor	Non-Farm Proprietor	Trapping
Skidegate	1252	10.6	6.7		21.6		4.9				70.3				3.24	
Caughnawaga	793	9.2	8.2							6.5	83.6	8.5			3.0	
Walpole Is.	715	6.16	5.9		2.9	3.0	6.5			55.4	8.0	8.1		8.7	3.5	3.8
Sheshaht, V.I.	664	10.7	10.7		.8	3.0		2.0		24.8	72.3		2.0			
Lorette	630	10.5	8.7			3.0	14.0			32.3	18.5	10.1			19.5	
Squamish	630	8.0	8.0		1.5		2.1			62.6	28.3	1.7			1.7	
Tyendinaga	516	8.3	8.0							24.5	36.5	12.0		17.5	4.6	
Curve Lake	350	7.3	3.1			6.8	8.1	10.2		30.6	28.5				8.1	8.0
Six Nations	350	7.5	4.0	8.1						35.8	26.8	2.1	8.5	12.9	4.7	
Mistassini	341	5.6	5.6		2.9	2.3			13.9	27.6	2.3	1.4			4.3	54.3
Masset	336	3.8	3.8		20.5		6.0			52.2	14.9			1.9		
Dog Rib Rae	332	5.67	4.35	8.0	12.3		4.0			28.6		4.0				42.5
Port Simpson	325	6.9			30.0					36.4	24.6				5.5	2.1
Kamloops	314	9.5		7.2					5.0	51.8	8.6	1.4		11.5		
Sarcee	302	6.7	2.82				10.7		17.8	21.4	10.7	6.9		23.5		
Fort William	298	8.1	6.45	31.7						40.1	16.9	8.4				
Williams Lake	291	7.5	3.23	13.3				26.6		23.9	10.6			25.7		
Moose Factory	284	6.24		6.1						48.0	24.6	4.9				12.3
Fort Alexander	255	7.1	1.7													
River Desert	250	4.9	3.5	53.4		15.4	2.7			5.6	5.1	6.2	2.5	2.6	3.7	6.2
St. Mary's	249	7.27	2.3	55.8						22.5	1.2				3.3	
Attawapiskat	247						3.3.	4.2	6.2							

Table A. Continued

Bands Ranked a/c Average Per Capita Real Income from Gainful Employment	Per Capita Real Income	Average Months Employment Per Worker	Average Months Employment Per Job	Forestry	Fishing	Guiding	Handicrafts	Food Gathering	Farm Labour	Casual Unskilled	Skilled	Clerical	Professional	Farm Proprietor	Proprietor Non-Farm	Trapping
Pointe Bleue	222	6.2	5.6	3.3		5.6				40.1	14.7	23.3			8.1	5.0
Tobique	215	10.6	3.7	10.3		11.0	12.9		41.2	16.5	8.2					
Pekangikum	197	6.3	3.4	6.8	19.8			15.1		13.5					9.1	57.4
Shubenacadie	180	4.3	2.5	8.8			22.7			26.5	6.0					
Oak River, Man.	176	3.6	3.6			10.4			8.7	31.2	10.4			32.3	8.7	8.7
Rupert House	174	3.2	2.5	7.8						5.2						62.3
Cold Lake	165		3.4	25.5	2.8		16.7		5.5	10.0	3.2			18.7		2.8
Fort St. John	161	5.0	5.0		18.7											
Deer Lake, Ont.	156	3.6	3.5				3.1			15.5	1.8	1.8			13.5	56.6
The Pas	140	6.6	6.6	3.4			5.6			58.2	4.8	4.8		2.4		4.8
James Smith	126	6.6	3.3							29.2		5.2		26.8		15.1
Peguis	99	4.6	4.6	13.7	6.8					18.3	5.6	13.7		37.0	1.4	
Big Cove	61	7.0	2.75	23.6			25.5		28.3	5.7		8.5			8.5	
Piapot	55		5.5	11.0						54.7	4.6			23.3	6.0	

H. B. Hawthorn, ed., *A Survey of the Contemporary Indians of Canada*, Vol. I (Ottawa: Indian Affairs Branch, 1966), pp. 49-50.

Table B. Durable Consumer Goods: Percentages of households in thirty-five sample bands with basic home facilities and automobiles

Band	Per Capita Income	Indoor Toilets % h.h.	Baths % h.h.	Telephone % h.h.	Automobiles % h.h.	Electricity % h.h.
Skidegate	$1252	74	83	55.5	54	100
Caughnawaga	793	33	33	33	88.5	92
Walpole Is.	715	13	13	43	33	56
Sheshaht, V.I.	664	80	80	45	25	86
Lorette	630	100	100	100	17.5	100
Squamish	630	75	99	21	36	100
Tyendinaga	516	2	2	35	81	73.5
Curve Lake	350	11.2	2.0	18	66	95
Six Nations	350	4.5	4.5	31	68.5	72
Mistassini	341	2.5	2.5	2.5	7.3	*2.5
Dog Rib Rae	332	0	0	0	0	0
Port Simpson	325	21	88	0	1.0	87
Kamloops	314	3	3	11	25.5	100
Sarcee	302	6	6	23	48.0	0
Fort William	298	2	2	11	42.5	82
Williams Lake	291	3.3	3.3	10	8.0	100
Moose Factory	284	1.6	1.6	45	33	4
River Desert	250	7	5	35	30.0	41
Attawapiskat	247	0	0	32	14	0
St. Mary's	249	n/a	n/a	n/a	10	0
Pointe Bleue	222	20	12.7	51	22.5	70
Tobique	215	33	28	10	34.6	98
Fond du Lac	200	0	0	0	0	0
Pikangikum	197	0	0	0	12.3	0
Shubenacadie	180	6	4	10	30.1	0
Oak River	176	0	0	2	72.1	33
Rupert House	174	0	0	0	0	1.2
Cold Lake	165	1.7	1.7	1.7	13	**1.7
Fort St. John	161	0	0	0	0	0
Deer Lake	156	0	0	0	7	0
The Pas	140	0	0	8	9	7
James Smith	126	0	0	2	14	2
Peguis	99	1	1	0	12.5	40
Big Cove	61	4	4	4	38.6	40
Piapot	55	0	0	0	46	2

Ibid., pp. 81-82.   *1 household out of 41.   **2 households.

Table B enables us to look at the concept of Indian poverty from another point of view. It consists of data on the extent to which the sample Indian bands have the use of basic home facilities (Indoor toilets, baths, telephone, electricity) and automobiles.

1. Identify the band located nearest to the community in which you live. Compare it in terms of each category with your community (or with the White part if there is an Indian section of the community).
2. What generalizations can you make about Indian living conditions from the data in the Table?
3. Imagine you are an Indian living on a reserve near a big city (e.g., Caughnawaga near Montreal), and that you are therefore exposed to the advertising of the affluent society. A commonly expressed view is that in a wealthy and democratic society there is no need for anyone to be poor, or any justification for it. Express what you think your attitudes might be towards the dominant White society.

Under-employment and low earnings are the general rule for Indians in Canada. From Table C it is possible to derive some idea of the extent to which they are dependent on welfare and other payments to supplement their income. Welfare or "relief" payments consist of grants made by the Indian Affairs Branch (in money or in kind). Transfer payments include unemployment insurance, family allowances, old age security, old age assistance, and welfare payments from band revenues.

Table C.   Summary of employment, earnings and dependency among thirty-five representative bands

Total Population	35,683
On reserves	73.2%
Off reserves	26.8%
Employable Males Aged 16-64	6,327
Employed more than 9 mos.	28.5%
Employed 6-9 mos.	10.6%
Employed less than 6 mos.	61.0%
Employed less than 2 mos.	23.6%
Annual Earnings of Workers	
Less than $1000	22.5%
Less than $2000	62.1%
Less than $3000	81.7%
More than $5000	4.6%
Welfare	
Total expenditure on Indians	$1,007,796
	9.3% of earnings
Coverage	33.5% of households
Total Transfer Payments to Indians	$3,407,887
	31.4% of earnings

Ibid., p. 48.

1. What percentage of employable Indian males were employed (a) less than nine months of the year, (b) less than six months of the year?
2. Compare the earnings of Indian workers with the overall Canadian national average of $4000.
3. What percentage of Indian households are in receipt of welfare payments? What percentage of average earnings do these payments represent?
4. What percentage of average earnings do transfer payments account for?
5. What percentage of average earnings do combined welfare and transfer payments amount to?
6. Develop some "educated guesses" as to the probable effects of dependency on welfare and transfer payments on Indian workers and their families.

Poverty can also be calculated in terms of disease, ill-health and life expectancy. The figures in the following excerpt from a government report illustrate the relationship between poverty and death.

. . . According to the Commissioner of the Northwest Territories, the Eskimo death rate in 1960 was 21 per 1000, nearly three times the national rate; fifty five per cent of all Eskimo deaths were infants under one year; the infant mortality rate was 193 per 1000 live births, against a national rate of 27. Even more graphic is a presentation of average age at death in the Yukon and Northwest Territories:

Average age at death	Yukon	N.W.T.	Canada
Males	44.8	26.0	59.7
Females	32.4	21.5	63.1

Indeed health conditions for the native people of the North are still among the worst in the world.

Compared with conditions in the North, the picture for Canadian Indians as a whole is brighter; but it is not good.

The infant death rate for Indians in 1963 . . . was 70.4 against an all Canada rate of 26.3. The average age at death was 33.3 for males and 34.7 for females. Expectation of life at birth for Indian men was about nine years less than for Canadian men generally, and was ten years less for Indian women.

A striking indicator of their poor living conditions is the fact that 19 per cent of all Indian deaths are due to pneumonia compared to four per cent for the country as a whole. Similarly, 17 per cent of deaths were due to accidents, compared to 8 per cent for the country generally.

The life tables on Indians compared to national tables reveal the increased risk to Indians of dying during the first three years of life. Infant mortality was 2.75 times the national rate. But, while rates are lower, mortality amongst toddlers is about 7½ times greater than amongst Canadian toddlers generally.

It is over three times as great among both Indians school children and teen-agers. The loss of life in the early years is very high. At the same time, because of high birth rates (40.0 compared to 24.6 in Canada), more than half the total Indian population is under the age of 17 years, and nearly 19 per cent is under the age of five.

The causes of death which particularly strike the Indians are the respiratory diseases, especially broncho-pneumonia; tuberculosis; accidents and violence; diseases of early infancy; and diseases of the digestive system, particularly gastro-enteritis. Clearly, much of the disease and death is related to poverty.

> "The Profile of Poverty in Canada," a paper presented to the Dominion Conference on Poverty by representatives of the Manitoba Government, 1966, pp. 4-5.

3.   Dependency and a Sense of Loss

On the face of it one might consider the Indians fortunate to have money and services given to them. There is no doubt that a great many Whites believe that "the Indian has it easy" or that "the Indian has it made," although it is doubtful whether, given the opportunity, many would change places with Indians.

In fact the situation is much more complex than might be assumed at first glance. Here is a speech made by a young chief at a recent meeting. As you read it, consider these two questions:

1. In what ways, according to the speaker, has welfare been a disservice to the Indians?
2. What kinds of policies does he think are needed to improve the conditions of the Indians?

Years ago our people were self-reliant. We made our living by trapping and from whatever nature was able to provide for us. Our life was hard. It was not an easy life – we had to use our minds continually to try and find means and ways by which to survive. But we lived like men.

Then the government came and offered welfare to our people. They also tried to give a little money through which we were to start something by which to make a new type of livelihood. When they offered us welfare, it was as if they had cut our throats. Only a man who was crazy would go out to work or trap and face the hardships of making a living when all he had to do was sit at home and receive the food, and all he needed to live. It seemed as if the government had laid a trap for us, for they knew that once we accepted welfare they would have us where they wanted us.

For a few years they provided welfare. During those years, our minds went to sleep, for we did not have to use them in order to survive. The years confused our minds. Then all of a sudden the government decided to cut off welfare assistance and also the economic development assistance that they were starting to provide. We found ourselves sitting in the middle of nowhere, for both our sources of survival had been taken from us and we had almost forgotten what it was like to make a hard living off the land.

I think this is where the government made its mistake. The government officials are white, and they are smart, but they, too, can make mistakes. I think they made a mistake when they gave us welfare for they did not seem to think of its consequences. The next time the government does something it should think twice. If it wants to give us welfare, then it should be prepared to give it to us for the rest of our lives or otherwise leave us alone. I, for one, will not have anything to do with welfare, for if I were to take it, then they would think that they owned me. They would come back later and say, 'at such and such a time, I gave you welfare.' I could never be a free man. I would first starve to death before I asked for assistance from them.

We do not want welfare assistance from the government. I would rather see the government put its money where it would help us most. There are resources in our land. There are some ways by which we could make a living. But we are Indians who are just emerging from the ways of trapping and hunting. We do not know the ways of the white man. We do not have the skills to make a living like the white man does. Instead of sending welfare, why does the government not send us men who would come and see our land, to see what forms of work it could provide? Why does the government not send us men who would come to teach us the skills we need to survive in the ways of the white man? Why does the government ignore our presence? Why do they not send men to sit down with us so that together we could lay down plans for the future of our people? Instead of sending us welfare, why does the government not send us the money to develop the resources that we have here so that people can make their living from these reserves?

I think that this would be better for our people. I think that this would help us regain our manhood. This is the only way that I can see for our people.

Maybe I am wrong, because these are only my thoughts. But one thing I do know, we will never get anywhere, the way the government is working.

Cardinal, *op. cit.*, pp. 62-63.

> The struggle by Indians to "regain their manhood" is bound to be difficult and exacting. Some of the problems facing them are brought out in this discussion between Dr. Gilbert Monture, Burton Kewayosh and Chief John Albany of the Songhees Band of the Coast Salish Tribe on Vancouver Island.

ANNOUNCER   The Indian races of Canada have always lived as a people apart from the immigrant settlers. So it's hardly surprising that they have a different outlook, different standards and different problems. One man who has surmounted most of the problems is Dr. Gilbert Monture, an eminent geologist, a Mohawk, brought up on the Six Nations Reserve near Brantford, Ont.:

DR. GILBERT MONTURE   The reserves today, even in the far north, are becoming depleted of game and fish. And this will grow progressively worse as the industrialization of the northland takes place. So that the opportunities for hunting and fishing and enjoying the primitive life will grow less and less. Consequently, what is the Indian to do? He is beyond the agricultural belt in most cases. He cannot supplement his living by raising a few vegetables or things of that sort. And so, for those types of food, he must pay money to buy them, either as canned goods or goods that come up from the agricultural area. Now, if he has no job opportunity, where is he going to find the money to maintain himself even at a very low standard of living? I would say that the opportunity for them to pursue their former natural way of life is rapidly disappearing and this presents the big problem that's facing the Indian.

BURTON KEWAYOSH   When I was a boy we had a reserve here which was all woods, all marsh. No white men. Which made it a very nice reserve. And these were some of the happiest times of my life when I was a boy, just wandering all over the reserve. Everything was just ideal — just trees and marsh and grass and wild plums and cherries and apple trees. There was no such thing as hurry, no idea of time — we didn't even have a clock. Now we have a reserve here, possibly 50,000 acres. We have a reserve here that's just as good as it ever was, but now it has to be farmed like the White Man's community. Even our muskrats and our ducks have to be farmed, whereas a long time ago we had broad expanses of duck marsh and the White Man never hunted there. Now we have to commercialize on everything we have in order to stay in the picture — like renting out the hunting to the White Man. But then, you see, you get to realize that these things have to be. You have to live with them. It's progress, you know.

CHIEF JOHN ALBANY   That's Burton Kewayosh of Walpole Island in Ontario. I think this is something that hits all of us. Times are changing. Living in the old ways, the ways of our grandfathers, isn't possible any more. The Prairie Indian can't live by hunting buffalo like he used to, because the wild buffalo are all gone.

ANNOUNCER   Many Indians in the northern areas still try to make a living by trapping, and they do still spend their lives very much as their ancestors did. Most of them are very insular, and not at all integrated into the non-Indian way of life. Quite a number are used as guides by fishing camp and hunting camp operators. These men still live in the woods and are well versed in woodcraft. But the old ways of hunting and living have for the most part been forgotten, and there are few Indians living today who could kill a deer with a bow and arrow of their own making.

CHIEF JOHN ALBANY   Yes, more and more the Indian is forced to live by following the White Man's way of life, and working at a White Man's job. Even if we live close to nature, like the trappers, we're still working for money to buy our groceries. Some work in fish-packing plants, or as miners or loggers. Or go berry-picking and beet-picking. In a few parts of Canada we're still trying to follow the old ways. On the West Coast we're still fishing just like our ancestors; on the Prairies the old buffalo hunters are growing wheat and raising cattle, what we call the White Man's buffalo.

ANNOUNCER   But farming isn't so popular nowadays. There are successful Indian farmers and ranchers but they are relatively few. There are hundreds of jobs that an Indian could hold, and yet the number of occupations they actually do follow is much smaller. Sometimes they lack the necessary training.

Very often their education is scanty. Sometimes they meet with prejudice and discrimination. So unemployment on the reserves is high.

DR. GILBERT MONTURE   When you come into the world of commercial enterprise, particularly in this day of mechanical invention and, I might say, automation, there's very, very little field of employment left for the man who has only a strong back to offer. And remember this, that if you're going to get even a simple job, there must be some means of communication. By that I mean ability to speak the English language, or French language if you're in a French-speaking community, and also the ability to write it. Even the simple job of a truck-driver, let us say. He may have the skill to drive the truck but if he can't read road signs for simple direction he loses out in the competition for that job of work.

CHIEF JOHN ALBANY   That's not only an Indian problem. There's whites got the same difficulty. But for generations the Indians have had poor education. We've spoken our own languages and we're only just beginning to be able to compete in the jobs. Then, here's another point of view, from Reeve Byers of Kenora, Ont.; he used to be the principal of the Indian school there:

REEVE BYERS   The average Indian doesn't want a steady job. He doesn't want to work week after week and month after month. He doesn't want to. He wants to work for a few days till he gets a pay cheque, and then the thing is to spend that before he gets any more money.

CHIEF JOHN ALBANY   Well, that's one point of view but it's not the whole story. The Indian never had any use for the ideas of time, or work, or saving. Time was a matter of days, and seasons. Work was matter of building a house or catching fish, not working regular hours for regular wages. And why save for the future when there was always enough to eat? Sure, these old ideas have got to change, it takes time to catch up with several centuries of White Man's progress.

> *The Way of the Indian*, pp. 8-9.

1. How has the advance of the White Man's world affected the lives of Burton Kewayosh and the Indians of the Walpole Island reserve?

2. What influence is the growing industrialization of the northland likely to have on the Indians of the outlying reserves? What choices seem to be open to them?

3. What traditional values of the Indians are mentioned by Burton Kewayosh and Chief John Albany that work against the success of Indians in a White-dominated society?

The Indians appear to have no choice but to come to terms with the rest of Canadian society. Their traditional ways of life have been disrupted and fragmented by the impact of the White Man and his culture. In the process they have lost not only their land and their traditional ways but also their independence and their identity. They are suspended between two cultures, their own, to which they cannot return, and that of the White Man, which they may fear and dislike through lack of understanding and into which they find acceptance difficult if and when they try to enter it.

To many Indians, accustomed to the idea of living with nature, the concept of exploiting nature which is a part of white urban-industrial culture is wrong-headed and unnatural. What to most Canadians appears as justifiable "exploitation of natural resources" appears to them as despoliation and an act of sacrilege. The following poem, written by a young Indian from British Columbia, expresses a sense of loss at the advance of "progress."

LOSS FOR PROGRESS

High in the mountains
Where sound is lost
And occasionally found
By a Blue Jay's cry
The murmuring tree tops
Seem to be saying,
       "I hear machines
       and noise approaching
       Which means we will soon die."
As time passed
Only the faint cry
Of the Blue Jay's
Discontent was heard.
Gradually the remains
On the barren ground
Were but little trees
Planted row on row
And to visualize all the
Magnificence of Nature's Past
Is possible only
For the unbiased sky.

Clarence Oppenheim

Kent Gooderham, ed., *I Am an Indian* (Toronto: Dent, 1969), pp. 38-39.

Similar sentiments were expressed by Chief Dan George in a poetic and moving address delivered at a centennial celebration held in Vancouver on Dominion Day, 1967.

How long have I known you – Oh Canada? A hundred years? Yes – a hundred years – and many many years more. Today, when you celebrate your hundred years Oh Canada – I am sad for all the Indian people throughout the land. For I have known you when your forests were mine. When they gave me food and my clothing. I have known you – in your brooks and rivers – where your fish splashed and danced in the sun, and whose waters said "Come and eat of my abundance." I have known you in the freedom of your winds and my spirit like your winds – once roamed this good land. But in the long hundred years since – the white man came – I have seen my spirit disappear – just like the salmon as they mysteriously go out to sea. The white man's strange ways and customs – I could not understand – thrust down upon me until I could no longer breathe. When I fought to protect my home and my land – I was called a savage. When I neither understood nor welcomed this new way of life – I was called lazy. When I tried to rule my people – I was stripped of my authority. My nation was ignored in your history text books. We were less important in the history of Canada than the buffalo that roamed the plains. I was ridiculed in your plays and motion pictures – and when I drank your firewater – I got drunk – very, very drunk – and I forgot. Oh Canada – how can I celebrate with you this Centennial Year – this hundred years? Shall I thank you for the reserves that are left me of my beautiful forests? Shall I thank you for the canned fish of my river? Shall I thank you for the loss of my pride and authority – even amongst my own people? For the lack of my will to fight back? Shall I thank you for my defeat? NO – I must forget what is past and gone. Oh God in Heaven – give me the courage of the olden chief. Let me wrestle with my surroundings. Let me once again as in the days of old – dominate my environment. Let me humbly accept this new culture and through it rise up and go on. Oh God – like the Thunderbird of old – we shall rise again out of the sea – we shall grasp the instruments of the white man's success – his education – his skill – and with these new tools I shall spirit my race into the proudest segment of your society; and before I follow the great chiefs that have gone before us – I shall see these things come to pass. I shall see our young braves and our chiefs sitting in the house of Law and Government – ruling and being ruled by the knowledge and freedom of our great land. So shall we shatter the barriers of our isolation. So shall the next hundred years be the greatest in the proud history of our tribes and nations.

1. In speaking of his experiences Chief Dan George is really giving an outline of Canadian history from an Indian point of view. Consult a standard Canadian history textbook. Does it present the Indian side of the story?

2. Consult a number of Canadian history textbooks in the school or local library to find out whether Chief Dan George is justified in claiming that: "My nation was ignored in your history textbooks."

3. What future does Chief Dan George predict for the Indians of Canada? Why do you think he is able to be so optimistic after the disastrous experiences of the past?

4.   Education

The way of the Indian has been a way of darkness. The Indian has been forgetting his traditional skills, but he hasn't been learning much of the White Man's knowledge to replace them. Education is one of the most important factors in anyone's life, and this applies more especially to the Indian.

Chief John Albany, *The Way of the Indian*, p. 44.

Education is a major key to Indian progress. Whether Indians are to compete successfully in the world of the White man (if that is what they wish) or whether they are to develop wisely the resources of their lands, education and specialized training are essential.

Table D gives details of the school enrolment of Indian children in the years 1964-69.

Table D.   Enrolment of Indian pupils in elementary and secondary schools classified by type of school and by grade, school years ended 1964-69

Year and Type of School	Grade Pre-1	1-6	7-8	9-13	Special	Absent from Reserve[1]	Total
	No.	No.	No.	No.	No.	No.	No.
1963-64	3,897	35,453	6,161	4,065	770	4,575	54,921
Federal[2]	3,575	24,791	3,089	750	506	–	32,711
Non-federal	322	10,662	3,072	3,315	264	4,575	22,210
1964-65	4,027	36,229	6,758	4,761	804	4,686	57,265
Federal[2]	3,422	24,067	3,292	768	509	–	32,058
Non-federal	605	12,162	3,466	3,993	295	4,686	25,207
1965-66	3,660	38,929	7,107	5,220	1,013	5,466	61,395
Federal[2]	3,093	24,566	3,203	716	462	–	32,040
Non-federal	567	14,363	3,904	4,504	551	5,466	29,355
1966-67	3,830	40,408	7,453	5,510	1,081	6,157	64,439
Federal[2]	2,939	24,672	3,093	427	210	157	31,498
Non-federal	891	15,736	4,360	5,083	871	6,000	32,941
1967-68	4,531	40,188	7,926	5,967	1,305	6,300	66,217
Federal[3]	3,513	24,524	2,879	307	359	–	31,582
Non-federal	1,018	15,664	5,047	5,660	946	6,300	34,635
1968-69	5,916	40,331	8,250	6,832	1,505	..	62,834
Federal[4]	4,363	21,845	2,720	209	346	..	29,483
Non-federal[5]	1,553	18,486	5,530	6,623	1,159	..	33,351

[1] Pupils (and parents) living off the reserves in communities with educational facilities usually attend non-federal schools but school records are not maintained by the Education Branch of the Department of Indian Affairs and Northern Development.

[2] Excludes non-Indian pupils.

[3] Includes 1,231 non-Indian pupils.

[4] Includes 1,030 non-Indian pupils.

[5] Excludes Yukon and Northwest Territories pupils.

Canada Year Book (Ottawa: Queen's Printer, 1968), updated information supplied by the Dominion Bureau of Statistics.

1. Looking at the total enrolments for the years 1963-68 (right-hand column) what generalization can you make about the numbers of Indian children enrolled during these years?

2. Read the enrolment figures by grades for the year 1963-64 (across the table). Approximately what fraction of the original enrolment has dropped out of school by Grades 7-8? Approximately what fraction stays in school until the secondary school grades? (9-13) How do you think these dropout rates compare with those for the overall Canadian school population?

3. Now look at the enrolment figures for 1968-69. Has the pattern of school attendance by Indian students changed significantly during the five years since 1963-64?

4. What tentative conclusions seem to be suggested by this data?

5. Would you expect to find large numbers of Indian students enrolled in institutions of post-secondary education? Why? Check your answer against the data in Table E.

Table E.   Indian students in post-secondary and vocational training, by province, school year 1968-69

(Exclusive of the Yukon and Northwest Territories)

Classification	P.E.I., N.S. and N.B.	Que.	Ont.	Man.	Sask.	Alta.	B.C.	Total
	No.	No.	No.	No.	No.	No.	No.	No.
University	16	51	40	33	35	26	34	235
Teacher training	2	15	15	1	2	–	3	38
Nurse's training	1	–	4	4	2	6	3	20
Vocational	155	212	408	118	522	156	548	2,119
Upgrading	129	116	218	107	493	57	323	1,443
Totals	303	394	685	263	1,054	245	911	3,855

Ibid., p. 216.

The dropout figures for Indian students are shown in greater detail in Table F in which the enrolment of the group registering in Grade I in 1951 is traced through a twelve-year sequence.

Table F.   Dropout figures for Indian students over a twelve-year sequence

Grade	Year	Enrolment	Loss (no.)	Loss (%)
1	1951	8782	–	–
2	1952	4544	4238	48.2
3	1953	3430	614	13.5
4	1954	3652	278	7.1
5	1955	3088	564	15.5
6	1956	2641	447	14.5
7	1957	2090	551	21.7
8	1958	1536	554	26.5
9	1959	1149	387	25.5
10	1960	730	419	36.5
11	1961	482	248	34.0
12	1962	341	141	29.3

Hawthorn, *op. cit.*, Vol. II, p. 130.

1. Of the 8782 students enrolled in Grade I, how many did not complete high school?
2. What percentage of the original 8782 do the 341 enrolled in Grade 12 represent?
3. What is the percentage dropout rate by Grade 12?
4. The national rate of dropout for non-Indian students is approximately 12 per cent. How many times is the Indian dropout greater than this?
5. Suggest reasons for the high Indian dropout rate.

In the following excerpts from the *Hawthorn Report*, sponsored by the Department of Citizenship and Immigration and presented to the Federal Government in 1967, some of the reasons for the failure of education to provide the help needed by the Indians are discussed.

It is difficult to imagine how an Indian child attending an ordinary public school could develop anything but a negative self-image. First, there is nothing from his culture represented in the school or valued by it. Second, the Indian child often gains the impression that nothing he or other Indians do is right when compared to what non-Indian children are doing. Third, in both segregated and integrated schools, one of the main aims of teachers expressed with reference to Indians is "to help them improve their standard of living, or their general lot, or themselves" which is another way of saying that what they are and have now is not good enough; they must do and be other things. In addition to these attitudes are the already cited problems of Indian children attending school.

One Indian informant, an attractive and charming 19 year old girl, had accurately assessed the atmosphere in her school and was determined to succeed in spite of it. She said, "I have to complete school because I am an Indian. Indians have to try harder to be better than everyone else because they are

Indians. If more Indians could succeed then maybe the idea that Indians can never do anything would be done away with and we wouldn't have to prove ourselves all the time."

Most human beings have a need to achieve. This is usually directed toward a defined goal. If the individual does not perceive that he has some possibility of achieving his goal, he substitutes a more accessible goal or he stops trying to reach the goal at all. Studies done in the course of the project indicated that there is little reliability to be placed in the common belief that Indians have less motivation than non-Indians. It is not true that Indian children, as a group, lack motivation in the elementary years to do well. However, it has already been established that young Indian children fail from the onset of their educational experiences. With each failure, motivation, self-image and level of aspiration drop.

It has already been stated that in general Indian people in reserves tend to have little faith in their own abilities to control their environment and lives. The Indian student comes to have these characteristics. He comes to accept his failures and to believe that there is nothing he can do to alter his status and proceeds to complete the self-fulfilling prophecy of the "inadequate and unmotivated Indian."

If the Indian student is faced with the decision of trying to complete school in lieu of obtaining low-level employment immediately he chooses the employment. Not only does it mean immediate income, it also fits his concept of "what Indians do" and is a more realistic choice when one considers his low expectations for academic success. The Indian's low level of aspiration agrees with his low self-image and his genuine belief that he cannot go beyond the limited range of goals established by the Indians he knows and by the additional restrictions imposed by non-Indians.

Apart from the beliefs of the Indian himself in relation to self-image, aspirations and vocational choices, the dearth of information available to him about alternatives seriously limits his choices. In only a few communities were Indians aware of the availability of funds and training programs through the Indian Affairs Branch and almost no Indians had any information about provincial facilities and opportunities. High school informants stated that the counsellor or principal had information available and gave it to those who asked. Most of them were too shy to go to the office of either principal or the councellor. Upper-elementary students had access to no information through the schools . . .

To summarize: attitudes of non-Indian personnel working with Indians determine the attitudes of Indians toward themselves and toward non-Indians generally. The range of attitudes of superintendents, health personnel, school personnel and others varies from very negative to slightly positive. Many officials are genuinely interested in working with Indians but many have become discouraged by their lack of progress and by their perceptions of the immensity of the job they have to do. Indians are sensitive to the discouragement of officials and they tend to react by withdrawing and by exhibiting their desperation or hostility. Indians faced with the attitude of "what can be done about the Indians" feel that there is not much to be done.

Children exhibit the same one-to-one type of response to non-Indian attitudes. When teachers expect Indian children to work well and succeed, and give them some additional help in the classroom, Indian children tend to perform adequately. When teachers class Indians as slow learners and non-achievers, the children do not try to succeed because they are convinced that they cannot. The penchant of some Indian groups for accepting the attitude of officials with regard to their capabilities results in their showing these capabilities. As long as Indians accept the limitations imposed upon them by White attitudes and as long as teachers and officials feel equally overwhelmed by the low expectancy for success of their programs, there is not likely to be any break-through. If each group could evaluate their own limitations and assets more objectively and if programs could be run cooperatively between agencies then hopes for success would be higher and quite realistic. In the final analysis, however, the one-to-one relationship between an Indian and a White appears to be the major determinant in the establishment of an atmosphere which allows seeking a comfortable and successful route to achievement.

Hawthorn, *op. cit.*, Vol. II, pp. 142, 147.

1. List the three factors mentioned as contributing to a low degree of confidence and a poor self-image in Indian students.

2. Take each of these factors in turn and discuss what might be done to make improvements. Give specific examples.

3. What is the effect of failure on the attitudes and behaviour of Indian students? Discuss ways and means by which this problem could be eliminated.

4. Why do Indian students choose low-level employment in preference to staying in school? Propose incentives which, in your opinion, might be used to influence their choice towards completing school.

5. In what way is the role of principals, counsellors, and teachers of Indian students extremely important? What implications does this have for the selection and training of their teachers?

5.   Rising Expectations

"To every thing there is a time; and a season to every purpose under the heaven." So says the Bible; and it does seem that there operates in human affairs what has been called "the law of the right time." In other words, there comes a moment when things are ripe for change and events are ready to take a new direction. After a long period of decline and dependence on the White Man, the Indians of Canada now seem ready to cast aside apathy and despair, and to shape their own future.

One sign of recovery is to be found in the population statistics.

Under the impact of the encounter with the White Man's culture, the Indian population declined alarmingly. Diseases such as smallpox and tuberculosis, malnutrition, debilitation through the abuse of alcohol, lowered vitality because of the destruction of the traditional culture – all contributed to the decline. Until this century it looked as though the Indians were doomed to extinction. The change which has reversed this trend is illustrated in Table G.

Another sign is the increased activity on the part of Indians. They are organizing conferences by means of which they seek to establish unity, develop policies, influence public opinion, and make their demands clear to political leaders. Indian spokesmen frequently address meetings of predominantly non-Indian groups, such as businessmen, church organizations, and university professors and students.

Newspapers are carrying more and more articles on Indian affairs. The following selections were found in a few newspapers during a very brief period. They convey some idea of the Indians' growing impatience with the *status quo* and the determination to achieve change.

B.C. Indian Leaders Urge Unity

KAMLOOPS – Which way are the Indians of British Columbia going to go?

Are they going to shuck the bonds of bureaucracy and strike out on their own?

Are they going to stake their future on hunting and fishing in an environment that is stacking the odds against them?

Or is there a compromise that will give each Indian band a chance to find its own future?

The questions came into focus Monday as the Conference of B.C. Chiefs got down to its week-long chore of considering the federal government's proposal to repeal the Indian Act and turn over Indian services to the provinces.

The questions weren't quite spelled out in the debate but the gap was pointed out by several delegates who said many of the chiefs attending the conference don't know each other, let alone each other's problems.

Officials of the conference, held at the former Indian residential school here, announced Monday night that 145 of 188 B.C. chiefs had checked in on the first day of the discussion.

The chiefs spoke for 38,323 B.C. Indians, which according to conference figures left only 8,673 not represented.

And more chiefs were expected today as the delegates listened to each other's views.

The call for unity was sounded over and over again Monday as B.C. delegates to the national Indian conference in Ottawa last April assailed the policy proposed by the government.

Philip Paul of the Tsartlip band in Saanich, representative to the National Indian Brotherhood and the Indian's national committee on aboriginal rights,

Table G. Indian population, by province, selected years 1949-68.

Province or Territory	1949	1954	1959	1961	1963	1965	1966	1967	1968
	No.	No.	No.	No.	No.	No.	No.	No.	No.
Prince Edward Island	273	272	341	348	374	393	399	409	418
Nova Scotia	2,641	3,002	3,561	3,746	3,935	4,099	4,183	4,287	4,411
New Brunswick	2,139	2,629	3,183	3,397	3,629	3,824	3,912	4,039	4,156
Quebec	15,970	17,574	20,453	21,793	23,043	24,446	25,033	25,650	26,302
Ontario	34,571	37,255	42,668	44,942	47,260	49,556	50,568	51,731	52,981
Manitoba	17,549	19,684	23,658	25,681	27,778	29,996	30,994	32,227	33,358
Saskatchewan	16,308	18,750	23,280	25,334	27,672	30,086	31,360	32,579	33,852
Alberta	13,805	15,715	19,287	20,931	22,738	24,587	25,434	26,440	27,322
British Columbia	27,936	31,086	36,229	38,616	40,990	43,250	44,205	45,152	46,046
Yukon Territory	1,443	1,568	1,868	2,006	2,142	2,292	2,337	2,477	2,562
Northwest Territories	3,772	4,023	4,598	4,915	5,235	5,569	5,739	5,911	6,082
Totals	136,407	151,558	179,126	191,709	204,796	218,098	224,164	230,902	237,490

Canada Yearbook, 1968.

branded the policy statement as "flowery words, distortion of the Indian's needs."

He said the government's declaration that it will not recognize aboriginal claims of Indians makes hunting and fishing a privilege instead of a right.

It also dismissed B.C. Indians' claim that they still own the land of the province because they made no treaties with the government, he declared.

He said B.C. Indians went to Ottawa to help revise the Indian Act, not throw it out as proposed by the government.

. . . a member of the Nishga tribal council which is seeking an appeal court declaration of title to its tribal lands, urged the chiefs to unite in the same way here.

"You and I should never forget we are the true owners of this country," he said.

"We owned it before anybody else came. We didn't have to fight anybody for it. We only had to battle the land.

"You and I will have to talk this out. Let history see that the Indians of B.C. are united. We are going to leave this conference united.

"We are going to have to speak with one voice. We did it before and we are going to have to do it again.

"Let it be known it is going to cost the two governments (federal and provincial) plenty of money to bring us up to the white man's level of living.

"We are very wealthy," he added, "B.C. real estate is as expensive as any in Canada. But I am fed up with the conditions under which my people have to live.

"We are going to deal with our problems. We are not going to back away from it."

Ron Rose in the *Vancouver Sun*, November 18, 1969.

Indian Leader Raps Ottawa's Proposals

SUDBURY, Ont.

"We want our birthright. This is our country, our hereditary home. We will not be treated as foreigners in our own land."

These words, and others like them, from Dave Courchene, president of the Manitoba Indian Brotherhood, drew sustained applause from delegates to General Synod. Mr. Courchene was theme speaker Aug. 20 at the start of a long session in which synod approved recommendations of the report "Beyond Traplines" urging changes in the church's relationship with native people.

Mr. Courchene was sharply critical of the recently-announced new Indian policy of the federal government, calling it a "white-man's white paper on Indians and as far as Indians are concerned conceived in isolation and aborted at birth."

Stating that publication af the proposals has raised Indian resentment to a new high, Mr. Courchene suggested that reaction among his people would probably take two forms. One group would be formed of conservative responsible persons represented mostly by the existing Indian organizations who already have retained legal advisors. The other he described as volatile militants, small, with little patience, and he warned that "violent reaction" can be expected.

Discussing the record of the Church in relation to native people, Mr. Courchene emphasized that he was not speaking of any particular denomination. He said that while Government had been guilty of administrative paternalism, the church in its own way "was guilty of both Christian paternalism and competitive conversion."

Mr. Courchene told delegates that because the Church is "literally invulnerable to external pressure" it can stand up and be counted on the issues of the day, and he urged that its members be converted from passive observers to active participants in the fight for social progress.

He called for a program of action by the church in three areas:

A crusade of enlightenment to tell the real story of Indian aspirations in every congregation – that Indians want to participate in development of Canadian society in a climate of mutual acceptance. "A shotgun marriage will not endure; Indians must be given the right to decide how such a marriage of interests will take place."

The Church should speak out and advise government that it does not subscribe to imposed social change, and should ask government to seek reconciliation and honorable negotiation.

The Church should consider diverting some foreign aid programs to assist Indian organizations in their search for solutions to problems of social and economic equality.

Bill Portman in the Canadian Churchman, September, 1969, p. 10.

Indians Declare Reserve Sovereign State

TORONTO – The Six Nations Iroquois Confederacy has declared that the Six Nations Indian reserve is a sovereign state and will not be governed by the Ontario or federal governments.

In a proclamation released Tuesday, the chiefs of the Six Nations said their demands for sovereignty have been sent to Ottawa and the United Nations.

They say they will not accept a federal proposal to have Indian matters transferred to provincial governments.

The Six Nations reserve, near Brantford, Ont., consists of about 50,000 acres of land and has a population of about 5,000.

The proclamation, signed by chiefs of the Mohawks, Senecas, Onondagas, Cayugas, Oneidas and Tuscaroras, reads:

" . . . The government of Canada has established a proposed statement of 'Indian policy' – which will no doubt be passed in the Parliament of Canada – to force Indians residing in Canada to become Canadian citizens. . . .

The chiefs said that under treaty "our lands were to be ours and for our posterity to enjoy forever, but within the centuries our lands have eroded, by trickery and deceit and theft, to small portions which are now in danger of being taxed and dissolved into oblivion.

Vancouver Province, November 12, 1969.

Red Power Means Indian-White Link-up to Nadjiwon

To Chief Wilmer Nadjiwon, Red Power means partnership between Indian and white.

The new president of the Union of Ontario Indians, chief of the Cape Croker band on Georgian Bay, accepts the fact the Indian must co-operate with the white man since the white man possesses the economic resources the Indian needs to progress.

In an interview last week, the 48-year-old Ojibway sculptor and former steelworker spelled out in considerable detail his ideas and proposals for Indian development. They are all keyed to the concept of partnership, but they nevertheless aim toward a greater degree of Indian autonomy.

The chief roadblock to successful Indian dealings with the federal and provincial governments has been the red tape resulting from the involvement of a multiplicity of departments in Indian affairs, the chief said.

Last week, the UOI came up with a proposal, submitted to Premier John Robarts, which they believe will cut through the red tape, and combine a fair degree of Indian autonomy with the need to maintain government control over public money.

The proposal is a Crown corporation to administer Indian affairs in Ontario. Chief Nadjiwon sees no constitutional reason for the province not being able to establish it. Under the 1966 federal-provincial agreement, Ontario took over complete responsibility for Indian community development, he said, and it is to this area that the corporation would be directed.

The corporation; as proposed by the UOI, would have at least a majority of Indian directors. Yet, like other Crown corporations, it would report to the Legislature through a particular minister and thereby be accountable for its expenditure of public money. Its finances would come from all Government departments currently providing sums for some aspect of Indian affairs. Instead of these departments spending their money separately, the money would be channeled to the corporation.

Chief Nadjiwon is willing for the Government to see how such a concept would work through a pilot project.

If the project is successful, it could become province-wide. And then, if that works, other provinces and the federal Government might become interested, Chief Nadjiwon said.

The Crown corporation concept reflects the growing determination among Indian leaders that the Indian must be involved, if not entirely responsible for, his own welfare and development.

"Unless the Indian approach is taken, there is bound to be failure," Chief Nadjiwon said. "There is no person better qualified to advance the Indian people than the Indian himself. Present government machinery is far too cumbersome."

Chief Nadjiwon said an important part of the Crown corporation concept would be insuring that the Indian maintained his ancient treaty rights and title to his lands.

"The Indian is very suspicious, and would want a watchdog over his treaty rights," he said. "The reserves, at least if they are economically viable, should be maintained at this point in history. The Indian must have some base from which to find his past and develop his pride."

Chief Nadjiwon, who finished his formal education at Grade 8, believes Indian education has been a total failure.

"Even if it means teaching in a poorer setting, Indian children should be taught their language, culture, past history, history of their own tribe and the role their ancestors played in the development of Canada. This could be in addition to their regular course of studies. At this point, the Indian must take a step back in history and build himself a cultural base so he can become aware of himself and his people."

The chief also thinks the province's Indian welfare program – much touted by the Government – is considerably short of being successful.

"The same cheque goes to Indians in the north as to Indians in the south. But the cost of living in the north, when you consider a bag of potatoes ranges from $15 to $60, is not even comparable. There are some Indian families in the north who have never seen a potato."

The chief agreed that many of his proposals could be criticized for affording the Indian a special status above other citizens.

"We always have had special status. No other people live in outdoor zoos. Before, it was a negative special status, and what we want now is to make it positive."

Frances Russell in the *Globe and Mail*, June 5, 1969.

Sask. Indians Protest New Gov't. Policy

PRINCE ALBERT – Saskatchewan Indian chiefs and band councillors expressed strong protests Tuesday against the new federally-sponsored Indian policy now before the House of Commons.

"When the Europeans came to our country, they took over our lands and left us nothing but reserves," said one delegate.

"Now they are trying to take our reserves away from us and still the white man is not satisfied. Now he wants to take over the moon. What next?" said the delegate to the two-day meeting called by David Ahenakew, chief of the Saskatchewan Federation of Indians.

The meeting is to formulate a policy, representing opinions of Saskatchewan Indians to present to the federal government.

"We're like a political football kicked from one government to another," said one of the 130 chiefs and councillors who interrupted a speech by Fred Clarke of Regina, regional director for the federal Indian affairs department.

Clarke said that from the early days of Canada a trustee relationship developed between the federal government and the Indian people. The Indian people should have the right to manage their own affairs to the same extent as fellow-Canadians.

The federal government has decided that now is the time to change long-standing policies, he said.

Several native speakers expressed doubts that the treaties and Indian rights would be recognized as lawful obligations of the provincial government.

Vancouver Sun, July 16, 1969.

Alberta Indian Leader Sees Civil Disobedience Coming

BANFF, Alta. – Warnings that widespread outbreaks of civil disobedience by minority groups can be expected in Canada during the 1970s were issued during the weekend at a meeting of the Western Association of Sociology and Anthropology.

Harold Cardinal, president of the Indian Association of Alberta, said there will be widespread non-violent civil disobedience by the mid-1970s.

He said the federal government's proposed new Indian affairs policy will only allow equality of treaty Indians with the poor people of Canada.

"It means that Indians can line up for their welfare cheques along with the rest of the poor people of the country."

The Indian must return to seeking cultural creativity from the medicine people of his tribe rather than from the educational system and religion of the white man, he added.

Howard Adams, president of the Métis Society of Saskatchewan, said Indians are a "conquered, colonized people" and must begin operating with this in mind.

"At the moment you (the white man) select which of us go into the mainstream. We want to make the decision ourselves. We believe that if we are going to move into the mainstream of society, we are going to move as a people."

Adams said the Canadian school system is racist and Indians may be forced to boycott schools, re-educate their children and seek confrontations to radicalize their populations.

Indians must begin a cultural, psychological and spiritual decolonization, a move towards liberation that may involve violence.

Tony Antoine of Vancouver said Indians must form their own police forces and get the needed medical and educational tools. Indian affairs agencies and their programs were insufficient "band aids" for what ails the Indian people.

Vancouver Sun, December 29, 1969.

Indian Act Liquor Sections 'Discriminate' Court Rules

OTTAWA – The Supreme Court of Canada called Thursday for a change in liquor sections of the federal Indian Act because they deny Indians equality before the law.

In a 6 - to - 3 judgment, the court said that Indians, by reason of the Indian Act, are treated more harshly than other Canadians for liquor offences, contrary to the Canadian bill of rights.

The bill of rights, a major piece of legislation passed by the Diefenbaker government, guarantees to all Canadians "equality before the law and the protection of the law."

Because the liquor sections of the Indian Act call for longer jail terms and higher fines for Indians than provincial laws do for others, they "abrogate, abridge or infringe one of the rights declared and recognized by the bill of rights," said Mr. Justice Roland Ritchie, who wrote the court's majority reasons.

Because of this, Section 94 of the Indian Act must be declared to be inoperative, he said.

Other sections of the act were not affected by the judgment.

It was believed to be the first time that the high court has decided an appeal on the bill of rights, passed by Parliament in 1961.

The court's declaration was contained in its judgment involving a Yellow-knife, N.W.T., Indian who was convicted in 1967 by a justice of the peace of being drunk while off a reserve.

Mr. Justice W. G. Morrow of the territorial court allowed Joseph Drybones to change his plea and later found him not guilty of the offence.

The territorial judge found that the Indian Act, under which Mr. Drybones was charged, was discriminatory.

The territorial court of appeal agreed and the Crown then took its case to the high court.

John Diefenbaker, now MP for Prince Albert, called the judgment a "landmark for freedom."

"It interprets it (the bill) in a manner to assure equality for Canadians whatever their color, creed and race and will bring about a tremendous change in the treatment of Indians."

Vancouver Sun, November 21, 1969.

Verbal Support From Federal Minister

Minister without Portfolio Robert Andras told the Indian-Eskimo Association of Canada on Saturday that Indian administration of their own affairs must be the federal Government's objective.

He added: "I say to those of the colonial mentality and to those despondent cynics in the Indian or near-Indian community that change is possible, that it is the only answer, that we must never give up."

Mr. Andras has been appointed to hold consultations with Indians across Canada on changes in the Indian Act. He has emerged as a kind of ombudsman for the Indian, carrying their complaints to Indian Affairs Minister Jean Chretien and the Cabinet.

One thing he has told the Cabinet, he said in his speech, is that Indians are more interested in the Government keeping its promises to them than in revising the Indian Act.

"It appeared (to me) that the establishment of an Indian Claims Commission, the fulfilment of treaty promises and restoration of hunting rights might be more urgent in substance and for re-establishment of good faith than revisions to the Indian Act.

"I made these views known in the councils of Government."

He said whites must support Indian organizations so they can become workable pressure groups. With all the changes, he said, it is important to avoid "substituting one form of paternalism for another, no matter how pure the motive might seem."

In an interview, he said Indian trust was a fragile thing, easily broken by rash Government action. He said the Government may have on hand drafts of proposed legislation but they would stand open to revision as long as Indian consultations are being held.

He said he would quit his job immediately if he felt his findings would not be taken seriously by the Cabinet. He does not hold any veto power over contents of the new act, he added, but he would try to negotiate within the Cabinet in the interest of the Indians.

Globe and Mail, September 30, 1968.

Province Urged to Adopt New Approach to Indians

NDP leader Donald MacDonald yesterday called for a new approach to Ontario's Indian problems as a first step toward dealing with "Canada's national disgrace." He said a number of federal Indian functions should be transferred to the provincial Government and criticized the Department of Indian affairs for its "bureaucratic paternalism."

He said the direction of community development should be entrusted to the Indians, with the Government providing outside assistance where necessary.

"Let us not forget we have lived with this unsolved problem for an inexcusable length of time," he said. Canada's own native population lives in economic and social conditions which are a match for those of underdeveloped countries. Here, surely, is a situation which should stir the national conscience."

Major emphasis, should be placed on education. "The education of Indians which has been left for the most part to the churches in the past, must become a public responsibility."

Globe and Mail, February 24, 1968.

SUDBURY, Ont.
When Edgar Bull rose to second the resolution on the Coalition for Development Report, delegates saw a man who was openly, deeply and agonizingly committed to the fight against poverty – poverty in all its aspects.

Bull is rector of St. Thomas' Church, Toronto, a wealthy Anglo-Catholic parish.

"I am in a personal agony because just now I am barely inside the church, and I speak for many more. Edinborough described us to a T – and it is *our* problem, not theirs. It's a white problem. It is how I see my soul and my fellow man. It is "we" – not "we" and "they" – but "we together.""

"I am a WASP, a White Anglo-Saxon Protestant. I am glad about it, but there are difficulties, painful difficulties.

"The Indians are not a minority problem – they are the North American representatives of a world-wide majority still being exploited by us whites.

"This is tremendously important for us to realize, and realize quickly.

"Through the exploitation of economic structures the majority are kept poor by the white minority."

Latin America was a case in point, he added. The poor there are supporting the growing affluence of the United States.

Along the same lines, Bull asked if delegates knew where church money was invested, and asked if it could be broken down and the investments evaluated.

What was at stake was our attitude to the poor, the Indians, the world's starving people.

The church must get into politics, as the report suggested, he went on, for "no man can be excluded from the gifts of God.

"Speak up now, and put the pressure on. We have been asked for a commitment of the heart.

"How many times can a man turn his head, and pretend he just doesn't see?" How many times?

> Carolyn Purden in the *Canadian Churchman*, September 11, 1969, p. 11.

Ottawa Threatens Status, Fulton Warns B.C. Indians

KAMLOOPS – Indians would lose their special status as Canada's native citizens under federal policy proposal, the B.C. chiefs' conference was told here Tuesday.

Lawyer and former justice minister E. Davie Fulton – retained by the conference to advise on the policy – said in giving up their status the Indians would shoulder all the disadvantages of other citizens, including land taxes.

Fulton, appearing before the chiefs to present an analysis commissioned by the conference planning committee, also said the policy announced in June by Indian Affairs Minister Jean Chretien did not deal adequately with the Indian claim to aboriginal rights.

Chretien proposed that the Indian Act be repealed, the Indian affairs department wiped out and Indian services be taken over by provincial governments.

He said these things could come in five years through negotiation between the Indians and the various governments.

He said the federal government would make grants to the provincial governments to take over essential services and that a new Indian land act would safeguard reserve titles while giving Indian bands autonomy in land development.

The chiefs conference applied by resolution Tuesday to the provincial First Citizens Fund for $3,000 to pay Fulton's fee for making the study and other legal services.

He told the chiefs the bill might not be as high as estimated.

On Indian status Fulton's report declared: "The avowed object of the new policy is the removal of 'legal and constitutional bases of discrimination.'

"On the face of it, the removal of discrimination sounds well, and anyone who opposes is apt to be branded as racist and reactionary. However, the implications in terms of the results must be studied before a decision is made on the acceptability of this policy.

"It is clear from the terms of the white paper that the practical result, and indeed the expressed intent, is to end the status of Indians.

"There would be no Indian Act, and no longer any constitutional authority for responsibility for dealing with the Indian peoples as an ethnic entity.

"This would be the end of discrimination but it seems difficult to see how it would be other than the end also of the Indians as a people."

On lands:

"The white paper . . . certainly implies that after title is transferred, the lands will be integrated and become subject to provincial taxation.

"It would seem desirable – indeed essential – that the title system for these lands after they are transferred be the same as for other lands, but the question of taxation requires full clarification.

"In British Columbia the provincial government has declined to extend full provincial services to Indian lands – even when substantial portions, in the hands of non-Indian leasees, are in effect subject to provincial land tax.

"Such services and public utilities as there are, are provided by the bands themselves from their own resources or revenues, or by the federal government."

The report questioned whether the provinces will claim and exercise the rights to tax all Indians lands as soon as title is transferred, and whether the federal government will discontinue such services and utilities as are now provided on the reserves.

On aboriginal claims:

"The matter of aboriginal claims is far too fundamental to be capable of dismissal in less than a paragraph, as the white paper attempts to do.

"History and experience in Canada and the United States and the expectations of the Indian peoples based on undertakings by successive Canadian governments indicates that the only effective way in which the Indian claims will be dealt with is by a commission based upon legislation."

Ron Rose in the *Vancouver Sun*, November 19, 1969.

Another example, I suppose, is the Indian problem. I think Canadians are not too proud of their past by the way in which they have treated the Indian population of Canada. I don't think we have very great cause to be proud.

They are not citizens of the provinces as the rest of us are, but they are wards of the federal government. They get their services from the federal government rather than from the provincial or the municipal governments. They have been set apart in law. They have been set apart in their relations with government and even set apart socially, too.

For years I've known this type of heckler: the easy thing was to say to the government, "What are you going to do to make the Indians equal to the rest of Canadians, and what are you going to do if they bring the Indians into our society, and when are you going to stop treating the Indians as outsiders and second class citizens?"

So this year we came up with a proposal. It's a policy paper on the Indian problem. It proposes a set of solutions. It doesn't impose them on anybody, it proposes them. It proposes not only to the Indians, but to all Canadians; not only to their federal representatives, but their provincial representatives, too, and it says we are at a crossroads.

We can go on treating the Indians as having a special status. We can go on adding bricks of discrimination around the ghetto in which they live. And at the same time, perhaps, help them preserve certain cultural traits and certain ancestral rites. Or we can say, you are at a crossroads: the time is now to decide whether the Indians will be a race apart in Canada, or whether they will be Canadians of full status.

This is a difficult choice. It must be a very agonizing choice for the Indian people themselves, because on the one hand they realize that if they come into the society as total citizens they will be equal under the law, but they risk losing certain of their traditions, certain aspects of their culture, and perhaps even certain of their basic rights.

It is a very difficult choice for them to make and I don't think we want to try and force the pace on them, anymore than we can force it on the rest of the Canadians.

Here again is a choice which in our minds – whether Canadians as a whole want to continue treating the Indian population as something outside, a group of Canadians with which we have treaties, a group of Canadians who, as many of the Indians claim, have aboriginal rights; or whether we will say we'll forget the past and begin today.

They should become Canadians as all other Canadians, and if they are prosperous and wealthy, they will be treated like the prosperous and wealthy, and they will be paying taxes for the other Canadians who are not so prosperous and not so wealthy, whether they be Indians or English Canadians or French or Maritimers, and this is the only basis on which I see our society developing.

But aboriginal rights – this really means saying. "We were here before you came and you took the land from us. And perhaps you cheated us by giving us some worthless things in return for vast expanses of land and we want to re-open this question. We want you to preserve our aboriginal rights and restore them to us."

And our answer – and it may not be the right one and it may not be one which is accepted, but it will be up to all of you people to make your minds up and to choose for or against it and to discuss with the Indians – our answer is no. We can't recognize aboriginal rights because no society can be built on historical might-have-beens.

Source: Prime Minister Trudeau, Vancouver, August 10, 1969.

1. From a reading of these newspaper clippings make a list of what seem to be the important issues.

2. Start a file of newspaper clippings on Indian affairs. You may wish to start a general file or you may prefer to concentrate on a major issue.

TWO

The Roots of the Problem

Enough has been said in Part One to show that there exists a basic problem in Canada with respect to its first citizens. With a few exceptions they are poor; they hold the most poorly-paid jobs and suffer high unemployment rates; they are relatively poorly educated; they are subject to prejudice and discrimination. In a real sense they live as strangers in the land that was owned entirely by their ancestors before the white man came. They are a people who have been robbed of their heritage. Small wonder then that some are apathetic and without hope, while many are bitter and cynical about the intentions of the white majority.

Such a state of affairs is wrong. It runs contrary to the ideals of justice and equality of treatment to which we in Canada are committed. It is also dangerous because in the growing discontent of Indians lies a threat to the peace and stability of Canadian society. It is therefore a moral problem as well as a political one, and it may be stated thus: what are the Canadian people going to do in order to provide the Indians in Canada with the opportunity to live a free and full life?

This is a difficult problem to which we will return later. Before doing so, we will try to answer another question: precisely how did the present situation develop? In tracing the experiences of Indians in their contact with the White Man and his culture, we should achieve a better understanding of the problem.

What then did happen in the collision between the culture of the White Man and the cultures of the various Indian tribes? We already know some of the answers to this question. We know, for example, that the Indians were displaced from ownership of most of the land known today as Canada. We also know that in some way these "first citizens" became second-class citizens. But there are other questions we need to ask and to answer if we are to have a genuine understanding of the present situation. Here are some of them:

1. Why were Europeans so successful in taking over the

country? Did the Indians resist? If so, why were they unsuccessful?

2. What were the effects on them of the introduction of European religion, contact with fur traders, and elements of European civilization such as alcohol, firearms, and smallpox and other diseases to which they had no immunity? How did these things affect their traditional ways of life – their economies, technologies, political organizations, their customs and their beliefs about life? In other words, what price, material and psychological, did the Indians pay for their encounter with Europeans?

3. What contributions did the Indians make, either directly or indirectly, to the establishment of the White Man in this part of North America?

As you study the selections that follow, bear these questions in mind. The answers to them help us to understand the difficulties in which the Indians of Canada find themselves today.

1.   The Beothuk Indians of Newfoundland

On September 14, 1829, the English newspaper *The London Times* contained an article which told a tragic story. It announced the death of a woman and the end of a people.

> DIED – At St. John's, Newfoundland, on the 6th of June last in the 29th year of her age, Shanawdithit, supposed to be the last of the Red Indians or Beothuks. This interesting female lived six years a captive among the English, and when taken notice of latterly exhibited extra-ordinary mental talents. She was niece to Mary March's husband, a chief of the tribe, who was accidentally killed in 1819 at the Red Indian Lake in the interior while endeavouring to rescue his wife from the party of English who took her, the view being to open a friendly intercourse with the tribe.

The story of the encounter of the Beothuk and the White Man has been summarized by a Canadian scholar, Diamond Jenness.

The word Beothuk meant probably "man" or "human being," but early European visitors to Newfoundland considered it the tribal name of the aborigines who were inhabiting the island. They gave them also another name, "Red Indians," because they smeared their bodies and clothing with red ochre, partly for religious reasons, apparently, partly as a protection against insects. They may have been lighter in colour than the Indians of the Maritime Provinces, from whom they differed in several ways. Thus, they had no dogs, and did not make pottery, but cooked their food in vessels of birch bark. For sleeping places within their bark wigwams they dug trenches which they lined with branches of fir or pine. Their canoes, though made of birch bark like those of other eastern tribes, were very peculiar in shape, each gunwale presenting the outline of a pair of crescent moons; and they speared seals with harpoons modelled on an archaic Eskimo type. Many of their graves contain bone ornaments of curious shapes and etched with strange designs. We know nothing concerning their political organization except that they were divided into small bands of closely related families, each with its nominal leader. Some meagre vocabularies of their language suggest that they spoke two or three dialects of a common tongue, although the entire tribe could hardly have numbered much more than five hundred individuals when Cabot discovered Newfoundland in 1497. . . .

Fig. 2-1 Approximate distribution of the eastern Algonkian tribes in A.D. 1525.

The European fishermen who settled around the shores of the island in the sixteenth, seventeenth, and eighteenth centuries resented their petty pilfering, and shot them down at every opportunity, the French even placing a bounty on their heads; and the Micmac who crossed over from Nova Scotia in the eighteenth century hunted them relentlessly far into the interior. The Beothuk attempted to retaliate, but, armed only with bows and arrows, they could not withstand the combined attacks of white and Micmac, and the last known survivor died in captivity at St. John in 1829. One or two families may have escaped from the island and found asylum among the Montagnais of Labrador, for an old woman, discovered by Dr. Frank Speck in 1910 among the Micmac of Nova Scotia, claimed to be the half-breed daughter of a Beothuk refugee. But Nancy Shawanahdit, the captive who died in 1829, was the last "Red Indian" ever seen by white men, and the year of her death marks the date of their extinction.

> D. Jenness, *The Indians of Canada* (Ottawa: the Queen's Printer, 1955), pp. 265-67.

1. Were Europeans alone responsible for the extinction of the Beothuks?
2. Suppose there had been no European settlement in this area. Do you think the Beothuks might have survived? Explain your answer.
3. Compare the weapons of the Beothuks and the Europeans. How did the difference between them lower the Beothuks' chances of survival?

---

2.   The Eastern Algonkian Tribes

Refer to Figure 2-1 for an identification of these tribes and their territories. These Indians have been influenced by continuous contact with the Europeans and their descendants over a period of more than four hundred years. During this time they have had dealings with, among others, fur traders, missionaries, settlers, fur traders, soldiers, administrators, and businessmen.

The Fur Traders

We are able to understand something of the nature of the Indians, as they were when Europeans first encountered them, from the accounts which Jesuits made in their regular reports, the *Relations*.

We see shining among them some rather noble moral virtues. You note, in the first place, a great love and union, which they are careful to cultivate by means of their marriages. Generally speaking, they are of lighter build than we are; but handsome and well-shaped, just as we would be if we continued in the same condition in which we were at the age of twenty-five. You do not encounter a big-bellied, hunchbacked, or deformed person among them; those who are leprous, gouty, affected with gravel, or insane, are unknown to them. Any of our people who have some defect, such as the one-eyed, squint-eyed, and flat-nosed, are immediately noticed by them and greatly derided, especially behind our backs and when they are by themselves. For they are droll fellows, and have a word and a nickname very readily at command, if they think they have any occasion to look down upon us. And certainly (judging from what I see) this habit of self-aggrandizement is a contagion from which no one is exempt, except through the grace of God. You will see these poor barbarians, notwithstanding their great lack of government, power, letters, art and riches, yet holding their heads so high that they greatly underrate us, regarding themselves as our superiors . . .

Their customs are different from ours, both in peace and in war, both in public and in private; they do not uncover in making salutation, having been always uncovered before knowing the French. But silence and obedience of the young men toward the elders, serve as marks of respect; and, for ordinary salutation, they content themselves with a "good day," which in their language is expressed by saying *Quoe.*

. . . They are not found either hunchbacked or dwarfed, or very corpulent, or with goiters, etc. They are affable to one another, exchange visits very frequently, and like to be regarded as liberal and disinterested. They are certainly worthy of particular admiration in four things: first, their senses, which are most perfect, – so that, although they spend nearly six months without seeing anything but snow outside, and in their cabins, nothing but smoke, – they have, nevertheless, exceedingly acute vision, excellent hearing, an ear for music, and a rare sense of smell, – differing from ours only in this, that they esteem musk ill-smelling, and are indifferent to the odors of things, which are not eatable . . .

Secondly, they have an admirable fortitude in hardships: they endure hunger for ten or fifteen days, – sometimes from superstition, mostly by necessity; fire they endure without crying out. The youth accustom themselves to this from the age of ten or twelve years, two of them binding their arms together, and then putting a coal between the two arms, to see who will shake it off the first; they despise him who loses . . .

Thirdly, they possess a marvellous faculty for remembering places, and for describing them to one another, and for guiding themselves in the woods where they hardly ever lose their way. I have several times tried, in cloudy weather, or by night, to lead some Barbarian astray, – using the compass, in the endeavor to confuse his notions of the four quarters of the World, and then questioning him where was the East, where the South, where the country of the enemy, where our own; yet I have never found that they were deceived, for they guided themselves just as securely by their senses as I by my compass . . .

Fourthly, a very tenacious memory. They have neither books nor writings; negotiations are carried on through embassies, in which I have been amazed to see how many things and how many circumstances they recollect. But this faculty shines forth still more in the Captains, who use little sticks instead of books, which they sometimes mark with certain signs, sometimes not. By the aid of these they can repeat the names of a hundred or more presents, the decisions adopted in the councils, and a thousand other particulars, which we could not rehearse without writing . . .

R. G. Thwaites, ed., *The Jesuit Relations and Allied Documents*, 3, (Cleveland: The Burrow Brothers Co., 1897), pp. 78-79.

1. Briefly describe the following Indian characteristics as portrayed in the above description: health; self-confidence; relationships with others.

2. How were the customs and skills described in this account useful to the Indians in their lives? Use the information in the following extract to add to your answer.

When the French reached Canada they found that the Indians were possessed of a knowledge of medicine and surgery that was in some ways the equal of their own. In their application of the medicinal properties of the vegetable kingdom the Indians were probably superior to the French physicians. They had remedies for each and every occasion. . . . Their system of medicine was an unwritten one that was handed down from generation to generation and, in spite of the manifold defects of such a system, was surprisingly complete. In the hands of the women of the tribe was placed the treatment and care of the sick.

J. J. Heagerty, *Four Centuries of Medical History in Canada*, Vol. I (Toronto: Macmillan Co., 1928), p. 268.

The Indians had developed a culture which enabled them to cope effectively with the problems of living. What happened to this culture when the Indians came into contact with the fur traders? The Indians became fur gatherers. In return for their furs they received payment in European goods – iron tools and cooking utensils, foods, firearms, gewgaws such as beads and mirrors, and brandy or rum. As early as 1616, the Jesuit, Biard, reports on some of the effects of these changes in the patterns of Indian life.

They are astonished and often complain that, since the French mingle with and carry on trade with them, they are dying fast and the population is thinning out. For they assert that, before this association and intercourse, all their countries were very populous and they tell how one by one the different coasts, according as they have begun to traffic with us, have been more reduced by disease; adding, that why the Armouchiquois do not diminish in population is because they are not at all careless. Thereupon they often puzzle their brains, and sometimes think that the French poison them, which is not true; at other times that they give poisons to the wicked and vicious of their nation to help them vent their spite upon some one. This last supposition is not without foundation; for we have seen them have some arsenic and sublimate which they say they bought from certain French Surgeons, in order to kill whomsoever they wished, and boasted that they had already experimented upon a captive, who (they said) died the day after taking it. Others complain that the merchandise is often counterfeited and adulterated, and that peas, beans, prunes, bread, and other things that are spoiled are sold them; and that it is that which corrupts the body and gives rise to the dysentery and other diseases which always attack them in Autumn. This theory is likewise not offered without citing instances, for which they have often been upon the point of breaking with us, and making war upon us. Indeed there would be need of providing against these detestible murders by some suitable remedy if one could be found.

Nevertheless the principal cause of all these deaths and diseases is not what they say it is, but it is something to their shame; in the Summer time, when our ships come, they never stop gorging themselves excessively during weeks with various kinds of food not suitable to the inactivity of their lives; they get drunk, not only on wine but on brandy; so it is no wonder that they are obliged to endure some gripes of the stomach in the following Autumn. . . .

. . . if they stay, their stores would soon be consumed; so they go somewhere else until the time of famine. Such are the only guards they leave. For in truth this is not a nation of thieves. Would to God that the Christians who go among them would not set them a bad example in this respect. But as it is now, if a certain Savage is suspected of having stolen anything he will immediately throw this fine defense in your teeth, We are not thieves, like you. . . .

> R. G. Thwaites, ed., *op. cit.*, pp. 105-109.

1. What reasons do the Indians give for the increased death rate?
2. What reasons does Biard give?
3. Which seems to you to be the most acceptable explanation?
4. What evidence is there in the document of malpractice by fur traders?
5. Make a list of the factors which might lead to a decline in the Indian population.

> The search for furs resulted in the dislocation of the traditional relationships among the tribes as one tribe trespassed on the territory of another. The complex effects of this process have been discussed by a scholar of the period.

Cartier's Indians were not great travellers beyond their own territories, nor did any of the natives spend their time in fruitless wanderings in pre-Columbian times to dangerous and mysterious regions beyond their view. In Cartier's words ". . . one could make one's way so far up the river that they had never heard of anyone reaching the end of it." But the possession of iron accelerated work and gave more time for getting furs, and as the supply decreased they were continually led farther afield. Therefore, the Indians acquired a knowledge of the country beyond their own territories which weakened their distinctive traits, hastened diffusion, and created a general instability of life. The search for furs led to an economical and political pressure on the tribes of the interior and was an important cause of the revival of inter-tribal warfare. Wars between tribes, which with bows and arrows had not been strenuous, conducted with guns were disastrous. As the colonists were leaving Port Royal in 1607 Membertou, the Micmac chief, returned from a war of revenge for the death of one of his own people. It is probable that fire-arms were first used here in inter-tribal war. Membertou and his men had them a year later. They were victorious, having killed twenty, and wounded ten or twelve. At this time a law was passed forbidding the sale of fire-arms to the Indians. It was ineffective, however, due to increasing competition in the trade, Indian

demand, and international rivalry which created the necessity for strongly
armed native allies. The hunt became more deadly when fire-arms and iron
weapons supplanted the stone spear and arrow, with the result that the food
supply became seriously diminished and the Indians were forced to rely more
and more upon European foodstuffs.

The new means of sustenance, together with the revival of warfare,
and the time consumed in the hunt for furs, led to a decline in husbandry
among the eastern Algonkians. "Our Souriquois formerly did the same (made
earthen pots) and tilled the ground; but since the French bring them kettles,
beans, biscuits, and other food, they are become slothful and make no more
account of those exercises." It is possible that Lescarbot was misled by Cartier's
account of the Laurentian Iroquois into believing that the Micmac practised
agriculture when he says, "The people of Canada and of Hochelaga . . . also
tilled the soil . . . and the land brought forth for them corn, beans, peas,
melons, squash and cucumbers; but since their furs have been in request, and
that in return for these they have had victuals without any further trouble,
they have become lazy, as have also the Souriquois, who at the same date
practiced tillage."

European foods tended to unbalance the diet of the natives, causing and
facilitating the spread of diseases, which resulted in a decline in the birth rate,
and the depopulation of the adult members of eastern Algonkian society.

> A. G. Bailey, *The Conflict of European and Eastern Algonkian
> Cultures* (Toronto: University of Toronto Press, 1968), pp. 12-13.

> 1. How did the expansion of the fur trade increase the amount of inter-
>   tribal warfare?
> 2. What were the effects of the introduction of firearms on (a) the
>   numbers of the animals on which the Indians depended for their food,
>   (b) the losses in human life in inter-tribal warfare?
> 3. What were the results of these changes on the Indians in terms of
>   (a) numbers, (b) morale?

> Along with new technology the White Man brought disease.
> ". . . There is little doubt," a medical historian has written, "that
> the infectious diseases, such as measles, scarlet fever, diphtheria,
> chicken-pox, small-pox, typhus, typhoid, malaria, and yellow
> fever, as well as the venereal diseases, and possibly tuberculosis,
> were importations."[1] The results for the Indians were disastrous.

> Whereas Europeans had acquired a degree of immunity from the
> worst effects of many of these diseases, the Indians had none at
> all. The Jesuit *Relations* are dotted with references to the toll
> the Indians suffered.

The most destructive of all the small-pox epidemics broke out at Tadoussac
in the winter of 1669-70. Midst cold and hunger, two hundred and fifty persons died of the Montagnais, Algonkins, Papinachois, and Micmac, from

[1] Heagerty, *op. cit.*, I, p. 268.

Sillery to Tadoussac. One shipload "all resembled Monsters rather than human beings, their bodies were so hideous, emaciated, and full of corruption." Whereas from a thousand to twelve hundred Indians had formerly frequented Tadoussac scarcely a hundred remained in the summer of 1670. It is said that six score had died at Tadoussac alone. Across the St. Lawrence at Ile Verte, theriac, described as a sovereign remedy, was administered to "living skeletons and bodies all disfigured. . . ." Nearby the missionary was forced to "live in a place infected with a horrible stench" while caring for a band of Micmacs. The French rendered efficient service

> by the assiduous attentions which they bestowed upon our sick Savages . . . in attending them, dressing their sores . . . burying them after their death . . . I have seen some of them with an admirable courage and zeal, load the dead bodies upon boats in the icy waters; and then unloading them, carry them on their shoulders, although the putrid matter ran from all parts upon their garments and cloaks.

That the French possessed a certain immunity may be gathered from the fact that, although one was slightly ill "none of them have experienced any injury." The Father was attacked but recovered.

Of the Abenaki at Sillery in 1682 the *Relation* declared that nearly all had been attacked by small-pox, but adds that "Not many persons have died This year in the mission." In 1684, at the instigation of LeClercq, a Micmac migration was made to Sillery, but "God has granted the favour to most of these Gaspesians to die at Sillery this year, some time after having arrived there."

Although Acadia had long been a fruitful soil for European diseases the small-pox encompassed great destruction in the last decade of the century. Great numbers of Penobscots and Malecite died in the regions of Pentagouet and Meductic. Gyles, who was a prisoner among the Malecite at this time, describes the epidemic that afflicted his band. The diseased person would bleed at the mouth and nose, turn blue in spots, and die in two or three hours. More than a hundred died among his immediate people. It caused the Indians to scatter and they were not reunited when he left them in 1698.

Although small-pox was perhaps the most lethal of all diseases that afflicted the eastern Algonkians it had sturdy companions in arms. In 1634 many were attacked by scrofula, or tuberculosis, the symptoms of which were sores full of pus, covered with a horrible looking crust, which attacked the ears, neck and arm-pits. Of the sick among the Montagnais in 1637 "nearly all die of consumption, becoming so thin that they are nothing but skin and bone. . . ." One of these, a woman, was stricken with paralysis and rawness of the loins. Another, the son of a sorcerer, having developed "a most horrible scrofulous affection near the ear, we were afraid he would give the disease to the little boys we have in our House, and so we refused him. Monsieur Grand . . . has this child's sores dressed, and dresses them himself." Pleurisy and consumption, which were perhaps induced by the wearing of European clothing, attacked the Christian Indians at Sillery in 1639. In 1644 an Indian was found to be suffering from an abscess in the head, worms issuing from the ears, rotting flesh, limbs falling away piecemeal, accompanied by great pain. Ten years later at Tadoussac a child with a scrofulous neck and throat eaten away, was noted. Again, what appears to have been tuberculosis was recorded at Quebec in 1658. Lahontan declared that consumption resulted from the use of brandy which had been adulterated in France. Moreover, after 1659, when the Saint Andre was stricken while on its way to New France, typhus became as frequent in the colony as the arrival of the king's ships from the Old World. Typhus may have been the epidemic which raged at Tadoussac in 1661, and which Menard declared was hitherto unknown, and which swept away all those whom it attacked. Death was accompanied by violent convulsions and contortions of the limbs. Other diseases of a minor nature, such as dropsy, were not infrequent results of the contact with European culture.

> Bailey, *op. cit.*, pp. 78-79.

> On top of these disasters there was the trade in hard liquor. Brandy was traded by the French and rum by the British for the furs that the Indians brought to them. Although in Acadia and New France, repeated efforts were made to control the brandy trade, they were unsuccessful. Missionaries repeatedly reported the ruinous effects on the Indians but to no avail.

Bishop St. Vallier declared that brandy had killed all the old men and great numbers of the young people among the cross-bearer Micmac. LeClercq said that the French made the Indians drunk and cheated them in the trade. They perpetrated a further fraud by diluting the liquor with water. The Indians were made to sell all their household goods to obtain brandy. The French seduced and practised indecency with the native women who were made drunk for the purpose. The liquor made the Indians kill each other and destroy their own property and that of the French. The most sordid picture of all is painted by Denys, and it is recommended to any who have any doubts concerning the degrading influence which liquor had upon every aspect of the native life. The Indians were trading themselves into destitution. Fraud in trade, the wholesale seduction of women by the fishermen, the promotion of disease and civil strife, the disintegration of the group spirit and the loss of the will to live, all resulted from the deliberate debauching of the Micmac with wine and brandy. The Jesuits had been forced to abandon the mission. Conditions were almost equally bad among the Malecite in 1690, who " . . . when they came in from hunting, they would be drunk and fight for several days and nights together, till they had spent most of their skins in wine and brandy, which was brought to the village by a Frenchman. . . . "

> Bailey, *op. cit.*, p. 71.

> Marie de l'Incarnation, who established a school in Quebec, describes in one of her letters the effects of the brandy trade.

I have spoken to you in another letter concerning a cross which as I said before is heavier for me to bear than all the hostilities of the Iroquois. It is this. There are in this country some French people so miserable and without fear of God, that they would destroy our new Christians by giving them strong drink, such as wine and brandy, in order to obtain beaver skins from them. This drink destroys all these unfortunate people; men and women and even boys and girls. Each of them eats and drinks as he or she desires. They become intoxicated very quickly and are then maddened. They run about naked, and with various weapons chase people by day and night. They run unchecked through the streets of Quebec. From this cause follow murders and violence and unheard of brutality. The reverend fathers have done their best to put a stop to this evil on behalf of the French as much as the Indians, but all their efforts have been in vain. We made plain to the Indian girls from outside who attend our classes, the evil toward which they were hastening if they followed the example of their relatives and since that time they have not entered our institution. The Indian nature is of that kind. Until they are well established in Christian morality, the Indians follow the customs of their own people. An Algonquin chief, a fine Christian man and the first baptized in Canada, when paying us a visit, complained saying, "Onontio, it is his Excellency the Governor who is killing us by allowing people to give us liquor." We replied, "Tell him to forbid it." "I have told him twice already," he said, "and still he does nothing about it, but do you beseech him yourself to have it forbidden. Perhaps he will listen to you."

P. F. Richeaudeau, ed., *Lettres de la Révérende Mère de l'Incarnation*, II (Paris, 1878), p. 220.

1. Explain how the brandy trade contributed to a decline in the numbers of the Indian population.
2. How, in your opinion, would it contribute to conflict among the Indians?
3. What effects would it have on the spirit or morale of the Indians?

The Missionaries in Acadia and New France

"One of the most potent weapons in the arsenal of New France was the zeal of the Jesuits." So says one writer. Sometimes these missionaries penetrated distant Indian lands before the earliest explorers and often they were there well ahead of the earliest trader. Their presence had an important effect on the Indians, and their teachings were yet another factor in the process which destroyed the Indians' traditional customs and beliefs.

The attitude of the Jesuits towards the Indians is expressed in the terms that they used to describe them. The Indians were "les sauvages" – the savages or barbarians. There was no hatred implied in this name. It expressed the Jesuits' belief that the Indians were not civilized, and particularly that they were pagans. If the Indians could be converted to Christianity, their souls would be saved from the eternal damnation that was the fate of the non-Christian.

Since there were no priests, temples, or images, the Jesuits could easily assume that there was no religion. In fact, of course, the Indians did have a set of religious beliefs which gave meaning to their lives. The persistent and devoted work of the Jesuits succeeded in converting some Indians, but it was difficult for others to accept the ideas of Christianity. One can imagine, for example, the frustration of the Jesuits in trying to explain, and the confusion of the Indians in trying to understand, the central Christian idea of the crucifixion for mankind's sake, of Christ, the son of God. On this point Red Jacket, an Iroquois chief, said:

> Brother, if you white men murdered the son of the Great Spirit, we Indians had nothing to do with it, it is none of our affair. If he had come among us, we would not have killed him; we would have treated him well. You must make amend for that crime yourselves.

To the Indians the concepts of Christianity were difficult to understand, even nonsensical.

When the priests first came "most all the Indians were witches. Some were willing to be christened, some were unwilling. They asked the priest. "What is Christening for?" . . . "If you are not christened, you are lost for good." . . . "Lost, in the woods?" . . . "No, in hell." . . . "Where is hell?" . . . "Black place, fire there burns the soul." . . . "How do you go there, by road?" . . . "No, your soul goes there." . . . "Where is my soul?" . . . "You might sicken and die. After you die you might see your soul." . . . "How can a soul go out from the birch-bark cover around the dead body, tightly bound?" . . . "You should dig a hole and put the dead in it." . . . "That would be even harder to get out of, couldn't go anywhere then." . . . "Yes, you could go to Heaven." . . . "Heaven? What is Heaven?" . . . Nice band (of music) in Heaven, nice berries there." . . . "How go there?" . . . "If you do not fight, do not talk bad, you can go there. If you murder, steal, you will go to Hell, for your sin." . . . "Sin? What is sin?" They knew nothing.

E. C. Parsons, "Micmac Folklore," *Journal of American Folklore, 38*, p. 90.

Imagine you are an Indian living at this time.

1. An essential part of your code of behaviour is that wrongs should be avenged: "an eye for an eye." How would you respond to the Christian idea of "turning the other cheek"? What would it mean to you in terms of (a) your manliness, (b) the survival of your people in inter-tribal warfare?

2. It is customary in your tribe for a man to have more than one wife. This is a social device for taking care of women who would otherwise be without means of support. A Jesuit missionary teaches that it is sinful to have more than one wife and that those who commit this sin will burn in hell fire forever after their death. Give your reactions.

3. A Jesuit missionary teaches that it is more blessed to give than to receive. You have seen that other white men – fur traders – use unscrupulous methods to get hold of furs; that they seem to be driven by greed. Describe the confusion in your mind. What questions would you ask the Jesuit in order to clear up the confusion?

4. A Jesuit mission has recently been established in your territory. Shortly after the arrival of the missionaries a small-pox epidemic decimates your people. What might be your attitude to the visitors?

If the Indians did not understand Christianity too well, the Jesuits had the same problem with the Indian religions. Indian practices and beliefs which did not accord with Christianity were understood by them as superstition or the work of the devil.

On the 2nd of March, and other days following the carnival, the devil was unchained here as well as in France. There was only deviltry and masquerading at that time throughout the Huron country; I will content myself with touching incidentally upon the deviltries of these peoples.

1. All their actions are dictated to them directly by the devil, who speaks to them, now in the form of a crow or some similar bird, now in the form of a flame or a ghost, and all this in dreams, to which they show great deference. They consider the dream as the master of their lives, it is the God of the country. It is this which dictates to them their feasts, their hunting, their fishing, their war, their trade with the French, their remedies, their dances, their games, their songs.

2. To cure a sick person, they summon the sorcerer, who without acquainting himself with the disease of the patient, sings, and shakes his tortoise shell; he gazes into the water and sometimes into the fire, to discover the nature of the disease. Having learned it, he says that the soul of the patient desires, for his recovery, to be given a present of such or such a thing, – of a canoe, for example, of a new robe, a porcelain collar, a fire-feast, a dance, etc., and the whole village straightway sets to work to carry out to the letter all the sorcerer may have ordered. As I was writing this, a Savage, greatly excited, came from a neighbouring village, and begged us to give him a piece of red stuff, because the sorcerer had said that one of his sons, who was sick, desired for his recovery this bit of stuff. It was not given to him; but one of our fathers immediately repaired to the place, and baptized the little patient.

3. Nearly all the Savages have charms, to which they speak and make feasts, in order to obtain from them what they desire.

4. The devil has his religious; those who serve him must be deprived of all their possessions, they must abstain from women, they must obey perfectly all that the devil suggests to them. The sorcerer of this village came to see us, and told us all these things.

The number of those baptized this year reaches fully 300 souls; in this village of la Conception, there have been baptized in sickness, both children and others, one hundred and twenty-two persons. Besides the sick, fifty persons in health were solemnly baptized. In the village of St. Joseph, one hundred and twenty-six; in the itinerant mission of St. Michel, twenty-six or seven. I speak only of this country of the Hurons; as concerns Kebec and Three Rivers, you have the Relation of those before we do.

I am with all my heart,
My Reverend Father,

your very humble and very affectionate brother in our Lord,
FRANÇOIS DU PERON,
surnamed in Huron
ANONCHIARA, S.J.

S. R. Mealing, ed., *The Jesuit Relations and Allied Documents*, (To-ronto: McClelland and Stewart, 1963), pp. 55-56.

1. If religion is defined as a set of beliefs about the universe which give meaning to people's lives, can it be said that the Indians referred to had a religion?

2. Why did Father Peron not see a religion here?

3. The Indians did not separate religion from the practice of medicine. The shaman (sorcerer) had both religions and medical duties: Why were shamans referred to as sorcerers or witches by the Jesuits?

4. Explain how the authority of the shaman was reduced by the appearance of diseases such as small-pox?

5. How might a decline in the belief in the powers of the shaman, together with the preaching of the Jesuits, affect the Indians' beliefs about supernatural forces in the universe?

Another legacy of exposure to a different set of religious ideas was a sense of sin and guilt in those Indians who accepted Christianity. For example, exposure of the body had traditionally been a natural thing. The readings of the missionaries emphasized modesty and thus made the Indians conscious of something which previously they had no awareness.

"A young Christian Savage, having awakened in the night, and seeing a woman immodestly covered in her sleep, was seized with fright, – Not knowing how to warn this woman, for fear of putting her to confusion, he bethought himself of roughly beating a dog, and making it yelp aloud, so that the woman on waking should again cover herself properly."

Ibid., pp. 20, 177.

"They are so modest that, if one of them has her throat even a little uncovered, the others tell her that she will drive away her good Angel. This is now so accepted among them that, to warn a girl to keep within the bounds of decorum, they say to her, 'Be careful that your good Angel does not leave you'; and the girl to whom this remark is made looks herself over, to see that there is nothing unseemly."

Ibid., pp. 19, 51.

"These children have such a regard for purity that, when they go out walking, they avoid meeting men, and they are so careful to cover themselves with decency, that their deportment is very different from the custom of the Savages."

Ibid., pp. 22, 185.

Settlers

> Wars and treaties deprived us of our land. Some of
> our people thought we were betrayed.
>
> Indian Pavilion Expo '67

> When the White Man came, we had the land and
> they had the Bibles; now they have the land and we
> have the Bibles.   Chief Dan George

The first influences on the Eastern Algonkian Indians were the fur traders and the missionaries. The effects of these contacts were to be supplemented by those of settlers. Increasingly the Europeans came to stay. Instead of working a lifetime in the service of the fur companies or the church, and then returning to the homeland, they settled on the land, where conditions of soil and climate were favourable. Settlers cleared the land, fenced it in, and farmed it. Already demoralized by the shock of collision with the White Man's culture represented by fur traders and missionaries, the Indians increasingly found that they had to make further adjustments in their way of life.

In New France farming made some progress, but the fur trade remained the most important industry. The defeat of the British in the American Colonies marked the beginning of a new emphasis on settlement and farming. Loyalists, displaced from the United States, flooded into the Maritimes and Upper Canada and took up land. They were joined by increasing numbers of immigrants from England, Scotland, and Ireland, and by soldiers of the British army who concluded their tour of duty in British North America by taking up grants of land.

The process whereby the Indians were displaced from their lands rapidly gathered speed. As the White Man moved westward, so the Indians surrendered their lands to him. The advance spilled over into the prairies, and as the White Man introduced his agriculture he destroyed those things that were essential to the life of the Indians of the plains, the great herds of buffalo and freedom of movement.

The White Man secured the land by making treaties with the Indians. Indian title to the land was recognized and then extinguished by treaty. The parties to the treaties were the representatives of the British crown on one side and the Indian chiefs on the other. Once the land was secured, the government could dispose of it as it saw fit.

The following is the text of a treaty concluded in 1806 whereby the Indians, in return for certain considerations, surrendered their title to land in the vicinity of what is now Toronto. Accompanying it is a list of the goods mentioned in the treaty and a map of the land being surrendered.

We, the Principal Chiefs of the Mississague Nation, for ourselves and on behalf
of our Nation, do hereby consent and agree with William Claus, Esquire,
Deputy Superintendent General and Deputy Inspector General of Indian
Affairs, on behalf of His Majesty King George the Third, that for the consideration of one thousand pounds Province currency, in goods at the Montreal
price, to be delivered to us, we will execute a regular deed for the conveyance
of the lands hereon marked pink: Commencing at the eastern bank of the mouth
of the River Etobicoke, being on the limit of the western boundary line of the
Toronto purchase in the year 1787; then north twenty-two degrees west six
miles; then south thirty-eight degrees west twenty-six miles, more or less, until
it intersects a line on a course north forty-five degrees, produced from the outlet
at Burlington Bay; then along the said produced line one mile, more or less,
to the lands granted to Captain Brant; then north forty-five degrees east one
mile and a half; then south forty-five degrees east three miles and a half, more
or less, to Lake Ontario; then north-easterly along the water's edge of Lake
Ontario to the eastern bank of the River Etobicoke, being the place of beginning, containing seventy thousand seven hundred and eighty-four acres, whenever the goods of the aforesaid value shall be delivered to us. Reserving to
ourselves and the Mississague Nation the sole right of the fisheries in the Twelve
Mile Creek, the Sixteen Mile Creek, the Etobicoke River, together with the
flats or low grounds on said creeks and river, which we have heretofore
cultivated and where we have our camps. And also the sole right of the fishery
in the River Credit with one mile on each side of said river.

This agreement done, signed and executed by us at the River Credit, this
second day of August, one thousand eight hundred and five.

J. W. WILIAMS, *Capt. 49th Regt.,*   W. CLAUS,
JNO. BRACKENBURY, *Ens. 49th Regt.,*   *Deputy Superintendent General,*
P. SELBY, *Assistant Secretary, I.A.,*   *on behalf of the Crown.*   [L.S.]
J. B. ROUSSEAUX.   CHECHALK, (totem)   [L.S.]
                                              QUENIPPENON, (totem)   [L.S.]
                                              WABUKANYNE, (totem)   [L.S.]
                                              OKEMAPENESSE, (totem)   [L.S.]

We do hereby certify that the following goods were delivered in our presence
to the Mississagua Nation, subscribers to the within deed, being the consideration therein mentioned, viz.:–

Articles	Quantity	Amount in Province Currency
		£ s. d.
Ball and shot	Nineteen hundred weight: 14 cwt. at 54s. 6d., 5 cwt. at 56s.	52 3 0
Blankets of 1 point	Thirty-one pairs at 10s. 6d. per pair	16 5 6
Blankets of 1½ point	Thirty-six pairs at 11s. 10d. per pair	21 6 0
Blankets of 2 point	Thirty-nine pairs at 14s. per pair	27 6 0
Blankets of 2½ point	Seventy pairs at 20s. 3d. per pair	70 17 6

Articles	Quantity	Amount in Province Currency
		£ s. d.
Blankets of 3 point	Fifty-two pairs at 29s. 11d. per pair	77 15 8
Calico	Seventeen pieces, 306 yds. at 53s. per piece	45 1 0
Caddee	Three hundred and fifteen yds. at 3s. 10d. per yd.	60 7 6
Cloth, broad	Forty-nine yards: 24 yds. at 14s., 25 yds. at 17s. 6d. per yd.	38 13 6
Flints	One thousand	0 19 7
Guns, common	Fifty-two at 28s. each	72 16 0
Guns, chiefs'	Eighteen at 56s. each	50 8 0
Guns, rifles	Sixteen at 77s. each	61 12 0
Gunpowder	Three hundred and seventy-five pounds at 203s. per barrel	38 1 3
Hats, plain	Sixty-three at 4s. 9d. each	14 19 3
Hats, laced	Fifteen at 10s. 3d. each	8 8 9
	Seven gross at 5s. 8d. per gross	1 19 8
Hooks, fishing	Four dozen at 50s. per dozen	10 0 0
Handkerchiefs, silk	Two hundred at 2s. 6d. each	25 0 0
Hoes	Thirteen, 65¼ lb. at 8½d. per lb.	2 6 2¾
Harrow pins	Two hundred eighty and three-quarter lb. at	
Kettles, brass	3s. 6d.	49 2 7½
Knives, butcher's	One and a half gross at 50s. per gross	3 15 0
Linen	Two hundred and fifty-four yds. at 2s. 10d. per yd.	35 19 8
Looking glasses	Seven doz. at 5s. 7d. per doz.	1 19 1
Molton	Nine pieces, 270 yds., at 81s. per piece	36 9 0
Ploughshare, Coulter hook and swivel	One, 37¼ lb. at 7½d. per lb.	1 3 3½
Ribbon	Fifty-two pieces, 18 yds. each, 22 pcs. at 8s. 10d., 30 at 9s. 10d. per piece	24 9 4
Serge, embossed	Two hundred and ninety-seven yds. at 2s. 5d. per yd.	35 17 9
Strouds	Fifteen pieces, 331½ yds., at 109s. per piece	81 15 0
Steels, fire	Five gross at 5s. 7d. per gross	1 7 11
Scissors	Seven and a half doz. at 8s. 4d. per doz.	3 2 6
Tobacco, carrot	Four hundred and eighty-six lb. at 11d. per lb.	25 5 6
Thread	Five lb. at 5s. 7d. per lb.	1 7 11
Vermillion	Twenty-two lb. at 4s. 11d. per lb.	5 8 2
	Amounting in the whole to one thousand pounds, 9 shillings and one penny three farthings, Province currency	£ 1,000 9 1¾

RIVER CREDIT, September, 1806. D. CAMERON, DONALD MACLEAN, *Commissioners on behalf of the Province,* GEO. R. FERGUSON, *Capt. Canadian Regiment,* WM. L. CROWTHER, *Lieut. 41st Regiment,* JAMES DAVIDSON, *Hospital Staff.*

Indian Treaties and Surrenders from 1680-1890, Vol. I (Ottawa: Queen's Printer, 1905), pp. 35-36. 41.

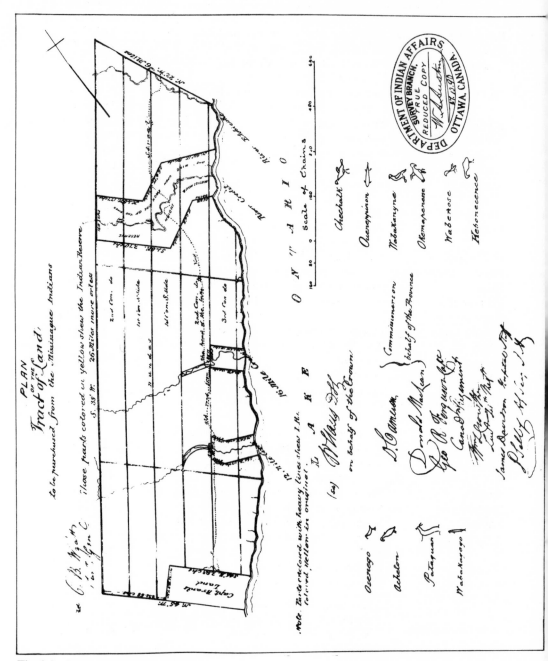

Fig. 2-2   Land purchased from Indians.

1. Consult the treaty and map. Trace the area purchased on the map. Calculate the approximate area in square miles (remembering to take account of land reserved for the Indians and Captain Brant's land). The purchase price was £1000. What was the approximate price per square mile? Per acre?

2. Notice how the Indians signed the treaty. What does this suggest about their understanding of it? (Knowledge of White Man's law, understanding of the implications of surrendering the land, etc.)

3. The traditional economy of the Indians was based partly on agriculture and partly on hunting. Consult the list of goods accepted by them. In what ways does the list suggest that they considered this would continue to be their way of life? How does the treaty represent an important step in ending this way of life?

4. Summarize the probable long-term effects of surrenders of this kind on the way of life of the Indians.

3.   Indians of the Plains

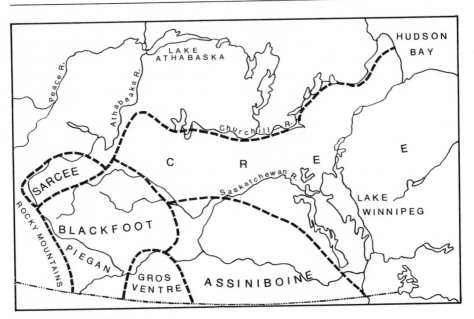

Fig. 2-3   Plains tribes.

D. Jenness, *op. cit.*, p. 309.

In the contact between the Eastern Algonkian Indians and Europeans, the culture of the Indians was fragmented and disorganized. The fur trade and new tools and weapons revolutionized traditional economic conditions. Indians neglected ancient skills as they gave their attention to the search for furs. They became increasingly dependent on White Man's food, and on his liquor.

Accompanying this revolution in economic conditions was a breakdown of the old systems of law, government, and religion on which their societies were based. A declining population and a weakened will to live were signs of the disintegration of the Indian cultures.

The following selections discuss the effects upon the Plains Indians of contact with Europeans.

The Fur Trade and the Indians

As the lands in the east were depleted of fur-bearing animals, the traders pushed westward seeking new sources of profit. David Thompson, explorer and fur trader himself, described the destructive march of the fur trade west and northwest of Lake Winnipegosis.

The Nepissings, the Algonquins and Iroquois Indians having exhausted their own countries, now spread themselves over these countries, and as they destroyed the Beaver, moved forwards to the northward and westward: the natives the Nahathaways (Cree), did not in the least molest them; the Chippaways and other tribes made use of traps of steel; and of the castorum. For several years all these Indians were rich, the women and children, as well as the men were covered with silver broaches, ear-rings, wampum, beads, and other trinkets. Their mantles were of fine scarlet cloth, and all was finery and dress. The canoes of the fur-traders were loaded with packs of beaver, the abundance of the article lowered the London prices. Every intelligent man saw the poverty that would follow the destruction of the beaver, but there were no chiefs to control it; all was perfect liberty and equality. Four years afterwards (1797) almost the whole of these extensive countries were denuded of beaver, the natives became poor, and with difficulty procured the first necessities of life, and in this state they remain, and probably forever. A worn out field may be manured, and again made fertile; but the beaver, once destroyed, cannot be replaced: they were the gold coin of the country, with which the necessaries of life were purchased.

> *Ibid.*, p. 255.

An important thing to note is that once the traditional ways had been changed, there was no returning to them. Change was irreversible.

Disease and alcohol demoralized and destroyed the Indians just when they needed all their energy and courage to cope with the new conditions that suddenly came into existence around them. The old order changed completely with the coming of Europeans. Stone tools and weapons gave place to tools and weapons of iron; cooking vessels of clay, skin, bark, and wood to metal pots;

the fire-stick to the flint and steel, and bows and arrows to firearms. Once a tribe had made these changes it could not revert to its former condition because it had lost most of its earlier skill in chipping knives and arrowheads of flint, in grinding out stone axes, and fashioning serviceable bows. Any withdrawal of the trading-posts upon which the Indians were now dependent would have caused endless hardships and widespread starvation. Firearms in particular could not fail to cause a complete revolution in a country so rich in game as Canada, for even with old muzzle-loading gun greatly simplified the food-quest. "With an arrow they killed only one Wild Goose; but with a shot of a gun they kill five or six of them. With the arrow it was necessary to approach an animal closely; with the gun they kill the animal from a distance with a bullet or two.

> *Ibid.*, p. 254.

> The following six selections are all extracts from the journals of fur traders. What evidence do they contain which supports the statements in the selection you have just read?

Friday, November 19, 1802, I have just returned from the lower fort, where I have been accompanied with part of my people, for goods. I find here a band of Indians, who have been waiting for my return, in order to procure such articles as they need, to enable them to make a fall hunt. The Indians in this quarter have been so long accustomed to use European goods, that it would be with difficulty that they could now obtain a livelihood, without them. Especially do they need fire arms, with which to kill their game, and axes, kettles, knives, &c. They have almost lost the use of bows and arrows; and they would find it nearly impossible to cut their wood with implements, made of stone or bone.

Thursday, December 25. Severe cold weather. This day being Christmas, our people have spent it as usual, in drinking and fighting. – My education has taught me, that the advent of a Saviour, ought to be celebrated in a far different manner. – Of all people in the world, I think the Canadians, when drunk, are the most disagreeable; for excessive drinking generally causes them to quarrel and fight, among themselves. Indeed, I had rather have fifty drunken Indians in the fort, than five drunken Canadians.

Daniel Harmon, *North-West Company* (1802), pp. 72-73.

... It is very probable, however, that the Indian doctors, like some apothecaries in the civilized world, sell some medicines, of little or no value. It is also well known to those acquainted with the Indians, that their physicians frequently effect cures with their roots, herbs, &c. in cases, which would baffle the skill and the drugs, of a scientifick physician.

The white people have been among the above mentioned tribes, for about one hundred and fifty years. To this circumstance it is probably to be attributed, that the knowledge of these Indians is more extensive, than that of the other tribes. But I very much question whether they have improved in their character or condition, by their acquaintance with civilized people. In their savage state, they were contented with the mere necessaries of life, which they could procure, with considerable ease; but now they have many artificial wants, created by the luxuries which we have introduced among them; and as they find it difficult to obtain these luxuries, they have become, to a degree, discontented with their condition, and practise fraud in their dealings. A half civilized Indian is more savage, than one in his original state. The latter has some sense of honour, while the former has none. I have always experienced the greatest hospitality and kindness among those Indians, who have had the least intercourse with white people. They readily discover and adopt our evil practices; but they are not as quick to discern, and as ready to follow the few good examples, which we set before them.

The Indians in general, are subject to few diseases. The venereal complaint is common to all the tribes of the north; many persons among them, die of a consumption; fevers, also, frequently attack them; and they are likewise troubled with pains in their heads, breasts and joints. Many of them, and especially the women, are subject to fits. For a relief, in nearly all of their diseases, they resort to their grand remedy, sweating.

Duncan Cameron, *North-West Company* (1804), pp. 270-271.

There are now eight Indians here, all drunk and very troublesome to my neighbour, who, I believe, is as drunk as themselves; they are all very civil to me, and so they may, for I am giving them plenty to drink, without getting anything from them as yet. They all take some credits from me and make very fair promises, but time alone will say whether they are sincere.

We are going pretty well with our building, but very poorly with the fishing, for we can hardly take what will make one meal a day, and I have already been obliged to give some flour to the men.

The Indians have lost all industry and are becoming careless about hunting and paying their credits, as they very well know that when one will refuse, another more extravagant will readily give. They now get a quantity of things so easily that they have grown quite extravagant and put no value on goods at all, supposing that, if those goods were so valuable, we would not so easily part with them, and begin to think that their skins are become so valuable that there is no possibility of satisfying them, for they will tell you that such a one offered them so and so, and that they expected you to give the same since you wanted skins.

It is now useless to tell them that those people only come to deceive them out of spite, against us, that they were all men we would not employ, that they would soon be pitiful and be obliged to leave the country, they answer that we told them so several years ago, but that instead of leaving the country they are getting more numerous every year, which would not be the case, if the few packs they made did not satisfy and pay them for all they gave for it. Although we always told them that those people were throwing away their goods to mislead the Indians, that, now, they begin to perceive that we were imposing upon them to get their skins for nothing as we did formerly, and render them poor and pitiful as they had always been till those charitable people came among them.

Notwithstanding all these complaints and arguments against us, we still get the three-fourths of the trade. But I am sorry to say that, even if there were no opposition at all in the country to spoil the trade, it is now getting so barren and poor that in a dozen years hence, the returns from it will be so trifling that, even if one company had the whole, on the cheapest terms, it will be little enough to pay the expenses of carrying on the business, for the hunt is declining very fast, and we are obliged every year to make new discoveries and settle new posts. Even with all that, we cannot keep the former average of returns, although the consummation of goods is increasing every year, and I believe that our discoveries are now about at an end, and that the trade cannot be extended much further than it is at present.

> Duncan Cameron, "The Nipigon Country" in L. R. Masson, ed., *Les Bourgeois de la Compagnie du Nord-Ouest* (New York: Antiquarian Press, 1960), pp. 294, 296, 297.

. . . he is supposed to be the most daring and intrepid Indian in this Department. He remained a considerable time in the Hall in a state of suspence revolving in his mind in what manner to proceed: at length he issued out in a transport of fury to make preparations for instant departure, threatening vengeance against me, but his relations flocking about him in numbers opposed his design and after many entreaties they persuaded him to relinquish it; – And next morning a general peace was concluded betwixt all parties, tho' this circumstance plainly shewed that he retained a lively sense of what had passed. – This discipline being the first instance of severity exhibited in this quarter has produced a very sensible effect in their manners – from being insolent and overbearing they are become entirely submissive and comport themselves with great circumspection to avoid giving offence: – they even deliver up their women to the unlawfull embraces of the men to purchase their lost favor – a custom hitherto held in some kind of dishonour among the tribe. – This treatment has also produced a wonderful alteration in their mode of trading. – I have seen one of this tribe employ a ½ hour in bartering a Dozen Wolves and twice as many *Depouilles*[1] and so unreasonable as to demand a Gun, Pistol, or any other article that attracted his attention for one Skin and yet seem but little disappointed on being offered 2 feet Tobacco for it. Now; they trade more expeditiously; accept whatever is given in return for their commodities with a good grace; and seem thankful and satisfied with any trifling present, tho' our usual liberality to them is greatly withdrawn. – During 3 days which they spent at the Fort was traded 16 Bales of 50 Wolves each, 800 lbs. Pounded meat with a sufficient quantity of Fat to employ twice as much, 20 Buffalo robes and 12 Bear Skins – a trade almost One half inferior to last year's, which shews that they had no inclination to hunt 'till a friendly intercourse with the Fort would be established. – The Inhabitants of the Plains are so advantageously situated that they could live very happily independent of our assistance. They are surrounded with innumerable herds of various kinds of animals, whose flesh affords them excellent nourishment and whose Skins defend them from the inclemency of the weather, and they have invented so many methods for the destruction of Animals, that they stand in no need of amunition to provide a sufficiency for these purposes. It is then our luxuries that attract them to the

[1] The fat on the ribs and back.

Fort and make us so necessary to their happiness. The love of Rum is their first inducement to industry; they undergo every hardship and fatigue to procure a Skinfull of this delicious beverage, and when a Nation becomes addicted to drinking, it affords a strong presumption that they will soon become excellent hunters. Tobacco is another article of as great demand as it is unnecessary. Custom has however made it of consequence to them as it constitutes a principal part of their feasts and Superstitious ceremonies, and in these treaties of peace and councils of War, a few whifs out of the medicine pipe confirms the articles that have been mutually agreed upon. As for amunition it is rendered valuable by the great advantage it gives them over their enemies in their expeditions to the Rocky Mountains against the defenceless Slave Indians who are destitute of this destructive improvement of War.

> A. S. Morton, ed., *Journal of Duncan M'Gillivray* (Toronto: Macmillan Co., 1929), pp. 46-47.

It has been remarked by those who first settled in the district, that the Indians are rapidly decreasing in numbers since their arrival – a fact which does not admit of a doubt: I myself have seen many villages and encampments without an inhabitant. But what can be the cause of it? Here there has been neither rum nor smallpox – the scourges of this doomed race in other parts. Yet, on the banks of the Columbia, which, when first visited by the whites a few years ago, literally swarmed with Indians, a disease broke out which nearly exterminated them. Has the fiat, then, gone forth, that the aboriginal inhabitants of America shall make way for another race of men? To my mind, at least, the question presents not the shadow of a doubt. The existence of the present race of Indians at some future, and by no means distant period, will only be known through the historical records of their successors.

The Indians to this day talk of their North-west "fathers" with regret. "Our old traders, our fathers, did not serve us so," is a remark I have frequently heard in every part of the country where the North-West Company had established posts. Had their rule been distinguished by oppression or injustice, the natives would rather have expressed their satisfaction at its suppression; had it been tyrannical or oppressive, it would not have been long tolerated. The natives in those times were numerous and warlike; the trading-posts were isolated and far apart; and in the summer season, when the managers proceeded to the dépôts, with the greater part of their people, were entirely at the mercy of the natives, who would not have failed to take advantage of such opportunities to avenge their wrongs, had they suffered any. The posts, in fact, were left entirely to their protection, and depended on them for support during the absence of the traders, who, on their return in autumn, found themselves surrounded by hundreds of rejoicing Indians, greeting their "fathers" with every manifestation of delight; – he who had not a gun to fire strained his lungs with shouting.

The native population has decreased at an extraordinary rate since those times. I do not mean to affirm that this decrease arises from the Hudson's Bay Company's treatment of them; but, from whatever cause arising, it is quite certain they have greatly decreased. Neither can it be denied, that the natives are no longer the manly, independent race they formerly were. On the contrary, we now find them gloomy and dispirited, unhappy and discontented.

As the country becomes impoverished, the Company reduce their outfits so as to ensure the same amount of profit, – an object utterly beyond their reach, although economy is pushed to the extreme of parsimony; and thus, while the game becomes scarcer, and the poor natives require more ammunition to procure their living, their means of obtaining it, instead of being increased, are lessened. As an instance of the effects of this policy, I shall mention what recently occurred in the Athabasca district.

Up to 1842 the transport of the outfit required four boats, when it was reduced to three. The reduction in the article of ammunition was felt so severely by the Chippewayans, that the poor creatures, in absolute despair, planned a conspiracy to carry off the gentleman at the head of affairs, and retain him until the Company should restore the usual outfit.

Despair alone could have suggested such an idea to the Chippewayans, for they have ever been the friends of the white man. Mr. Campbell, however, who had passed his life among them, conducted himself with so much firmness and judgment, that, although the natives had assembled in his hall with the intention of carrying their design into execution, the affair passed over without any violence being attempted.

The general outfit for the whole northern department amounted in 1835, to 31,000*l.*;[1] now (1845) it is reduced to 15,000*l.*, of which one-third at least is absorbed by the stores at Red River settlement, and a considerable portion of the remainder by the officers and servants of the Company throughout the country. I do not believe that more than one half of the outfit goes to the Indians.

While the resources of the country are thus becoming yearly more and more exhausted, the question naturally suggests itself, What is to become of the natives when their lands can no longer furnish the means of subsistence? . . . People of Britain! the Red Men of America thus appeal to you; – from the depths of their forest they send forth their cry –

"Brethren! beyond the Great Salt Lake, we, the Red Men of America salute you:–

"Brethren!

"We hear that you are a great and a generous people; that you are as valiant as generous; and that you freely shed your blood and scatter your gold in defence of the weak and oppressed; if it be so, you will open your ears to our plaints.

"Brethren! Our ancients still remember when the Red Men were numerous and happy; they remember the time when our lands abounded with game; when the young men went forth to the chase with glad hearts and vigorous limbs, and never returned empty; in those days our camps resounded with mirth and merriment; our youth danced and enjoyed themselves; they anointed their bodies with fat; the sun never set on a foodless wigwam, and want was unknown.

"Brethren! When your kinsmen came first to us with guns, and ammunition, and other good things the work of your hands, we were glad and received them joyfully; our lands were then rich, and yielded with little toil both furs and provisions to exchange for the good things they brought us.

"Brethren! Your kinsmen are still amongst us; they still bring us goods,

[1] Pounds sterling.

and now we cannot want them; without guns and ammunition we must die. Brethren! our fathers were urged by the white men to hunt; our fathers listened to them; they ranged wood and plain to gratify their wishes; and now our lands are ruined, our children perish with hunger.

"Brethren! We hear that you have another Great Chief who rules over you, to whom even our great trading Chief must bow; we hear that this great and good Chief desires the welfare of all his children; we hear that to him the white man and the red are alike, and, wonderful to be told! that he asks neither furs nor game in return for his bounty. Brethren! we feel that we can no longer exist as once we did; we implore your Great Chief to shield us in our present distress; we desire to be placed under his immediate care, and to be delivered from the rule of the trading Chief who only wants our furs, and cares nothing for our welfare.

"Brethren! Some of your kinsmen visited us lately; they asked neither our furs nor our flesh; their sojourn was short; but we could see they were good men; they advised us for our good, and we listened to them. Brethren! We humbly beseech your Great Chief that he would send some of those good men to live amongst us: we desire to be taught to worship the Great Spirit in the way most pleasing to him: without teachers among us we cannot learn. We wish to be taught to till the ground, to sow and plant, and to perform whatever the good white people counsel us to do to preserve the lives of our children.

"Brethren! We could say much more, but we have said enough, – we wish not to weary you.

"Brethren! We are all the children of the Great Spirit; the red man and the white man were formed by him. And although we are still in darkness and misery, we know that all good flows from him. May he turn your hearts to pity the distress of your Red Brethren! Thus have we spoken to you."

Such are the groans of the Indians.

> W. S. Wallace, ed., *John McLean Notes of a Twenty-five Years Service in the Hudson's Bay Territory* (Toronto: The Champlain Society, 1932), pp. 79, 325, 326, 354-357.

Samuel Hearne, Hudson's Bay Company, 1769-72

In my opinion, there cannot exist stronger proof that mankind was not created to enjoy happiness than the conduct of the miserable wretches who inhabit this part of the world, for few of the Northern Indians, except the aged and infirm, or those who are indolent or unambitious, will any longer submit to remaining in the parts where food and clothing are procured in the easy manner of impounding deer; for the reason that they get no fur for trade, and therefore cannot purchase what they will.

What then, do the industrious gatherers of fur gain for their trouble? The real wants of these people are few and easily supplied. A hatchet, ice-chisel, file and knife are all that is required to enable them to procure a comfortable livelihood. Those of them who endeavour to possess more are always the most unhappy and may, in fact, be said to be only slaves and carriers to the rest, whose ambition does not lead them beyond the need of procuring food and clothing for themselves.

It is true that the more industrious Indians who carry the furs gathered by themselves and other Indians to the Factory, pride themselves upon the respect which we show them at the Fort. Yet to gain this respect they frequently run great risks of being starved to death in their way thither and back. Furthermore, all that they can possibly get from their year's journeying and toil seldom amounts to more than is sufficient to yield a bare subsistence; while those Indians whom we call indolent, live in a state of plenty, without trouble and risk, and consequently must be the most happy, and the most independent also. Indeed those who take no concern about gathering furs, generally have an opportunity of providing themselves with the trade goods they require by exchanging for provisions and ready-dressed skins with their more industrious countrymen.

It is undoubtedly the duty of every one of the Company's servants to encourage a spirit of industry among the natives, and to use every means in their power to induce them to procure furs; and I can truly say that this has ever been the grand object of my attention. But at the same time I must confess that such conduct is by no means for the real benefit of the poor Indians, it being well known that those who have the least intercourse with the Factories are by far the happiest. . . .

At the time this journal was written, the peace with the Southern Indians had redounded greatly to the advantage of our Northern Indians, and of the Company. The good effect of this harmony increased the trade from that quarter to the amount of eleven thousand Made Beaver per annum. In addition to the advantage which arose to the Company, the Northern Indians reaped innumerable benefits from having access to the fine and plentiful country of the Athapuscow Indians.

However, though it is no part of the record of my journey, I must here carry forward in time and interject a tragic addition to the account of the ultimate results of the peace between the Northern and the Southern Indians.

Some years after my journey was concluded, the Northern Indians, by visiting their Southern friends, contracted the smallpox from them. In a few years this disease carried off nine-tenths of them; and particularly those who composed the trade at Churchill Factory. The few survivors afterwards followed the example of the Athapuscow tribe, and traded with the Canadians who were then becoming established in the country of those Indians.

Thus it is that a very few years have proved my short-sightedness; for it would really have been much more to the advantage of the Company, as well as having prevented the depopulation of the Northern Indian country, if they had still remained at war with the Southern Indians. At the same time it is impossible now to say what increase in trade might not have risen in time from a constant and regular traffic with the Copper and Dog-ribbed peoples. But these, having been cut off from our Factory by the decimation of the Northern Indians, soon sank into their original barbarism, and a war ensued between the two tribes for the sake of a few remnants of iron-work that was left amongst them; with the result that almost the whole Copper Indian race was destroyed.

Farley Mowat, *Coppermine Journey* (Toronto: McClelland and Stewart Ltd., 1958), pp. 43-44, 90-91.

Evidence from the Indians themselves is not so abundant. Since they had no written language, they were not able to set down their observations and thoughts. But there is some evidence; first in records of fur traders and others who reported what Indians said; and, second; in the stories passed down by word of mouth among the Indians themselves.

David Thompson recorded this story, told by an old chief of the Piegan Indians, about an attack by Piegan warriors on a camp of Snake Indians with whom they were at war.

At the dawn of day, we attacked the tents, and with our daggers and knives, cut through the tents and entered for the fight; but our war whoop instantly stopt, our eyes were appalled with terror; there was no one to fight with but the dead and dying, each a mass of corruption. We did not touch them, but left the tents, and held a council on what was to be done. We all thought the Bad Spirit had made himself master of the camp and destroyed them. It was agreed to take some of the best of the tents, and any other plunder that was clean and good, which we did, and also took away the few horses they had, and returned to our camp.

The second day after this dreadful disease broke out in our camp, and spread from one tent to another as if the Bad Spirit carried it. We had no belief that one Man could give it to another, any more than a wounded man could give his wound to another. We did not suffer so much as those that were near the river, into which they rushed and died. We had only a little brook, and about one third of us died, but in some of the other camps there were tents in which everyone died.

When at length it left us, and we moved about to find our people, it was no longer with the song and the dance; but with tears, shrieks and howlings of despair for those who would never return to us. War was no longer thought of, and we had enough to do to hunt and make provision for our families, for in our sickness we had consumed all our dried provisions . . .

Our hearts were low and dejected, and we shall never be again the same people . . .

R. Glover, ed., *David Thompson's Narrative, 1784-1812* (Toronto: The Champlain Society, 1962), p. 246.

1. What does this story tell us about vulnerability of the Indians to smallpox?
2. Smallpox epidemics were recurrent. What do you thing the long-term effects on the Indians would be?

The desolation of the survivors of smallpox is expressed in a story told by the Kootenay Indians.

I will tell the story of what happened long ago. The Kootenays were living together. Once they fell sick, sickness spread to everyone. They died, they all

died, all but a very few. And it was everywhere the same. Those who were
left travelled to tell the news, they travelled without finding anyone alive. At a
village far away the Kootenays had died. The only one left was a man. He was
alone. So he also decided to travel and look for people: 'I must go all around
the world,' he said. Then he started in his canoe around the lakes. Now he
landed at a camp of the Kootenays, their last camp. But there was nobody. As
he went about he saw only dead ones, the bodies piled up inside the tents. No
sign of any one living. He cried and went back to his canoe, thinking to himself, 'I am the only one left in this country, for the dogs also are dead . . .' "

> Marius Barbeau, *Indian Days on the Western Prairies*, Bulletin No.
> 163, Anthropological Series No. 46 (Ottawa: National Museum of
> Canada, 1960), p. 42.

An Indian view of two other elements of European culture first
brought by the fur traders – metals tools and hard liquor – is to
be found in the following stories.

The tale of Big-Raven

The rumour for a long, long time was that things would soon be different, that
the world would be made easy to live in. Chief Maloolek (Walking-Skeleton)
became very excited when he heard that the change was about to come. He
gave up work – he would hunt no more. His nephews left him sitting at the
back of the house, waiting for the change to come, while they themselves
resorted as usual to the far distant hunting grounds in the mountain passes
to the east. The hunters knew that the chief was lazy, so they only laughed at
him.

While most of the people were away, some Indians of a neighbouring tribe
came over; they came to Maloolek's village; not only that, but to his own
house. He was still there waiting for the things that would make life and the
world easy. He awaited the coming of the White Man for five years, sitting
without working, without hunting. As he spied the strangers at long last, he
put on his dancing-robe, sang and danced to welcome them. He knew that the
moment had come and his heart was glad. While singing his song, 'Who am I
to fight with?' he waved his stone axe in the air and threw it away on the
dump heap.

The strangers had an iron axe to trade. This was the purpose of their visit.
But the axe was so precious that they would not unwrap it yet. Maloolek invited
them and the few people left in the village to a feast. The guests were to witness
the ceremony of unwrapping what was to make life easy ever after. When
finally the axe was unwrapped, the people looked at it as if it had been a
manitou; they looked at it for a long while. Then one of the Indian strangers
invited Maloolek and the other people to follow him outside, to learn the
magic power of the axe.

The holder of the axe selected a small poplar to his own liking and asked
the people to stand around at some distance; but he was not yet ready for the
ceremony. The old men, the old women, and the cripples leaning on their
sticks had plenty of time to gather round the ring. Word then passed round,
'He will hit it five times and it shall fall.' Those who had faith in the tool

echoed, 'Yes, it shall fall.' But this seemed incredible, as the people always had to chop a tree all around like beavers, for ever so long, with their stone axe. The incredulous ones insisted, 'No, he will have to hit it ten times, twenty times, and then, maybe, it will not fall.' They stood there looking and discussing, almost coming to blows among themselves, until the holder of the axe feared bloodshed. He grew excited, raised the axe, and brought it down upon the poplar. Four times only, twice on each side, he hit the tree, and it fell down upon some women before they had time to move. Shouts of joy greeted the event. Maloolek now traded for the (iron) axe, and the strangers left with huge packs of moose hides and other furs.

Now then, there were only two trails leading in and out of the village, one named "the Moving Trail," and the other, "The Travelling-Trail." Both were used by the hunters. Maloolek started out with his new iron axe, all by himself, and he chopped trees down, chopped trees down all along the trail just in sight of the village on both sides. The chips he gathered in heaps, in the middle of the footpath, and the ends of the trees he dragged across the trail.

When the absent hunters arrived on the spot they were thunderstruck; they "fell dead" with surprise. "Look at it all," they exclaimed; "what was to make life and the world easy has come in our absence!" They stayed there gazing at the chips and the trees; they could not move; they could not leave those chips and those trees. They camped right there, awaiting for the other hunters to return, also to be thunderstruck in their turn.

The next day the hunters moved in a body into the village. It was Maloolek's turn to laugh at them, and the people thought it was a great joke. They asked, "What were you doing along the trail last night? What kind of men were you, not to be able to end the journey when you were just in sight of your very houses?"

Here is how the first appearance of two white hunters – possibly French coureurs-des-bois or half-breeds – had been remembered at Hiding-in-Mountain village, to the north of the Big Bend of the Columbia River.

This took place long ago, in the mountains. Two hunters of our own tribe were travelling along the trails, in the passes. The name of one was Rain-drop, and of the other, Cloven-hoof. As they were preparing to ford a deep creek, two men unlike anybody else approached them. 'These are People from the Sky,' they thought to themselves. But they could not move away; their legs were as if stiffened by the cold. Rain-drop said, 'I will kill them'. Cloven-hoof retorted, 'Beware! it means disaster for us!' They had only hafted stone axes in their hands. When they saw that the ghost-like strangers were not afraid but drew nearer, they thought, 'We cannot do anything, we cannot help ourselves.'

One of the two men – they were white like peeled logs – took a cup and a crystal-like bottle from his pocket and poured out a drink. Rain-drop was too frightened to try the cup. So was Cloven-hoof. The white man then swallowed a mouthful himself. 'If he can drink it,' thought Cloven-hoof, 'it may not be hurtful.' Rain-drop's idea was, 'If we drink it, we may become as white as they are. We may get the power of spirits.' Now they were both willing. Rain-drop took the cup first. Then it was his friend's turn. They found it good, very good, much better than anything they had ever known. After one cupful, an-

another. They felt jolly. 'We will turn into white beings from the sky.' The change was so wonderful that they clamoured for more. They sat down to rest and fell into a stupor. When they knew no more, the white men departed.

They must have stayed there a long while, a day or more. Their limbs were stiff and cold and their stomachs sick when they came to. Rain-drop was the first to stand up. What he did was to look at one of his hands. It was not white, but the same shade as before. The other hand was not different. He had not had enough to drink. The change had only begun. Cloven-hoof was sick when he came to. He fell to sleep again, and when he awoke his friend was gone. 'It is all very strange,' he said; 'Rain-drop is surely gone to the sky, and I am left alone here. I did not get enough to drink; that is the whole trouble. He was disappointed to find the shade of his skin unchanged. After crawling a short distance, he found his friend asleep on the trail. 'He stopped only half-way,' he thought; 'not enough drink!' And he also lay down to sleep again.

Before a few days had passed, they were much disappointed. The change had left nothing but regret to them. When they reached home and told their experience, the old men laughed and said, 'You fools! These were not ghosts, but white men.'

> *Ibid.*, p. 7.

1. In these stories what do the Indians seem to expect from their contact with the White Man?

2. Explain the ideas held by the Indians that led them to these expectations. How are these ideas different from those of white men?

3. Read the story which follows.
   a) Explain how it shows the difference between the ideas and beliefs of Indians and those of white men.
   b) List some effects on Indians of their introduction to Christian ideas as these are suggested by the story.

Hector Crawler: Early Whites and Preachers (informant: Daniel Wildman, his nephew)

I remember well the old days, an old man named Kahotadohan (Face-Anything). He was a big medicine-man, about eighty years ago, a Stony. In those days the Stonies lived on the Saskatchewan (Wapthamnoza: River-Boiling). This old man, in the early days, had with him a big tribe of Stonies. He said that he had a spirit, and he could talk to the eagles as they were flying in the air. He could see or hear ahead what was going to be. So all the Indians depended on him. His prophecies always came true. He was like that all his life.

One fall, he told the Indians, "These things my spirits tell me, that there is going to be the greatest news ever heard in the Indian history. The Spirit told me there is one who owns the moon and stars, all the creation on earth. There is one God who owns all these things. He is the Spirit of the white man. He is going to come next summer, some time next summer." At that time the white man had never been seen here. But the Indians had heard of the Hudson's Bay (Company). Yet they had not seen any of the Hudson's Bay (traders).

When the winter was over, young fellows went in canoes down the Saskatchewan River. They travelled east. They went a little ways and found men who had hair on their faces [beards]. So they ran away, believing them to be men eaters. One of those white men laughed at them and told them to come forward. They started to talk in signs to one another. Then they found out these men had something like water in a little barrel. They offered a drink to these young Indian fellows, who were afraid it might be bad medicine to kill them. One of the young braves tried it. He said the water was just like fire. Another fellow tried it too. And they all tried it, after a while. And they felt a different spirit. By and by they rejoiced and were happy, the happiest they had ever been. Then they went back home, believing that the spirit of the white men had come. And they told the medicine-man about it, 'Oh,' he said, 'I heard of this water before. The Indians have told me,' And he added, 'This is not the Spirit men.'

They all moved toward the white men. These were Hudson's Bay folk. They had been told that the spirit white man would come about the middle of the summer. And in the middle of the summer, the white man really arrived. Their leader was a middle-sized man, fair faced. He started to tell the people about the Great Spirit. He asked the Indians to come to one place to the biggest tent there was. All the eldest assembled in the medicine lodge, where they had bear-heads and images mounted, numerous things like that, and birds. They painted their faces; some were in war costume. The spirit white man faced them. "What are these images for?" they asked. They answered: "Those are our spirit images, they are gods." And their medicine-man tried to explain in the best way he could.

The white man [a preacher] had a half-breed interpreter. He told the Indians, "Make a big fire and burn all these images." They were surprised. "How could we do that? Ask him if he has got a god that possesses more power than these gods." The spirit man [preacher] said, "These images are only animal heads. If you die with them, you never go to another country [above]." They talked together but could not understand one another. He [the preacher] tried to explain, "All your relatives who have died, they have gone to another place." This they understood and firmly believed.

These were the first Stonies who met a white man's [missionary] on the western prairies. He was a Presbyterian preacher. Ever since, the Methodists, Presbyterians, and Catholics have tried to explain to the Prairie Indians about religion. They, the Indians, laughed at them. They said, "They are trying to get us into the corral. They put us down as babies. They are trying to tell us that the fire water is wrong. How is that – the happiest thing they have brought to us! They try to keep down all the happiness of life. They are greedy; they tell us to have only one wife. And see, some of us have ten wives. They fear the Indians, because they have lots of horses. Big feeling! Everybody is afraid of the chief, because he is big. I think the white people are jealous of him, so they talk like that."

Ever since the preacher came to the Stonies, they never want to fight, because the elders tell the young fellows not to do any harm to anybody. But many a time the young fellows don't pay any attention. They want to kill a Blackfoot, a Cree, or a Piegan. But Stonies would not fight the Sarcee. They are the best of friends; yet they cannot speak each other's language; they cannot understand each other. They use the Cree language – broken Cree. Still they cannot understand the Cree people.

Ibid., pp. 100-102.

Settlers

One page of entries in the Canadian government's list of Indian treaties and land surrenders tells an interesting story.

TREATY No. 1 –
3rd Aug., 1871. By Chippewa and Cree Indians. Part of Manitoba. To Wemyss M. Simpson.
23rd Aug., 1875. Adhesion and amendment by Chippewa and Cree Indians.
23rd-28th Aug., 1875. Adhesion and amendment by Chippewa and Cree Indians.
8th Sep., 1875. Adhesion and amendment by Chipewa and Cree Indians.

TREATY No. 2 –
21st Aug., 1871. By Chippewa Indians. Parts of Manitoba and Assiniboia District. To Wemyss M. Simpson.
23rd Aug., 1875. Adhesion and amendment by Chippewa Indians.
23rd-28th Aug., 1875. Adhesion and amendment by Chippewa Indians.
8th Sep., 1875. Adhesion and amendment by Chippewa Indians.

TREATY No. 3 –
3rd Oct., 1873. By Saulteaux or Chippewa Indians. Part of Manitoba and Thunder Bay, Rainy River and Keewatin Districts. To Lt. Gov. Morris.
13th Oct., 1873. Adhesion by Saulteaux or Chippewa Indians.
9th June, 1874. Adhesion by Saulteaux or Chippewa Indians.
12th Sep., 1875. Adhesion by Half-breeds of Rainy River and Lake, Rainy River District.

TREATY No. 4 –
15th Sep., 1874. By Cree and Saulteaux or Chippewa Indians. Part of Manitoba and Assiniboia and Saskatchewan Districts. To Lt. Gov. Morris.
21st Sep., 1874. Adhesion by Saulteaux or Chippewa Indians.
8th Sep., 1875. Adhesion by Cree, Saulteaux or Chippewa and Stony Indians.
9th Sep., 1875. Adhesion by Cree, Saulteaux or Chippewa and Stony Indians.
24th Sep., 1875. Adhesion by Cree and Saulteaux or Chippewa Indians.
24th Aug., 1876. Adhesion by Saulteaux or Chippewa Indians.
25th Sep., 1877. Adhesion by Stony Indians.

TREATY No. 5 –
20th-24th Sep. 1875. By Saulteaux or Chippewa and Cree Indians. Parts of Manitoba and Keewatin and Saskatchewan Districts. To Lt. Gov. Morris.
27th Sep., 1875. Adhesion by Saulteaux or Chippewa Indians.
28th Sep., 1875. Adhesion by Saulteaux or Chippewa Indians.
26th July, 1876. Adhesion by Saulteaux or Chippewa Indians.
4th Aug., 1876. Adhesion by Saulteaux or Chippewa Indians.
7th Sep., 1876. Adhesion by Saulteaux or Chippewa Indians.
7th Sep., 1876. Adhesion by Saulteaux or Chippewa and Cree Indians.

TREATY No. 6 –
23rd-28th Aug., and 9th Sep., 1876. By Cree Indians. Parts of Saskatchewan, Assiniboia and Alberta Districts, N.W.T. To Lt. Gov. Morris.

9th Aug., 1877. Adhesion by Cree Indians.
25th Sep., 1877. Adhesion by Cree Indians.
19th Aug., 1878. Adhesion by Cree Indians.
3rd Sep., 1878. Adhesion by Cree Indians.
18th Sep., 1878. Adhesion by Cree Indians.
2nd July, 1879. Adhesion by Cree Indians.
8th Dec., 1882. Adhesion by Cree Indians.
11th Feb., 1889. Adhesion by Cree Indians, including also 11,066 square miles
   north of Treaty No. 6.

TREATY No. 7 –

22nd Sep., and 4th Dec., 1877. By Blackfoot, Peigan, Carcee and Stony Indians.
   Parts of Assiniboia and Alberta Districts, N.W.T.

Indian Treaties and Surrenders, pp. lix-lx.

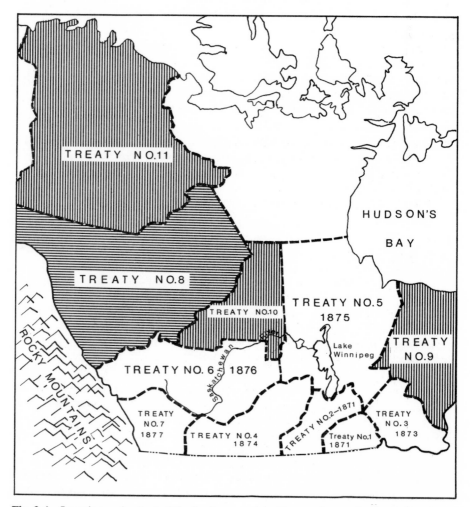

Fig. 2-4 Location and extent of the lands surrendered by treaties on the list (1-7)
and, in addition, Treaties 8, 9, 10, 11.

1. How many years elapsed between the signing of Treaty No. 1 and Treaty No. 7? Comment on the time taken for the transfer of the lands.

2. Which of Canada's provinces are comprised mainly of lands surrendered in Treaties 1 to 7?

These treaties represent a rapid and massive transfer of land. A question that arises is: Why did the Indians enter into these treaties? Before attempting to answer this question, consult references on Canadian history to find why the Canadian government and people wished to acquire this land. (What were John A. MacDonald's ambitions for the young dominion? What steps had his government taken to achieve these ambitions? What threats were there to these ambitions? Was there need for rapid action by the government of Canada?)

One reason why the Indians entered into the treaties may be found by considering the effects on them of the fur trade.

1. How had the Indian way of life been changed by contact with fur trade?

2. What effects had exposure to smallpox and other diseases had on the Indians?

3. Summarize the effects of the contact on the morale of the Indians up to the time the treaties were signed.

4. How are all these changes related to the making of the treaties?

Some further clues may be gained from a letter written in July, 1871, by Governor Archibald to the Honorable Joseph Howe, at this time Secretary of State for the Provinces in the federal government. Archibald is reporting on the negotiations which led shortly afterwards to the signing of Treaties 1 and 2.

LOWER FORT GARRY, July 29th, 1871.

SIR – I have the honor to inform you that on Monday last I came to this fort with the Commissioner to meet the Indians called here with the view to negotiate a treaty, intending to open the business on Tuesday morning.

It appeared, however, on enquiry, that some bands of Indians had not arrived on Tuesday morning, and we were therefore obliged to postpone the opening of the meeting till Thursday. On that day, the Indians from all the sections of the country to which the invitation extended were found present, to the number of about one thousand. A considerable body of half breeds, and other inhabitants of the country, were also present, awaiting with some anxiety to learn what should be announced as the policy of the Government.

I enclose you a memorandum of the observations with which I opened the meeting. On reading them, you will observe one or two points which may require some explanation.

At the time of the treaty with Earl Selkirk, certain Indians signed as chiefs and representatives of their people. Some of the Indians now deny that these men ever were chiefs, or had authority to sign the treaty.

With a view, therefore, to avoid a recurrence of any such question, we asked the Indians, as a first step, to agree among themselves in selecting their chiefs, and then to present them to us, and have their names and authority recorded.

Furthermore, the Indians seem to have false ideas of the meaning of a reserve. They have been led to suppose that large tracts of ground were to be set aside for them as hunting grounds, including timber lands, of which they might sell the wood as if they were proprietors of the soil.

I wished to correct this idea at the outset.

Mr. Simpson followed me with some observations in the same strain, after which the Indians retired to select their chiefs and spokesmen.

On Friday morning, the chiefs and spokesmen were duly presented, and, after their names were recorded, the Indians were invited to express their views. . . .

A general acquiescence in the views laid down by Mr. Simpson and myself was expressed; but it was quite clear by the proceedings of today that our views were imperfectly apprehended. When we met this morning, the Indians were invited to state their wishes as to the reserves; they were to say how much they thought would be sufficient, and whether they wished them all in one or in several places.

In defining the limits of their reserves, so far as we could see, they wished to have about two-thirds of the Province. We heard them out, and then told them it was quite clear that they had entirely misunderstood the meaning and intention of reserves.

We explained the object of these in something like the language of the memorandum enclosed, and then told them it was of no use for them to entertain any such ideas, which were entirely out of the question. We told them that whether they wished it or not, immigrants would come in and fill up the country; that every year from this one twice as many in number as their whole people there assembled would pour into the Province, and in a little while would spread all over it, and that now was the time for them to come to an arrangement that would secure homes and annuities for themselves and their children.

We told them what we proposed to allow them was an extent of one hundred and sixty acres for each family of five, or in that proportion; that they might have their land where they chose, not interfering with existing occupants; that we should allow an annuity of twelve dollars for every family of five, or in that proportion per head. We requested them to think over these propositions till Monday morning.

If they thought it better to have no treaty at all they might do without one, but they must make up their minds; if there was to be a treaty it must be on a basis like that offered.

That, under some such arrangements, the Indians in the east were living happy and contented, enjoying themselves, drawing their annuities, and satisfied with their position.

The observations seemed to command the acquiescence of the majority, and on Monday morning we hope to meet them in a better frame for the discussion and settlement of the treaty.

I have, etc.,

ADAMS G. ARCHIBALD.

The Honorable the Secretary of State
   for the Provinces.

                  Alexander Begg, *History of the North-West*, Vol. II (Toronto: Hunter Rose & Co., 1894), pp. 48-50.

1. What evidence is there in this letter to suggest that the Indians were not fully clear about what they were involved in?

2. If the letter presents a true account of the discussion, what can we say about the negotiations? Were both sides equally free to make decisions or not to make them? Give examples from the text of the letter to support your conclusion.

3. What were the attitudes of Archibald and Simpson in the negotiations?

4. If this bargaining procedure was typical, what inferences can you draw as to why the Indians signed the treaties?

5. Evaluate the argument put forward by Archibald and Simpson about the conditions of the Indians in the east after you have read the following extracts from official reports of officials at about this time.

NOVA SCOTIA,
INDIAN DISTRICT NO. 1,
BEAR RIVER, 20th November, 1876.

The Honorable
   The Superintendent-General of Indian Affairs,
Ottawa.

SIR, – I have the honor, as Indian Agent for District No. 1, N.S., to submit for your information the following Report of the state of the Indians and the Reserves within this Agency.

The population I believe to be gradually on the decrease. I account for this by the careless and exposed manner in which they live; in fact, their habits generally have a tendency to make them weakly and short-lived.

The last year has been very hard on the Indians here; they have not been able to obtain more than half of the former price of their porpoise oil, and the game laws greatly interfere with their hunting. I think it unjust to deprive the Indians from hunting wild game . . .

I find a growing desire among many to settle down and give up their roaming habits. They often say to me, "Give me a deed of my lot and I will have some courage to work;" this would do in some cases, but in the majority of instances it would not do, as they would very soon, by their foolish trading, be deprived of their land entirely.

> I have the honor to be, Sir,
> Your obedient servant,
> JOHN HARLOW,
> *Indian Agent.*

> NOVA SCOTIA,
> DISTRICT No. 5,
> POMQUET, ANTIGONISH,
> 9th, August, 1876.

The Honorable
    The Superintendent-General of Indian Affairs,
Ottawa.

SIR, – In compliance with the request of the Department, I beg to transmit the following report of the Indians of this District.

It can be seen by the Tabular Statement that no marked change in the status of Indians of this Agency has taken place since the last Report. A number of deaths occurred last winter which diminished their number by two.

Our poor Indians here are at best a thriftless and improvident class of people. With little or no care to provide for the future, many are at times reduced to extreme want. This happens especially during long-continued storms and deep snows in winter, which prevent them from going about to dispose of their handiwork.

Of late years there has been a very perceptible improvement among them with regard to temperance. With very few exceptions they are of sober habits. Many of them are teetotallers.

Cases of gross immoralities are of rare occurrence among them.

They have a thorough and hearty aversion to work their land. The men during the winter months and part of the summer are occupied in making firkins and butter tubs, the women in making baskets and fancy bead-work.

The $150 received from the Department each spring is expended, not alone in seed, but also in paying to plow and manure the land to put the seed in. Out of the blanket money in the Fall I reserve small sums for the occasional relief of the aged and infirm members of the Band.

> All of which I respectfully submit,
> WM. CHISHOLM, P.P.,
> *Indian Agent.*

> ONTARIO,
> NORTHERN SUPT. 3RD DIVISION.
> SAULT STE. MARIE, 26th Sept., 1876.

The Honorable
    The Superintendent-General of Indian Affairs,
Ottawa.

SIR, – I have the honor to enclose herewith statistics for the year ended June 30th, 1876, as required by your circulars of 3rd July last.

And I also beg to report as follows: That during the past winter a great deal of sickness prevailed among the Indians of the Augustin and the Nubenaigooching Bands, residing on the Garden River Indian Reserve, and in several instances I regret to say terminated fatally.

The complicated form of the disease from which they suffered, became epidemical, and its severity was much intensified by the want of proper nourishment.

Great want during the winter prevailed generally on the Garden River Reserve.

Owing to the saw mill of Messrs. McRae, Craig & Co. not having worked, there was little or no employment for the Indians on the Garden River Reserve. A few obtained employment in taking out cordwood on the American side, where it can be brought to the shore for sale considerably cheaper, than when cut on the Garden River Reserve, owing to the dues and charges for licenses, and the distance it has to be drawn to the shore . . .

The prospect of the potato crop this year is very favorable, though the market value will not be as high as former years. Hay is likely to be scarce, the unusual height of the water on Bush Lake and River having flooded nearly all the marsh lands.

The attendance at the schools, I am sorry to say, is not so large as might be wished; the teachers complain of the difficulty in getting the parents to insist on the regular attendance of their children.

Only two instances have occurred in which persons have been convicted and fined for selling alcoholic liquor to the Indians.

I am happy to say that there seems this year to have sprung up among the Indians a seemingly stronger inclination towards agricultural pursuits.

> I have the honor to be, Sir,
> Your obedient servant,
> WM. VAN ABBOTT,
> *Indian Lands Agent.*

Indian Affairs, 1875-79, pp. 21, 26, 28.

Treaty I

Articles of a Treaty made and concluded this third day of August, in the year of Our Lord one thousand eight hundred and seventy-one, between Her Most Gracious Majesty the Queen of Great Britain and Ireland by Her Commissioner, Wemyss M. Simpson, Esquire, of the one part, and the Chippewa and Swampy Cree Tribes of Indians, inhabitants of the country within the limits hereinafter defined and described, by their Chiefs chosen and named as hereinafter mentioned, of the other part.

Whereas all the Indians inhabiting the said country have pursuant to an appointment made by the said Commissioner, been convened at a meeting at the Stone Fort otherwise called Lower Fort Garry, to deliberate upon certain matters of interest to Her Most Gracious Majesty, of the one part, and to the said Indians of the other, and whereas the said Indians have been notified and informed by Her Majesty's said Commissioner that it is the desire of Her Majesty to open up to settlement and immigration a tract of country bounded and described as hereinafter mentioned, and to obtain the consent thereto of her Indian subjects inhabiting the said tract, and to make a treaty and arrangements with them so that there may be peace and good will between them and Her Majesty, and that they may know and be assured of what allowance they are to count upon and receive year by year from Her Majesty's bounty and benevolence.

And whereas the Indians of the said tract, duly convened in council as aforesaid, and being requested by Her Majesty's said Commissioner to name certain Chiefs and Headmen who should be authorized on their behalf to conduct such negotiations and sign any treaty to be founded thereon, and to become responsible to Her Majesty for the faithful performance by their respective bands of such obligations as should be assumed by them, the said Indians have thereupon named the following persons for that purpose, that is to say:—

Mis-koo-kenew or Red Eagle (Henry Prince), Ka-ke-ka-penais, or Bird for ever, Na-sha-ke-penais, or Flying down bird, Na-na-wa-nanaw, or Centre of Bird's Tail, Ke-we-tayash, or Flying round, Wa-ko-wush, or Whip-poor-will, Oo-za-we-kwun, or Yellow Qaill, — and thereupon in open council the different bands have presented their respective Chiefs to His Excellency the Lieutenant Governor of the Province of Manitoba and of the North-West Territory being present at such council, and to the said Commissioner, as the Chiefs and Headman for the purposes aforesaid of the respective bands of Indians inhabiting the said district hereinafter described; and whereas the said Lieutenant Governor and the said Commissioner then and there received and acknowledged the persons so presented as Chiefs and Headmen for the purpose aforesaid; and whereas the said Commissioner has proceeded to negotiate a treaty with the said Indians, and the same has finally been agreed upon and concluded as follows, that is to say:—

The Chippewa and Swampy Cree Tribes of Indians and all other the Indians inhabiting the district hereinafter described and defined do hereby cede, release, surrender and yield up to Her Majesty the Queen and successors forever all the lands included within the following limits, that is to say:—

Beginning at the international boundary line near its junction with the Lake of the Woods, at a point due north from the centre of Roseau Lake; thence to run due north to the centre of Roseau Lake; thence northward to the centre of White Mouth Lake, otherwise called White Mud Lake; thence by the middle of the lake and the middle of the river issuing therefrom to the mouth thereof in Winnipeg River; thence by the Winnipeg River to its mouth; thence westwardly, including all the islands near the south end of the lake, across the lake to the mouth of Drunken River; thence westwardly to a point on Lake Manitoba half way between Oak Point and the mouth of Swan Creek; thence across Lake Manitoba in a line due west to its western shore; thence in a straight line to the crossing of the rapids on the Assiniboine; thence due south to the international boundary line; and thence eastwardly by the said line to the place of beginning. To have and to hold the same to Her Majesty the Queen and Her successors for ever; and Her Majesty the Queen hereby agrees and undertakes to lay aside and reserve for the sole and exclusive use of the Indians the following tracts of land, that is to say: For the use of the Indians belonging to the band of which Henry Prince, otherwise called Mis-koo-ke-new is the Chief, so much of land on both sides of the Red River, beginning at the south line of St. Peter's Parish, as will furnish one hundred and sixty acres for each family of five, or in that proportion for larger or smaller families; and for the use of the Indians of whom Na-sha-ke-penais, Na-na-wa-nanaw, Ke-we-tayash and Wa-ko-wush are the Chiefs, so much land on the Roseau River as will furnish one hundred and sixty acres for each family of five, or in that proportion for larger or smaller families, beginning from the mouth of the river; and for the use of the Indians of which Ka-ke-ka-penais is the Chief, so much land on the Winnipeg River above Fort Alexander as will furnish one hundred and sixty acres for each family of five, or in that proportion for larger or smaller families, beginning at a distance of a mile or thereabout above the Fort; and for the use of the Indians of whom Oo-za-we-kwun is Chief, so much land on the south and east side of the Assiniboine, about twenty miles above the Portage, as will furnish one hundred and sixty acres for each family of five, or in that proportion for larger or smaller families, reserving also a further tract enclosing said reserve to comprise an equivalent to twenty-five square miles of equal breadth, to be laid out round the reserve, it being understood, however, that if, at the date of the execution of this treaty, there are any settlers within the bounds of any lands reserved by any band, Her Majesty reserves the right to deal with such settlers as She shall deem just, so as not to diminish the extent of land allotted to the Indians.

And with a view to show the satisfaction of Her Majesty with the behaviour and good conduct of Her Indians parties to this treaty, She hereby, through Her Commissioner, makes them a present of three dollars for each Indian man, woman and child belonging to the bands here represented.

And further, Her Majesty agrees to maintain a school on each reserve hereby made whenever the Indians of the reserve should desire it.

Within the boundary of Indian reserves, until otherwise enacted by the proper legislative authority, no intoxicating liquor shall be allowed to be introduced or sold, and all laws now in force or hereafter to be enacted to preserve Her Majesty's Indian subjects inhabiting the reserves or living elsewhere from the evil influence of the use of intoxicating liquors shall be strictly enforced.

Her Majesty's Commissioner shall, as soon as possible after the execution of the treaty, cause to be taken an accurate census of all the Indians inhabiting the district above described, distributing them in families, and shall in every year ensuing the date hereof, at some period during the month of July in each year, to be duly notified to the Indians and at or near their respective reserves, pay to each Indian family of five persons the sum of fifteen dollars Canadian currency, or in like proportion for larger or smaller family, such payment to be made in such articles as the Indians shall require of blankets, clothing, prints (assorted colours), twine or traps, at the current cost price in Montreal, or otherwise, if Her Majesty shall deem the same desirable in the interests of Her Indian people, in cash.

And the undersigned Chiefs do hereby bind and pledge themselves and their people strictly to observe this treaty and to maintain perpetual peace between themselves and Her Majesty's white subjects, and not to interfere with the property or in any way molest the persons of Her Majesty's white or other subjects.

In Witness Whereof, Her Majesty's said Commissioner and the said Indian Chiefs have hereunto subscribed and set their hand and seal at Lower Fort Garry, this day and year herein first above named.

Signed, sealed and delivered in the presence of, the same having been first read and explained:

WEMYSS M. SIMPSON,   [L.S.]
   Indian Commissioner,

MIS-KOO-KEE-NEW, or RED EAGLE
                                      his
   (HENRY PRINCE),   x
                                      mark

ADAMS G. ARCHIBALD,
   Lieut.-Gov. of Man. and N.-W.
   Territr's.
JAMES MCKAY, *P.L.C.*
A. G. IRVINE, *Major.*
ABRAHAM COWLEY,
DONALD GUNN, *M.L.C.*
THOMAS HOWARD, *P.S.*
HENRY COCHRANE,
JAMES MCARRISTER,
HUGH MCARRISTER,
E. ALICE ARCHIBALD,
HENRI BOUTHILLIER.

KA-KE-KA-PENAIS (or BIRD FOR EVER),
                                      his
   WILLIAM PENNEFATHER,   x
                                      mark

NA-SHA-KE-PENNAIS, or
                                      his
   FYLING DOWN BIRD,   x
                                      mark

NA-NA-WA-NANAW, or
                                      his
   CENTRE OF BIRD'S TAIL,   x
                                      mark

KE-WE-TAY-ASH, or
                                      his
   FLYINGROUND,   x
                                      mark

WA-KO-WUSH, or
                                      his
   WHIP-POOR-WILL,   x
                                      mark

OO-ZA-WE-KWUN, or
                                      his
   YELLOW QUILL,   x
                                      mark

Memorandum of things outside the Treaty which were promised at the Treaty at the Lower Fort, signed the 3rd day of August, A.D. 1871.

For each Chief who signed the treaty, a dress distinguishing him as Chief.

For braves and for councillors of each Chief a dress; it being supposed that the braves and councillors will be two for each Chief.

For each Chief, except Yellow Quill, a buggy.

For the braves and councillors of each Chief, except Yellow Quill, a buggy.

In lieu of a yoke of oxen for each reserve, a bull for each, and a cow for each Chief; a boar for each reserve and a sow for each Chief, and a male and female of each kind of animal raised by farmers, these when the Indians are prepared to receive them.

A plough and a harrow for each settler cultivating the ground.

These animals and their issue to be Government property, but to be allowed for the use of the Indians, under the superintendence and control of the Indian Commissioner.

The buggies to be the property of the Indians to whom they are given.

The above contains an inventory of the terms concluded with the Indians.

> WEMYSS M. SIMPSON,
> MOLYNEUX ST. JOHN,
> A. G. ARCHIBALD,
> JAS. MCKAY.

Indian Treaties and Surrenders, pp. 282-85.

Since the other treaties with the Indians of the plains are similar in form to this treaty, it is useful to study this one. These treaties are in force today (except for some amendments, for example, those relating to liquor).

1. What did the Indians give up by the terms of this treaty?
2. What did they receive in return? (land, money, goods, and services)
3. The memorandum attached to the treaty is a list of articles to be given or made available to the Indians. What does the list suggest about the way in which the Indians were intended to make a living in the future?
4. By the treaties, the Indians were placed on reserves. What effects do you think this had on their morale particularly on those tribes whose traditional life was hunting?

The treaties were a necessary preliminary to the settlement of the prairies. But that settlement meant that the land would be fenced and farmed, and that roads and railways would have to be built to connect centres of population and to carry goods back and forth. This in turn meant the end of the great herds of buffalo which had wandered in their thousands over the vast natural grazing lands of the prairies. The culture of the plains Indians was based on the use of the buffalo. When the buffalo disappeared, as it did in a very short time – the buffalo herds were almost annihilated by 1880 – the Indian way of life collapsed. The skilled hunter sat on the reserve and recalled the great days of the hunt that were gone forever. He was no farmer, nor did he wish to become one. Scratching a living from the reluctant soil was in his view a poor and contemptible way of life. The attitude to farming was summed up by a chief who said: "Who wants to be a servant to a cow?"

The effects of the treaties and the changes that followed from them have been described by a noted Canadian anthropologist.

The roving herds of buffalo on the prairies are no more. Their disappearance, which has meant so much to the Plains tribes, dates back to 1878–1880, when the troops of the American Government undertook to clear the prairies of all encumbrances – buffaloes and Indians alike. If a massacre of the Indians was not contemplated, as in the case of the Oregon and Washington campaigns in the thirties, it was because the day had passed when such a bare-faced policy could be openly confessed. Opinion at home was divided; the murder of innocent Indians would leave a blot on the national escutcheon. To provoke an insurrection might prove embarrassing. Why resort to antiquated methods when a subtle distinction was enough to save face and lead to the same results? Why not simply remove the food supply of the undesirables? And so it was done. No sooner had the buffalo vanished than the Plains Indians, to their consternation, found themselves face to face with starvation. The corner-stone of their very lives had been taken away. Two winters of dire famine played havoc with their numbers; a band of Sioux actually fled across the border into Manitoba, where they received rations from the Canadian Government. Following an outcry, a policy of artificial support was inaugurated. But from that day, starvation has never ceased to stalk over many western reservations, where it has developed into a chronic disease slowly smothering life.

About the time when their food supply was giving out, and their physique, in consequence, was being undermined, the Indians of the northwest suffered the most painful experience of the century, what to them meant no less than exile. They were forced to renounce their territorial rights, to give up the hunting grounds they knew and loved so well, the lands where their forefathers had lived and were buried. In return they accepted gifts, small reserves with treaty annuities; and in the case of the British Columbia tribes, reserves only and a forlorn hope of redress. With heavy hearts they had to acknowledge the inevitable and pass into comparative confinement, henceforth to find ample time to dream of their past glories and ponder over the future.

Some means had then to be provided to keep them from absolute starvation. The Stonies and the Kootenays, like the rest, were advised to go to school, to cultivate the land, raise cattle, seek day employment with their white neighbours, in other words to shift for themselves. An existence traditionally nomadic is a poor farming instructor, especially when ill-fortune and discouragement linger on the door-step; the old life had bred an unsteadiness that was fatal to success. Nursing "food out of sand and rocks" after the manner of the white man still seems too tedious to the Indian, used to the thrills of the buffalo hunt, to the arduous chase of the wild goat on the mountain sides, or to the bounties of the salmon run. Yet; real progress towards adaptation is to be noticed in more than one place. Weaning the Red Man from his inveterate habit of "mushing the trails" has become a settled policy, and the aid of the Mounted Police has been more than once invoked. It must be discouraging for government inspectors, however, to find so many ploughs rusting in unfinished furrows, and improved machinery, bought with treaty money, going to waste in untilled fields.

When still undisturbed, these natives had elaborate customs of their own. Marriage was regulated, and licence was almost unknown in most parts. . . . The children, loved by their parents, underwent systematic training in a way that fitted them for the pursuits of later life. Bravery was associated with gentleness, native indifference to uncleanliness, and evil smells did not preclude health and endurance. If thievishness prevailed among the prairie tribes in their dealings with the white men, it was excused on the ground that the strangers themselves were cheats. The mountain dwellers were more scrupulous in this respect, and their reliability was proverbial. Authority was paternal and friendly; it rested in the hands of the parents and elders, and in the wise men gathered in council. Peace in intertribal trade and intercourse was based upon mutual respect, goodwill, and the acknowledgment of territorial rights. It came to an end only at the time when firearms ushered in the period of transgressions and opened the door to the ultimate doom of the race.

Now after more than a century of association with the "superior" race, matters have taken a different turn. The ancient customs have disappeared imperceptibly, one by one. The thread of tradition was broken long ago. Marriage in the pagan style was condemned as unworthy by the early educators and missionaries. The seclusion of girls before puberty and premature betrothal were branded as barbaric. A church ceremony, following a semi-promiscuous education, was substituted, though in itself it considerably weakened the sexual taboos. Now, after years of gradual transition, church weddings on many reserves in the Northwest are going out of fashion. There can be no thought of reviving the old system. Some of the government agents are attempting to restore order out of chaos, but their efforts, on the whole, remain fruitless. The marital bond, when it snaps, is not one that can be welded by a blacksmith. It belongs to the mind and the heart and cannot hold firm when morality has strayed away from its sign-posts. Free unions, lasting for a moon or a year, or facile promiscuity are now coming to the fore, as all signs of restraint fade away. If this social phenomenon is worth the notice of theorists and eugenists, let them wait for a few years and behold the result. When marriage is abolished, parental duties are neglected and education is placed in jeopardy, in spite of government schools, which at best can enlist only a small minority of Indians.

The truth is that there are no longer any regular chiefs, and tribal councils are institutions of the past. Indian youth, like our own, is unruly. It knows too much, or else too little, to submit to age and experience alone, for it has grown impatient of training and control. Civil authority in the hands of the elders was firm and generous in the old days; it was wholesome, to quote the term of Father de Smet. It presided over the various phases of daily life. Why then should it have been allowed to disappear among the western tribes? The missionaries and government agents had come there to stay, to establish the new rule, the new standards of existence. The resistance they often encountered on the part of old chiefs was denounced as heathenish and noxious. As the newcomers had the upper hand, they succeeded in casting discredit on the old "pagan" leaders and soon established themselves as the only masters. On some reserves – as in the Kootenay country, for instance – the new authority has upheld its prestige and retained the reins of power for the good of their wards. But, unfortunately, this did not happen in most places. Many posts have been vacated altogether, or else strong personalities have given way to perfunctory successors. The influence of the missionaries has been decidedly on the wane in recent years. The government agents, as a rule have not felt competent to take the lead or to do more than dole out relief and annuities or to call in the police and prosecute delinquents. At the present day the sole vestige of authority is the white man's law, sitting conveniently far away out of sight and usually also out of mind.

Deprived of his former hunting grounds and food supply, the Indian might still become an agriculturist. Denied the moral comfort of his ancient customs and government, he might still stand up and look for a ray of hope in the sky. He is by no means devoid of physical strength, ability, and endurance. His sagacity and shrewdness have always been proverbial. It seems only natural that he should desire to adapt himself to modern conditions for the preservation of the race. Why then does he remain sullen, discontented, voluntarily stooping, as it were, over the edge of an open grave? Why does he not feel impelled to fight his way definitely through life, as so many white men have done in the forlorn wastes of the new world?

The problem now resolves itself into one of mob psychology. It involves fundamentally the spiritual fibre and stamina of the race. There is no doubt that the Indian mind has lost its bearings on a starless sea. The ancient beliefs, notions, and myths have been shaken to the roots; the ancestral cosmogony has fallen to the ground, and the path to salvation can be found by no one, whether he be seer or sorcerer, wise man or fool.

Barbeau, *op. cit.*, pp. 44-46.

1. List the principal changes and their effects detailed by this writer.

2. What is the ultimate result of all these changes as far as the Indians are concerned?

3. The writer states that "the Indian mind has lost its bearings on a starless sea." Can this situation be remedied? If so, how? If not, explain what you think will probably happen in the future.

The takeover of Indian lands was much more peaceful in Canada than in the United States where bloody wars marked the resistance of the Indians to the westward advance of the White Man. The treaties contributed to a peaceful takeover. But the advance of settlement did not go entirely unchallenged. The Métis, offspring of Indian mothers and European fathers, attempted to stem the tide. In 1870 and again in 1884, they challenged the advance of a way of life which threatened to disinherit them and destroy their culture. Failing on the Red River in 1870 they moved north and west into Saskatchewan, where in 1884 they found themselves at bay. In the North-West Rebellion, they failed to get the support of the Blackfoot Confederacy and were defeated. Gabriel Dumont, a Métis leader with Riel, expressed his disappointment in a statement about the Indians and the Métis as he saw them.

You would not know the Canadian Indian. He is all changed. Pride, vigour and sturdy independence all gone. The loss of the buffalo made the change. His living is gone. His very life is gone. He does not like the rotten pork the government gives him. He is sick. Smallpox and other white men's diseases kill them in hundreds. He talks of uprisings but he does not have it in him any more. He is just full of grievances. The only difference between the Métis and the Indian is that the Indians have a treaty.

> Ethel Brant Monture, *Canadian Portraits: Famous Indians* (Toronto: Clarke Irwin Company, 1960), p. 123.

> Many white men who had dealings with the Indians were moved by honest and generous impulses. Missionaries did not try to do harm. Administrators often tried to make decent provisions for the Indians. Why then were all efforts so disastrous in their effects? Could it be that none of them – fur traders, missionaries, treaty negotiators, government administrators had the slightest idea of what the results of their actions would be? That they did not understand the fragile nature of Indian cultures? In the excerpt below read "Canadian" for "American."

Americans had always felt that the process of acculturation, of throwing off one way of life for another, would be relatively simple. To be civilized the Indian would have merely to be made into a farmer; this was a matter of an education for a generation or two. Christianization would follow inevitably; perhaps Christianization itself was the way to civilization. But acculturation was not a simple process, as we know now, at least. For a culture is a delicately balanced system of attitudes, beliefs, valuations, conditions, and modes of behavior; the system does change and reintegrate itself overnight, or in a generation or two. This is what those Americans who were trying to civilize the Indians inevitably discovered, although they did not know it precisely as this. Civilized, Christian life did not raise up all savages as it should have. Rather it lowered some savages and destroyed others. This was the melancholy fact which Americans understood as coming inevitably in the progress of civilization over savagism.

> Roy H. Pearce, *The Savages of America* (Baltimore: The Johns Hopkins Press, 1953), p. 66.

1. Note the definition of culture in this extract. Explain how the work of fur traders *or* missionaries *or* treaty negotiators, *or* white administrators might upset the culture balance of an Indian tribe.

2. How does a culture change of the kind we have been considering affect the way a person in that culture thinks and feels?

4. The Indians of British Columbia

The acculturation process has been of a shorter duration in British Columbia than elsewhere in Canada. Here Indian contact with white men began about two hundred years ago.

There have been three main phases in the history of culture contact in British Columbia:

The era of exploration and the fur trade, 1774–1849. In this period, especially in the twenty years after 1785, contact was stimulated by a busy trade in sea otter furs between the coastal tribes and British and American ships. A little later, men of the North-West Company such as Alexander Mackenzie, Simon Fraser, and David Thompson, reached the area by land and established fur trading posts in the interior. After the North-West Company was taken over by the Hudson Bay Company in 1821, the whole area was,controlled by the Company until 1849. In that year, the British government established the colony of Vancouver Island. In 1858, the mainland area became the colony of British Columbia, and the era of fur trade dominance was ended.

The colonial period, 1849–1871. During this short period several important developments took place. Governor Douglas laid the foundation of an administrative structure for dealing with the Indians. This was particularly necessary after the Gold Rush, which began in 1858, drew thousands of fortune seekers to the mainland, and it was found that the methods used by the Hudson's Bay Company were no longer adequate for the new situation.

In 1871, the colony of British Columbia entered Confederation to become the fifth province. Administrative arrangements continued to develop after this time under the control of the Federal government.

The period of growing white colonization and industrialization. In the post Confederation period, the Province was settled and its resources exploited by a growing white population. Farming, fishing, mining and logging became important industries, while at the same time towns and cities sprang up. During this period, the Indians were challenged more than ever before by the expanding White culture.

The three maps which follow (Figures 5, 6, and 7) contain information on the location and population of the main tribal groups in British Columbia.

Use the maps to answer these questions:

1. What are the main coastal tribes?

2. Which were more numerous in 1835, the Coastal Indians or those living in the interior?

3. What was the British Columbia Haida population in 1835? in 1963? Make similar calculations on the Nootka Indian population in 1835 and 1963. What changes took place in the population of the coastal tribes between 1835 and 1963? What generalization can be made about the numbers of the coastal tribes between 1835 and 1963?

4. What sites were chosen by Indians not living on the coast? Would this selection of sites tend to bring them into contact with fur traders?
5. Consult both population maps again. Does there seem to be a population increase in any of the Indian tribes?

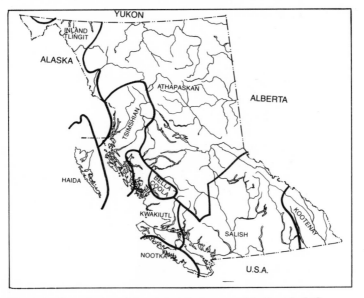

Fig. 2-5 Boundaries of the main tribal areas of Indians in B.C.

Wilson Duff, *The Indian History of British Columbia*, Vol. 1 (Victoria, B.C.: Provincial Museum of Natural History and Anthropology, 1964), p. 13.

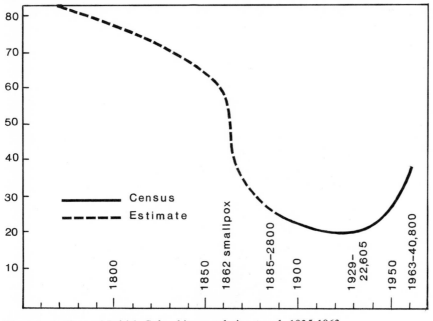

Fig. 2-6 Indians of British Columbia, population trend, 1935-1963.

Adapted from: Duff, *op. cit.*, p. 44.

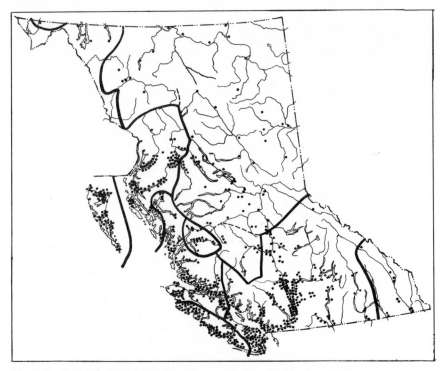

Fig. 2-7 Indians of British Columbia, population distribution, 1835
(one dot represents 100 persons)

Adapted from: Duff, *op. cit.*, p. 41.

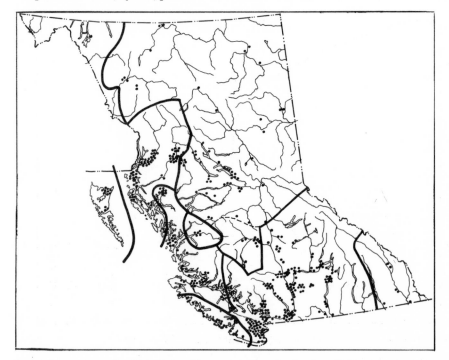

Fig. 2-8 Indians of British Columbia, population distribution, 1963
(one dot represents 100 persons)

Adapted from: Duff, *op. cit.*, p. 51.

1. What was the estimated population about 1800?

2. Between which years did the most rapid decline take place?

3. When was the low point reached? What was the population at this time?

4. What is the present population?

5. How would you describe recent trends of population growth? Refer also to Table G on page 26.

6. In the light of the information in the maps and the chart above, and of the patterns you have studied in eastern Canada and the prairies, make a list of educated guesses as to what happened to the Indians of British Columbia as a result of two centuries of culture contact.

The Fur Trade

The fur trade in British Columbia began on the coast. In 1778, Captain James Cook stayed at Nootka during which time he traded with the Indians. The furs of the sea otter were found to fetch high prices in China. The news soon spread and the rush began. At first most of the traders were English (King George men); later Americans (Boston men) came in increasing numbers. The rush started in 1785 and soon reached a high level of intensity. Blankets, muskets, powder, shot, cloth, molasses, rice, bread, and biscuits became the staple items of trade. Other items such as tobacco, beads, buttons, brass wire, chisels, needles, thread, knives, scissors, stockings, and apples were used as "presents." At first the Indians were repelled by alcohol; but once they had acquired a taste for it, it was in constant demand. The Indians were selective in their choice of goods, for example, when they had a sufficient number of iron chisels, they refused to trade for them, and demanded other goods. Moreover, they were hard-headed traders who drove hard bargains. Sometimes, misunderstanding and bad faith led to bloodshed.

The immediate effects of trading produced no great changes in the way of life of the Indians. A scholar has summarized it as follows:

The fur trade produced no major revolution in coast Indian life, compared, for example, to the effects of the horse and the gun on Plains Indian life. But it brought prosperity, an increase in wealth in a society already organized around wealth. The new tools and guns increased the Indians' productive efficiency, and the outlet of the European market for furs brought them increased returns. The new wealth strengthened the existing social and economic systems rather than weakening them. The chiefs, who controlled sea otter hunting and trade relations, became richer and more secure. More wealth meant more and bigger potlatches and a more active ceremonial life, with more need for artistic products.

Ibid., pp. 57-58.

The Indians at first did not know what to think of the bearded, light-skinned strangers. Some, for a while, thought they were supernatural creatures like those known from ancient traditions. Near Yale the Indians told Simon Fraser that someone like him had once come up the river and left scratch-marks on the rocks, a local story that refers to the mythical Transformer Haylse. The new-comers were strange in many ways. For one thing, they were all males. They owned many wonderful things – "magic sticks" (as the Kwakiutl called muskets), clocks, uniforms with buttons and buckles. Telescopes seemed magical, too: one Haida chief asked Captain Ingraham to look around a point of land to see if enemies were approaching. The Haida called white men "Yets-haida" ("iron men") because they were so rich in that valued metal; the Nootka called them "Mamathni" ("their houses move over the water").

Once the novelty wore off, however, the Indians gave further thought to dealing with these new men. They were not relatives, so perhaps should be treated like members of distant tribes, as potential enemies. Then it would be fair to steal from them or even kill them if there was an advantage to be gained. Some of the white traders, for their part, used unfair methods with the Indians and were touchy and suspicious, ready to use their guns to put the natives in their place. Inevitably, clashes occurred, and several bloody fights dot the history of the maritime fur trade period.

> *Ibid.*, pp. 56-57.

A writer has skilfully reconstructed an incident which actually occurred in 1789. This account illustrates how a lack of cultural understanding led to bloodshed.

It was two years later that the *Lady Washington* arrived in Haida waters.

The *Lady Washington* was from Boston.

The first time she stood off the fortified island in front of Koyah's village, on June 11th, 1789, she was commanded by courteous young Captain Gray, whose senior officer was Captain John Kendrick of the *Columbia,* currently trading elsewhere for the same Boston shipowners.

Chiefs Koyah and Skulkinanse traded with Captain Gray for their people. Now experienced traders, they demanded clothing as well as metals and trinkets, a request that caught the Boston men unprepared.

Eager for the fabulous furs, however, seamen offered the very shirts off their backs. And so, unwittingly, they started a new rivalry in the village. Every man desired a garment made of the cloth that was so much finer than the material Haida women made from shredded cedar bark.

Unfortunately, seamen could spare no more shirts when the *Lady Washington* came back again during the same trading voyage.

This second time she anchored off Koyah's village, the *Lady Washington* was under the command of Captain Kendrick, who had handed his bigger ship *Columbia* over to Captain Gray.

Captain Kendrick was a huge man with reddish hair and an unreasonable temper. This day he had been drinking. And in spite of anxious protests from his officers, he let Indians swarm aboard the *Lady Washington*, contrary to the custom. At the same time, he insisted on having his personal laundry hung out on deck to dry. No young whippersnappers were going to tell him how to run his ship! No dirty savages were going to upset his private arrangements!

So, while the chiefs bartered, Indians explored the tempting wonders of the Iron Man's canoe. One of them filched a shirt from the captain's laundry and disappeared overboard.

Captain Kendrick was livid when the theft was discovered. "I'll teach these thieving devils a lesson they'll never forget," he thundered. "Arm every man!"

Muskets bristled on all sides. Warning shots blazed. Sea-gulls dropped, dead. And fierce warriors trembled.

"Man that gun! . . . FIRE!"

A tree on shore splintered.

Staggered by the power of his thundersticks, the Haidas watched Captain Kendrick.

"Grab the chiefs!" he roared, red-faced with fury.

Koyah and Skulkinanse were seized. A cannon was dismounted, and a leg of each chief was clamped into the iron mounts.

Shamed eyes turned away from his humiliation of the chiefs; for it was not the Indian way to leap into battle while the odds were hopeless. The wilderness had taught them that only patience assured final victory, that a time always came for boldness. Then you struck without mercy.

Meanwhile, the chief's hair was cut like slaves' hair. Horrified eyes watched this new indignity. The chiefs were further pinioned by ropes around their necks; ship's paint was daubed on their faces; and they were flogged.

Neither chief moved a muscle. But the eyes of both burned with a fire that was never to be quenched. Hatred smouldered in the eyes of every watching Indian, too. But theirs was a patient hatred. They could wait the right moment for revenge.

"Now!" Captain Kendrick roared at the Indians. "Bring back my shirt or your chiefs will be blasted to bits!"

The shirt was handed up; other pilfered articles appeared as if by magic. At the same time, furs were picked up defiantly.

Even the captain's bleary eyes saw that trading was finished here.

No! It was not finished. Not while he held the chiefs captive.

"Bring me every last skin in the village!" he yelled. "Every last skin, or your chiefs will be killed. Your village will be blown to pieces!"

The Haidas understood him. Alert eyes could read the threat of the muskets and the menace of the big guns. They brought every pelt to the ship.

"Now!" Captain Kendrick boasted. "I'll show you how civilized men do things." And to prove what a fair-minded fellow a civilized man was, he paid for every skin at the prevailing rate in chisels.

Then he released the chiefs. And training his guns on the Haidas, Captain Kendrick fled from their waters.

Maada was horrified. Almost in disbelief she stared at her husband's shorn head, at the paint on his face, at the welts on his body.

"This is an insult not to be borne!" she declared.

She looked again at his shorn head, shrinking visibly from it. This was the utter stigma, the sign of a social outcast; and welts, unlike the honorable scars of battle, were as vile a stigma.

"*You* were captured. *You* were made a slave by the Iron Men," she whispered, as though needing to convince herself that this dreadful thing could be true. "*You* were ridiculed."

Her towering pride was shattered. Koyah, her husband, had been utterly humiliated. Word would spread through the tribes; and wherever he moved, people would turn their heads away not to see his humiliation; chiefs would turn their heads away also, and not seat him in the old, honored places.

The very name itself, Koyah, had been dishonored. It had been degraded among the proud, ancient Haida names. Her eyes chanced on Chisalgas, who was destined to wear the name next. Hero of a dozen raids, the young chieftain was heir now only to a bitter shame.

Maada's eyes sought her son. Even he was shamed. Only blood could wipe out a shame such as this.

"This is an insult not to be borne!" she said again.

"The insult will be wiped out," Koyah fiercely assured her.

"It will be wiped out in blood," Koyah's heir vowed.

But all in good time.

Indian revenge could be patient. Patient, but sure. Sure as the turning of the tide. Sure as the coming of the winter gales.

> Christie Harris, *Raven's Cry* (Toronto: McClelland and Stewart Ltd., 1966), pp. 30-33.

> The introduction of firearms caused changes in the relations between the tribes. Inter-tribal warfare was traditional. The use of guns made it more costly in human life.

Noisy and short-ranged, the first muskets obtained by the Indians did not wholly replace the bow and harpoon for hunting purposes. But they did to a great extent replace the club and dagger for purposes of war. Warfare suddenly became much more deadly. On the coast some villages were practically wiped out, and in at least one instance a warlike tribe decimated its neighbours and moved into their territories. This happened in the vicinity of Cape Mudge and Campbell River. When Vancouver passed this way in 1792 on his survey of the coast, he found the area occupied by Salish-speaking people who had no guns. Farther north on Vancouver Island, at "Cheslakee's Village" at the mouth of the Nimpkish River, he noticed that the Kwakiutl chief had eight muskets, obtained from Nootka. Soon after that date the Kwakiutl raided and terrorized the Salish tribes along Georgia Strait and Puget Sound. In the extensive warfare that followed both sides suffered heavy losses, but the end result was that the Southern Kwakiutl displaced the decimated Comox Indians of Cape Mudge and Campbell River.

> Duff, *op. cit.*, p. 59.

> With the White Man came the diseases against which the Indians had little or no resistance. Even the medicine men of the greatest reputation were not immune. The confusion and fear of the Indians emerges in the following story.

It was in the middle of the winter that a strange message came from Tanu, a message that recalled again the words of Mr. Green.

Tanu was an east coast village with a famous medicine man, Condo-hahtgha.

Condohahtgha had achieved marvelous cures with herbs and charms, rattle and incantations (and with powerful psychic suggestion). Now, like lesser men, he was defeated by the new sicknesses that had come with the Iron Men.

But he did not accept defeat. He merely needed another power, he said, to combat these new evil spirits. And being dedicated to his own fame as well as to tribal health, he prepared himself to acquire this power.

He cleaned himself ceremonially with devil's club juice and with sea water. He fasted until he seemed to be a cadaver, until his long, uncombed, unwashed hair straggled over scarred, ghastly emaciation. Then he laid aside his crown of carved horn tips, and the carved bone charms that no longer served him.

He would go into a deep trance, he announced. His soul would leave his body and climb up the long Sky Ladder. And there, above, he would gain the new power to drive out the new evil spirits.

Before he lay down, he instructed the Tanu people. He showed them a long strip of cedar bark treated to burn very slowly, and marked into sections by bands of paint.

"Between these strips is one hour," he told them.

"*Hour*?" They repeated the strange word, and wondered.

When the bark had burned through four hours, they were to wake him, he said. By that time his soul would have returned to his body, and he would know what it was the tribe must do to be rid of the new pestilences.

The people agreed solemnly.

The spirit self of Condohahtgha left his body and climbed up the long Sky Ladder (he told them later). He came to a village surrounded by a wall, and there was a gate, through which he must enter. The gate of silvered cedar was so richly inlaid with abalone mother-of-pearl that it glistened with iridescent rainbows, like a leaping salmon. And guarding this shining gate was a man with a gigantic musket. The man was black; his hands were grown to the musket.

This black man looked at him and sniffed, as if he smelled a rotting carcass. Then he spoke angrily. "Look down at the villages!"

Condohahtgha glanced down.

But where were the villages?

The inland wilderness of mountain and forest had crept to the very shores of Lak Haida. Everywhere waves lapped at empty beaches.

Alarmed, his spirit self flew right around the Haida islands. But where were the villages? There were no houses at Tanu. No totem poles. Nor at Skedans, or Cumshewa.

Moving north along the east coast, he came to Skidegate. Here there were poles and houses. Here there were canoes. Here there were people moving, but the people did not seem happy.

His spirit self flew on, northward, more and more aghast at the aching silence. There was nothing even at Tlell, nothing but the long, lonely, lovely beaches. There was nothing at Nai-koon, the long nose jutting through the

ocean. He rounded the spit and flew west. There was nothing at Tou Hill . . .
Ya-kan . . . Skou-an. Only silent stretches of hard packed sand.

There was a town at Masset! But none at Yan . . . Klaskwun . . . Yaltetze.
Nothing at Kiusta . . . Dadens.

Trembling with dread, he flew south along the west coast of the islands.
Here the wild sea hurled itself angrily against the rocks and reefs; but nobody
saw it. Nobody heard its fury. Only seagulls screamed and ravens cried out
and eagles circled high above them. Only the dorsal fins of killer whales sliced
through the lonely ocean.

"What has happened to the villages?" he implored the black man whose
hands were grown to the musket.

"God has wiped them out because He does not like two things: the
heathen totem poles of the Haida, and the smell of the corpses in the mortuary
totem poles."

"God?"

"The Old-Man-with-the-Beard," the black man explained, "as mighty as
Power-of-the-Shining-Heavens." He opened the gate to show him.

But Condohahtgha could not see God, at first. He saw only a burning lake.
People screamed in the flames; screamed to die in the burning lake, but they
could not die.

> Harris, *op. cit.*, pp. 75-77.

1. What is the significance of the medicine man's dream? What does
   the dream foreshadow? How does it show that his ideas have been
   influenced by the teachings of missionaries?

2. In the next part of the story, what evidence is there that his fears
   would be realized?

Then, in 1857, gold was discovered in the sands of the Fraser River, in Salish
lands on the mainland, just north of the Oregon Country.

During the summer of 1858, 33,000 men rushed north from San Francisco.
They docked first at Fort Victoria on the southern tip of Vancouver Island.
And here the Hudson's Bay Company's James Douglas became alarmed at
the extent of the American invasion.

With his help, Her Britannic Majesty moved fast. She proclaimed the whole
wilderness the Gold Colony of British Columbia. Magistrates and policemen
were sworn in to enforce English law. Soldiers arrived from England. Royal
Navy gunboats patrolled the waters. Miners' licenses were imposed to
emphasize British possession.

Haidas, as curious as the rest of the local residents, paddled the six
hundred miles south to see if all the fantastic rumors could be true. *The British
Colonist* reported their arrival at Victoria in its April 23rd issue, 1859:

> "HAIDAH INDIANS — About eighty canoes containing
> nearly 1,000 Indians arrived on Thursday from Queen
> Charlotte's Island. They have pitched their lodges at the
> end of the town. They have brought several very fine speci-

mens of gold-bearing quartz and some fine gold. We are
not informed as to what part of the Island they obtained
their gold from."

The fine gold was from Stastas lands.

"Why did you bring gold here?" Chief Edinsa demanded of Masset Town
Chief Wiha when he heard the report.

"The Skidegates brought gold quartz," Wiha answered defiantly; and his
eyes smouldered with resentment.

"Do you want this to come to Lak Haida?" the chief retorted, encom-
passing Victoria with a sweep of his arm.

This was a tent town full of Iron Men, saloons, and muddy streets. This
was crowded ships arriving from San Francisco, and even more crowded ships
leaving for the diggings on the mainland. Worst of all, this was a fringe of
Indian encampments exploited by the whiskey trader. In the Indian camps,
burned out tribal feuds were being rekindled by firewater. . . .

Suddenly the Governor sent an urgent summons to all the chiefs encamped
near Victoria. "A man arrived from San Francisco with smallpox," he told
them. "An epidemic is sweeping the town. Go home! Take your people back
to their villages!"

"Smallpox?" a chief retorted contemptuously. "So you have finally learned
that 'measles' will no longer scare us off the land you Iron Men want. Now
you try 'smallpox'."

"There is smallpox," Governor Douglas insisted.

"There's something new every year," the chief agreed. "First it was measles.
Then it was rent, Indians must pay rent to the intruders or else go home! Now
you try yet another ruse to make us obey you."

Governor Douglas, whose own wife had Indian as well as Scottish fur-
trader blood, begged them to go.

But they were adamant.

"If we obey him," they reminded one another, "we acknowledge his right
to give orders to us." This situation was like a potlatch. Public acknowledgment of a claim made it valid, by the custom of the country.

They refused to go home.

"Then I will make you go home," the Governor thundered at them.

He ordered out the Police, the Royal Marines, and the Navy gunboats.
Warning cannon shots splintered cedar huts. And while muskets and big guns
held the natives at bay, canoes were tied in long lines behind Navy craft;
people were forced into the canoes; they were towed out of Victoria harbor, and
north along the coast.

Edinsa's magnificent canoe was towed by a gunboat, with the canoes of
his people.

It was an indignity not to be borne!

The chief did not bear it long. Suddenly he leapt along the canoe. He
slashed the towrope. His men followed his lead, and the whole Stastas fleet
headed back for Victoria, chanting triumphantly. They landed with the traditional flourish of the Eagles. Entering the harbor, all the crews stroked in
unison, without sound or ripples, symbolizing the stealthiness of an approach

upon an enemy. Then, with a war-whoop, they dashed their paddles deep into the water in simulated attack. A paean of triumph followed. And then, like weary eagles, they nosed shoreward with two strokes, a rest; three strokes, a pause; alternating the pattern and keeping time to a chant. As they touched shore, they crossed paddles. These were the mighty Eagles! These were the Lords of the Coast!

They stayed only long enough to establish their right to stay. Then they chose to go home.

As they moved northward along the coast, they saw people dying. Before they reached Haida waters, people were sickening in their own canoes. And now, wanting only to put space between themselves and the new pestilence, they rushed to their hereditary haven, Lak Haida.

> *Ibid.*, pp. 75-77.

> The Indians of the interior had been exposed to contact with white men through the establishment of a chain of fur trading posts throughout the territory. By the time of the Gold Rush of 1858, they had experienced about fifty years of contact, first with the North-West Company, and after 1821, with the Hudson's Bay Company. The Gold Rush intensified this contact as large numbers of miners swarmed up the Fraser River and beyond to the diggings at Barkerville. A steady and continuous traffic of men and supplies developed to and from the gold-fields. Governor James Douglas was soon aware of the dangers in the new situation. In a letter to the Colonial Secretary in London, dated April 6, 1858, he wrote:

The search for gold and prospecting of the country had, up to the last dates from the interior, been carried on by the native Indian population, . . . and who are extremely jealous of the whites, and strongly opposed to their digging the soil for gold. . . . It is, however, worthy of remark, and a circumstance highly honourable to the character of those savages, that they have on all occasions scrupulously respected the persons and property of their white visitors, at the same time that they have expressed a determination to reserve the gold for their own benefit.

Such being the purpose of the natives, affrays and collisions with the whites will shortly follow the accession of numbers, which the latter are now receiving by the influx of adventurers from Vancouver Island and the United States territories in Oregon.

> William C. Hazlitt, *British Columbia, and Vancouver Island* (London: G. Routledge & Co., 1858), p. 131.

1. Why do you think the Indians were "strongly opposed" to the whites digging for gold? Do you think they were justified in adopting this attitude?

2. How would you describe the Indians' behaviour towards the white prospectors in the circumstances?

3. What trouble does the Governor predict for the near future?

An English observer, who happened to be in this area at the time, gave another view of relations between Indians and miners.

But, worst of all the ills of the miner life in New Caledonia, are the jealousy and the audacious thieving of the Indians, 'who are nowise particular in seizing on the dirt of the miners.' 'The whites,' being in the minority, and the Indians being a fierce athletic set of rascals, 'suffered much annoyance and insult' without retaliating. What a trial to the temper of Oregon men who used to shoot all Indians who came within range of their rifle as vermin in California in 1848 and 1849!

The difficulties of access to the mines will soon be ameliorated, as small steamers are to be put on the river, to ply as far up as the rapids will permit them; but as to the Indian 'difficulties,' it is much to be feared they will increase until a military force is sent into the country to overawe them.

Ibid., p. 143.

1. In what way is the behaviour of the Indians, as described here, different from that portrayed by Governor Douglas?

2. Which description, in your opinion, is nearer the truth? Support your answer with argument and examples.

Administrative Controls Established

The influx of settlers to Vancouver Island and, after 1858, the arrival of large numbers of gold miners, made urgent the problem of establishing machinery for regulating the relations of Indians and Whites. Governor Douglas did not neglect this problem. Between 1850 and 1854 he made fourteen treaties with Indians living near Victoria, Nanaimo and Fort Rupert. By the terms of these treaties, the land became "the entire property of the white people forever," and reserves were set aside for the Indians. However further treaties were not signed in Douglas's administration because of lack of finances, and his successors chose not to make treaties with the Indians. Moreover, where Douglas had been generous in the matter of reserve lands, his successors were much less open-handed. The land situation in British Columbia is thus different from that in the prairie provinces where Indian title to the land was recognized and then extinguished by the treaties. The difficulties which arose from this policy have been traced and explained in an Indian history of British Columbia.

The Indian policies of British Columbia differed from those of the rest of Canada most sharply on matters involving land. First there was the question of recognizing and extinguishing the aboriginal possessory rights or "Indian title." In North America it had been the usual practice, started by Britain and continued by Canada and the United States, to make treaties with the Indian tribes as the country was opened up for settlement. In return for their ownership rights, the Indians received tracts of land for Indian reservations and compensation in the form of money and gifts, services, and perpetual annual payments. The practice was given Royal sanction in 1763, when King George III issued a Proclamation (which had the force of a statute in the colonies) saying in effect that the Indians were not to be dispossessed of their lands without their own consent as well as that of the Crown, and that Indian lands were to be ceded only to the Crown. . . .

The Colonies of Vancouver Island and British Columbia, on the other hand, despite the intentions of all concerned in the beginning, evolved a policy that ignored or denied the existence of any native title and therefore any need to make treaties. This oversight has not, probably, resulted in any relative hardship on the Indians of the Province, but it has kept the land question in the category of unfinished business, providing a focus for their sense of grievance and a rallying point for the native spokesmen and inter-tribal organizations which have appeared to present the Indians' case.

The second problem, closely related, was that of Indian reserves: how much land were the Indians to be given for their own use, and how was it to be safeguarded? Elsewhere in Canada it was the policy to allot each tribe a single large tract of land (either 160 acres or 1 square mile per family), on which they were expected to settle and establish farms. British Columbia's system was better suited to the coast Indian way of life: each local band was allotted several small reserves which it used intermittently in the course of its migratory activities. In terms of total acreage, however, these compared poorly with the Canadian standard. On entering Confederation, how much land was the Province to convey to the Dominion for new reserves? Ottawa maintained that at least 80 acres per family of five was required. The Province replied that the coast tribes would not use that much land, and set a maximum of 20 acres per family for future reserves (and double that amount in the agricultural areas east of the Cascades): The Province also insisted on its "reversionary interest" in reserve lands: if at any time land was cut off a reserve, or a band gave up reserve land, its ownership was to revert to the Province.

While the two governments argued, the Indians became more and more agitated. By 1877 the situation in the interior was so tense that an Indian war seemed imminent. In Ottawa the Minister of the Interior thought the situation serious enough to warn the Provincial authorities by telegram that his government would side with the Indians in any trouble: "Indian rights to soil in British Columbia have never been extinguished. Should any difficulty occur, steps will be taken to maintain the Indian claims to all the country where rights have not been extinguished by treaty. Don't desire to raise the question at present but Local Government must instruct Commissioners to make reserves so large as to completely satisfy Indians." He enlarged on these views by letter (Mills to Powell, August 2, 1877). Like James Douglas, he hoped that the vexing question of title could be circumvented by a generous policy of allotting reserves. The commissioners to which he referred were the three members of a Joint Committee on Indian Reserves appointed in 1876. They were empowered to lay out reserves, using no fixed basis of acreage, and subject to the reversionary interest of the Province. The Commission was active for more than 30 years. In 1877, however, it was reduced to a single member, Gilbert Malcolm Sproat. Sproat resigned in 1880 and was replaced by Peter O'Reilly, who served until his retirement in 1898. Commissioner Vowell then added this to his other duties, and served until 1908, when all reserve allotments were halted by Provincial protests. It was during these three decades that most of the reserves in the Province were laid out.

The Province now asked for an adjustment downward in the size of existing reserves. Also, the reversionary interest clause, by which the Province immediately became the owner of any land surrendered by the Indians, was causing difficulties of administration. It meant, for example, that the Dominion was not able to sell reserve land for the benefit of the Indians involved, because the land could not be sold until surrendered, and once surrendered it was the property of the Province. In 1912 a special Dominion Commissioner, Mr. J. A. J. McKenna, was appointed and met with Premier Richard McBride to settle these problems. The result was the "McKenna-McBride Agreement." A five-man Royal Commission was to be appointed to make the final and complete allotment of Indian lands in the Province. Upon settlement of the number and size of reserves, title was to be conveyed to the Dominion free of any reversionary interest, except in the case of lands belonging to bands which might become extinct. This Royal Commission on Indian Affairs, now usually referred to as "the Reserve Commission," was named in 1913, and laboured for three busy years, travelling to all parts of the Province and interviewing virtually all bands. Some of the northern coastal people refused to discuss their reserve requirements until the question of Indian title had been settled, and their needs had to be judged from information given by the Indian agents. In most cases the Commission confirmed the existing reserves, but it also added about 87,000 acres of new reserve land and cut off some 47,000 acres of old. Its report, in four volumes, was published in 1916, and was ratified by both governments in 1924. The reserve lands were formally conveyed to the Dominion by Order in Council No. 1036 in 1938. With some minor adjustments since then, this was the final settlement of Indian land questions between the two governments. In 1963 British Columbia's 189 bands owned a total of 1,620 reserves (of 2,241 in the whole of Canada) with a total area of 843,479 acres.

To return to the question of Indian title, it was the Nass River Indians, encouraged at first by missionaries, who took the lead in agitating for a proper hearing of the Indian case. In 1887 a three-man Joint Commission was sent up the coast to inquire into the causes of their unrest. The Nass chiefs presented their case with eloquence and dignity, but were met by statements of legal technicalities which they could not comprehend. Again and again they explained that they owned all the land and had never given it up, and they objected to being given a few small reserves. How was it that the land no longer belonged to them, but to the Queen? . . .

> "What we don't like about the Government is their saying this: 'We will give you this much land.' How can they give it when it is our own? We cannot understand it. They have bought it from us or our forefathers. They have never

> fought and conquered our people and taken the land that way, and yet they say now that they will give us so much land – our own land."

The chiefs asked for a treaty recognizing their aboriginal title, for large reserves, and compensation for the land outside the reserves. The Commission had no power to grant any of these; it had only come to get the facts and make recommendations (British Columbia, 1888).

The Indians began to realize that they had to organize and learn new ways of presenting their case. In 1906 a delegation representing the Squamish and other southern coast tribes went to London; they received a hearing but no real satisfaction. The Nass Indians formed the "Nishga Land Committee" to raise funds and obtain professional legal advice. In 1913 they adopted and sent to Ottawa the "Nishga Petition" stating their land claim, and asked that it be tested before the highest court, the Judicial Committee of the Privy Council in London. But that body can hear only cases appealed from lower courts; the Indians refused to have their case tried first in a lower (Canadian) court, maintaining truthfully that they had been promised a direct hearing before the Privy Council. Nishga delegations travelled to Ottawa in 1915 and 1916 in unsuccessful attempts to win this concession. In 1916 the Nishga joined with the Interior Salish and southern coast tribes to form the "Allied Tribes of British Columbia," a powerful inter-tribal organization led by the two outstanding Indian leaders of their generation, Peter Kelly and Andrew Paull. Meetings were held, funds raised, and petitions sent to Ottawa. Rejection by the Allied Tribes of the 1916 report of the Reserve Commission delayed its ratisfication by the governments until 1924. In 1923 they presented Ottawa with a set of demands in return for which they would drop the issue of Indian title. These included a cash settlement of about 2½ million dollars, an increase in the size of reserves to 160 acres per person, certain hunting and fishing rights, and extensive educational and medical benefits. The Dominion Government thought these demands beyond reason, and delayed no longer in ratifying the Reserve Commission report (as the Provincial Government had done a short time before).

The Allied Tribes continued to press for a hearing before the Privy Council. In 1926 the Government appointed a Special Joint Committee of the Senate and House of Commons to examine their claims. This was a major climax in the history of the Indian title question. The Joint Committee met in haste near the end of the parliamentary session. Although Peter Kelly and Andrew Paull were well received and made a good impression on the members, their legal counsel succeeded in nothing more than antagonizing and infuriating them. The Committee's report has been called "the Great Settlement of 1927." It found that the Indians "have not established any claim to the lands of British Columbia based on aboriginal or other title," and decreed that the question of Indian title should now be regarded as closed.[1] Although, they said, the treatment of the Indians of British Columbia was at least as generous as that received by treaty Indians, they recommended that a grant in lieu of

---

[1] The Nass Indians have kept the question of their aboriginal title open. A ruling has yet to be made by the Supreme Court of Canada.

treaty payments amounting to $100,000 a year be expended for their benefit, over and above the normal costs of administration.

>Duff, *op. cit.*, pp. 65-69.

1. What do you understand by the term, "aboriginal title"? On what grounds would a claim to aboriginal rights be based?
2. Is the reasoning of the Nass River Indians sound? If not, show how it is fallacious. If it is, explain why they do not own the land.
3. The claims of the Nass River Indians are still before the courts. If you were judging the case, what would be your decision? How would you arrive at it?
4. In the "Great Settlement of 1927" it was decided that the Indians "have not established any claim to the lands of British Columbia based on aboriginal or other title." Consider the wording of this decision carefully. As an Indian, how would you criticize it?

Missionaries

The opening up of British Columbia to exploration and settlement came at a time when there was intense Christian missionary activity. It is not surprising to find, then, that throughout the nineteenth century, the Indians of British Columbia were subject to the attentions of missionaries whose principal aims were to convert them from their heathen ways to Christianity and to set their feet on the path to civilization. Many denominations were represented including Roman Catholic, Anglican, Methodist, Salvation Army, and the Shaker Church. In terms of numbers of Indians converted, the missions were extremely successful. By 1939, only 28 Indians were recorded as still retaining their aboriginal beliefs. 57 per cent were Roman Catholic, 20 per cent Anglican, 20 per cent United Church, and the remaining 3 per cent mostly Salvation Army.

There is disagreement as to the effects of the missionaries' work on the Indians. They attacked many practices and institutions that they found abhorrent – cruelty, slavery, intertribal warfare, the potlatch and winter dance ceremonies, the "sale" of brides, the avenging of one murder by another, and so on. To missionaries, these things were evil and inhumane and ought to be ended. The trouble with this action, much of which was successful, was that in carrying it out, they were destroying the fabric of Indian culture. The potlatch, which seemed only to be a feast for giving away or destroying property, was important for defining social relationships and for redistributing property. It also stimulated oratory, dancing, singing, and other forms of artistic expression, and provided an important ceremonial occasion which gave meaning to life. The "sale" of brides was a device whereby marriages between social groups were arranged. The "sale" was a traditional exchange of gifts which accompanied the arrangement. The overall effect of the changes was to weaken the social institutions on which Indian life was based – kinship and rank. Kinship determined what rank a person could attain, what social class he belonged to, whom he could marry, and so on. The old ways lost their meaning and fell into disuse. The question is, did the Indians gain more or lose more as a result of the changes?

In this extract from *Raven's Cry* the author enables us to see how the Haidas perceived the Christian missionaries and their teachings. They had their own religion and their shamans. They see the Reverend Mr. Green as another shaman, one who brings confusing ideas. Could these ideas have contributed to the demoralization of the Indians?

"Before you go," Gao implored Edinsa, "come and hear the words of an Iron Man who is not a fur trader. I think he's a sorcerer." Gao scowled before he went on. "Edinsa, I want to know what you think of Mistagheen."

Gwai-gwun-thlin accompanied the chiefs to the Rev. Mr. Green's barque, *Volunteer*. And the Indian youth could see that Mistagheen was indeed a sorcerer. He held a charm that he called *The Book*. It was a packet of ghost leaves. And before he could gaze at *The Book*, Mistagheen put twin circles of the-ice-that-does-not-melt before his eyes. *The Book,* an interpreter said, revealed that men must not steal, nor kill, nor drink rum.

"Then why did the Iron Men bring rum?" Edinsa demanded to know. "Why did they change the good way we lived?" In the old days, he claimed, people did not steal and kill and drink the poisoned water that drove skillful young seamen out onto the ocean while the storm spirits were angry. "Why did they bring rum?" he challenged.

Because *money* was the root of all evil, the interpreter explained to the Haidas.

Money?

Money was strings of dentalium shells.

Dentalium shells were evil? Gwai-gwun-thlin found it most confusing.

"God is not Power-of-the-Shining-Heavens," commented Chief Gao, who had talked before with the missionary. "He is the Old-Man-of-the-Sky, an old man with a beard, Edinsa."

"And God does not like heathen idols," the Rev. Mr. Green told them. *The Book* revealed that people should not make a graven image. The totem pole was a graven image. And a graven image was heathen and wicked. People with a graven image would be thrown into a burning lake, he assured them. People with totem poles would be hurled into the lake to burn forever.

The Haidas were astounded. They consulted one another with anxious faces. If Edinsa had no totem pole, they argued, how could people know he was of the tribe descended from Copper Woman? How would Eagle strangers know they could find brothers in this lodge? How could Raven visitors know that here they could find husbands for their nieces? How could the young people remember the tribe's history if there were no emblems to remind them of the important events in the lives of their ancestors? If you could not carve Killer Whale or Eagle or Frog or Bear, how could anybody tell whose canoe was whose canoe; whose fish-club was whose fish-club; whose house was whose house? How could a society manage without identifying totems? How could a graven image be wicked?

The potlatch was evil, also, Mistagheen assured the Haidas. And the dancing was evil also.

The chiefs raised surprised eyebrows again. They consulted again, together. How could these things be evil when they were the very things Power-of-the-Shining-Heavens had given them to live by? Even as God had given white men *The Book!* How could you possibly manage life without the public witnessing of claims at a potlatch? And without paying the witnesses for their service? And without first reassuring those witnesses by having the chiefs dance the dance of welcome and scatter the eagle-down of peace and friendship? How could you gain the spirit power you needed if you couldn't honor supernatural beings with a ritual dance? How could you ensure the harvest of the waters if you did not dance reverently to honor the Chief of the Salmon People when he arrived? How could you live spiritually?

Gwai-gwun-thlin found it all more and more confusing.

A particular thing troubled Gao. He could understand God. He could understand prayer; prayer was part of his own life. But, he wanted to know, why did the Iron Men pray without reverence? He had heard them, many times, calling on God. But they didn't do it with the trembling respect of the Indian supplicator. They called angrily, and they usually added the word "Damn!" What did it mean?

"It means that Iron Men are often wicked," the Rev. Mr. Green said, wiping his forehead with his big bandana.

Chief Edinsa invited him to come to Kiusta to talk more about these things, but Mr. Green had other commitments. So the chief and his nephew went back to Lak Haida confused, as well as unhappy over Skoual.

Harris, *op. cit.*, pp. 72-74.

In this next extract, Chief Edinsa of the Haidas visits the village of Metlakahtla on the mainland. At Metlakahtla an energetic missionary, William Duncan, had set up with his Tsimshian converts a model Christian, self-supporting, industrial mission. There was a population of 1,100, a church large enough to seat 800 people, and a school to accommodate 500. There was a sawmill, a sash factory, a blacksmith shop, bakery, carpenter shop, and trading post. The people lived in uniform houses with two rooms downstairs and three bedrooms upstairs. Each house had its fenced garden. To live there, the people had to obey 15 laws of the "Christian City."

1st. They were to give up their "Ah-lied," or Indian deviltry.
2nd. To cease calling in conjurors when sick.
3rd. To cease gambling.
4th. To cease potlatches or giving away their property for display.
5th. To cease painting their faces.
6th. To cease drinking intoxicating liquors.
7th. To rest on the Sabbath.

8th. To attend religious instruction.

9th. To send their children to school.

10th. To be cleanly.

11th. To be industrious.

12th. To be peaceful.

13th. To be liberal and honest in trade.

14th. To build neat houses.

15th. To pay the village tax.

Indian Affairs, 1875-1879, p. 33.

Entering Metlakahtla Pass that same morning, Chief Edinsa was sad. When he had come here as a boy, nine handsome villages had nestled along the meandering channel. Now there was only the stark town where Mr. Duncan ruled his thousand converts.

"It's so bleak!" the chief said, dismayed by the long, straight row of ugly, unpainted, two-story houses made of whipsawed lumber. There were no projecting, carved beams to relieve the plainness, no colorful crest-poles standing against the forest.

A few flags were whipping out in honor of a visitor, Rear Admiral Prevost, retired. People wore their Sunday clothes, and their Sabbath manners.

"They look so awkward in those clothes," Edinsa remarked to his son. He longed for the beauty of muscles rippling in wet skin; he sighed for the flash of bracelets and anklets on now soberly garbed women.

People answered to strange foreign names like George and Henry. Brash young commoners snapped out orders to men who had been chiefs. And no one danced in welcome, or wafted the eagle-down of peace and friendship. "It's so bleak without the old ways and the old totems," he protested to Kahu.

"But nobody died at Metlakahtla," Kahu pointed out; and his tone surprised his father.

Mr. Duncan and his converts had moved to Metlakahtla in May, 1862, just before the terrible smallpox summer. Their deliberate isolation from the "heathen" had saved them from infection.

"There were no totem poles here," Kahu continued, "and people didn't die here."

Metlakahtla poles had been burned with righteous enthusiasm.

Mr. Collison came up to them at that moment. "Just see the vegetable gardens!" he said.

There was a neat little garden in front of each ugly house. There were precise picket fences to keep out playing children and dogs.

Edinsa glanced at them coldly. For some reason he could never quite fathom, white men thought that great virtue lay in gardens. To dig the soil seemed to be a superior thing to do; though Power-of-the-Shining-Heavens had clearly ordained this as a land of rock, forest, moss, and sea; and had bountifully provided for the people with sea foods and fruits. Why should it be so worthy to dig a garden? True, the Haidas grew potatoes and valued them. But why should they be tied to gardens when there were clams to dig and salmon to catch and seaweed and berries to gather? What was so good about gardens?

He was genuinely impressed by the blacksmith shop, astounded by the sawmill and bakery. But he concealed his disapproval of the town's weaving industry, except from Kahu. "Why don't they weave beauty into their blankets?" he said to his son as he fingered shoddy woolen cloth. "Why don't they design them with patterns, like the Chilkats?" Surely any Indian knew that Chilkat blankets were greatly increased in value by the beauty of their pattern, an intricate pattern of flattened ovals.

"God doesn't like totem patterns," Kahu answered. A glint of defiance brightened his eyes.

Edinsa turned a startled look on his son. "Handsome blankets would sell better," he retorted. But maybe they wouldn't now, he thought, recalling the ugly plainness of spoons, dishes, storage boxes, and even canoes in this model Christian village. God did not like totem poles. Apparently He did not like decoration in any form.

He could see that Admiral Prevost considered Metlakahtla vastly superior to any native village. But what a white man thought was unimportant to Edinsa. It was Kahu's thoughts that perturbed him, and the way Kahu sailed in the wake of the missionaries.

Harris, *op. cit.*, pp. 146-148.

1. What did the Indians of Metlakahtla gain from membership in Duncan's community?

2. What does Chief Edinsa see as being lost?

3. In what ways does Kahu seem to be influenced by the missionaries?

Perhaps the most important result of all the work of the missionaries was the contribution it made to the growth of Indian dependence. In their relations with the Indians they assumed without question their own superiority. After all, they had come to show the Indians a better way of living and believing. The Indians accepted their role in the relationship. They were converted. When the missionaries built schools, the Indians allowed their children to be sent away to them, to learn English and the White man's ways. As their culture decayed they looked to the missionaries for help and guidance in a new and confusing situation. The missionaries were kind and helpful. They were also paternalistic, fatherly in their attitudes towards the natives. Paternalism and dependence are two sides of the same coin.

Read the following extracts from the annual report on Indian Affairs in the Victoria Superintendency for the year ending June 30, 1876. List evidence of attitudes of dependence you perceive in the extracts.

At Fort Simpson, where the Wesleyan Methodists have a successful mission, and at Metlakahtlah, where Mr. Duncan of the Church Mission Society has presided for many years, the beneficial effects of Christian teaching may be especially seen.

These results are, however, exceedingly limited, and hardly extend beyond the settlements alluded to. Even as they are, the Indians of this Province are its best consumers, and contribute much more to its wealth and vital resources than we have any idea of; but under the expanding and beneficent influence of civilization how much greater their value would be to us as inhabitants, I believe can scarcely be imagined.

This process of Christianizing Indians scattered over such an extensive coast line is, however, exceedingly difficult, mainly from the baneful influence of White men, whose principles are not all in accord with such designs, and who live among and freely mingle with them chiefly for the gratification of evil desires. It is no doubt greatly due to the many untoward effects arising from this circumstance, that the present race of Coast Indians is fast disappearing, and at the rate with which they are now being swept from light and life, it will not be long hence ere they exist only in memory. Even in such a field of labour, instances of failure either from the want of funds or fitness for the position, are not wanting among Missionaries, who have from time to time tried their hand at redeeming the savage in various parts of the Province.

Having taken in some coal purchased of the Cannery Company, at Inverness, we sailed on the afternoon of the 10th for Metlakahtla, where we arrived about five o'clock, p.m.

Mr. Duncan came out with his Indian crew, and acted as pilot into the harbour, which, though difficult to enter on account of the number of rocks which appear at low water in dangerous proximity to the channel, is nevertheless very pretty and picturesque. The village itself was gaily decorated with any quantity of bunting and evergreens, and the Indians who had been anxiously expecting our arrival during the day, were impatient to extend their hearty welcome. At the landing we were received with a grand salute of big guns and small arms, and escorted to the platform in front of the church where there were assembled in a most orderly array the whole population of the village.

Seats had been already provided for the officers and myself, and the following address was presented to me, and read very well, indeed, by Mr. Duncan's interpreter, David Leash:

> We, the council of Metlakahtla, desire to tell our hearts. We are happy to see you on our shores. We have heard of your name for a long time, and wanted to see your face, now we are happy to express our feelings in seeing you amongst us. We all heard of your work in helping the Indians, therefore we desire to tell you what troubles our hearts.
>
> Our forefathers were brought up on fishing, &c., and their work is still in our hands, and we claim the fishing places as our property.
>
> We do not want white people to take these places from our hands, or to be driven from our stations where our forefathers have lived.
>
> Before the gospel came to us we considered these places of more value than life, and they were not allowed to be touched

without the permission of the owners, but now the light of the gospel has showed that we are brethren, therefore we are happy to ask your favor to assist us and all the Indians to keep our rights.

(Signed)   PAUL SEBASSAH

DONALD BRUCE

ABRAHAM LINCOLN

LEEGAIC

SEMION DELANY

MOSES VENN

PETER SIMPSON

Having replied to this, a few words were then addressed to the Indians by Capt. Orlebar and Mr. Inspector Anderson. Most hearty cheers were then given for the party, with three rousing ones for Her Majesty, and we dispersed to look about the village.

The morning of the next day was devoted to hearing private complaints, and at noon all assembled in the large school-house for the grand meeting, where I spoke to them generally on the purpose of my visit, and the intentions of the Government towards them.

I was glad to congratulate them upon the very creditable appearance of their village, which, I may truly add, exceeded my most sanguine expectations.

My address, throughout, was listened to with profound attention, and was followed by congratulatory remarks and sensible advice by Capt. Orlebar.

The different chiefs and members of the village council then address me in turn, viz.:

Paul Sebassah: "Chief, What have we further to say beyond this, that we are very happy. We have already written on our address what our hearts say to you. We have also heard for ourselves, and find to be true what Mr. Duncan has often told us.

"Yes, many have spoken lies to us about the Government (chief).

"Many have tried to estrange (make different) our hearts, and trouble us by evil reports. We have listened (opened our ears) to strange (different) men, and so we have been troubled, just as some have sown lies among our brethren of the interior (up the Fraser River) of which you have spoken, so have they done amongst us. We now hear from you what we are to believe, and we are made happy by what you have told us.

"It was God who gave our forefathers and us the small streams which supply us with food. Our rights are being invaded, but you tell us that we are not to fear as we shall not suffer injury or loss.

"Your work for us is good. We feel strong, should evil reports again reach us we shall know how to treat them."

Moses Venn: "Chief, it is as Paul has said. Many chiefs have visited us from time to time, but they only examined or looked at us and then went away, but you came to help us, and settle and arrange for us our affairs. It is God again blessing us to which we trace your coming. We have fully listened to your words to us, and we thank you for your words and work for us and all our brethren.

"We are still weak and poor but you have added happiness to us to-day, and we feel we cannot satisfy ourselves in thanking you."

Simeon Wahdeemesh: "Chief, You have heard the words of Paul or Moses. They have spoken rightly. What further should we ask from you? You have in your address anticipated our requests, and we are satisfied and made happy.

"We are very happy to meet you; long have we heard of your name, but we have never seen you before, and now, as children are gratified in meeting a father, so are we gratified in meeting you, and not ashamed to speak in your presence.

"We have listened to your words and will obey them.

"We have received God's word and that is our strength.

"Some white men would have us disregard the word, but we are happy that you are not one of them, and we will remember this."

Neashack: "Well, sir, what can we ask for more than what you have promised us. This is the way with the birds – the young ones open their mouths and the mother bird feeds them.

"We are like the young birds to-day, and you have fed our hearts with your words. I am poor, but though I am poor I have been made happy by seeing you and hearing you to-day. And I may tell you that I and my brethren here are determined to go right on our way, and persevere in following what is good."

John Tait (elder in Metlakahtla church): "Though I am neither wiser nor older than others here, yet I cannot refrain from speaking.

"We have heard and are happy to learn that we are no longer to listen to unauthorized reports which reach us. This strengthens our hearts. At last, sir, you have come to examine our village. We have long expected you, having heard of your work. You now see us, and you have acknowledged the work of God amongst us is good.

"Just, however, as there are evil men among the whites, so there are evil men yet amongst the Indians.

"We are not all good, nor are we all yet strong enough to stand by ourselves. Nor can we by ourselves withstand the evil white men around us.

"The good news (Gospel) has come to you, and it has come to us, and we embrace it as you do, and we want to be saved as you do. Yet there are white men that would frighten us into breaking the Sabbath.

"They come to earn money in our country, but not content, they try to injure us and lead us wrong.

"Mr. Duncan has stopped intoxicating liquor from coming amongst us, not only here but all around Metlakahtla; but now he has to contend with those who would lead us to violate the Sabbath (referring to Canneries desiring Indians to commence fishing at 6 o'clock, p.m., on Sunday). We are glad you came to help us in the right way. We beg you to persevere in your good work of mercy in helping the poor Indians in what is for their good."

The proceedings then terminated with great cheering on the part of the Indians, and the remainder of the day was devoted to visiting and prescribing for the sick of the village, and it was midnight before I was able to return to the ship.

Indian Affairs, 1875-1879, pp. 33, 114-116.

By the end of the nineteenth century, it looked as if the Indians
were travelling rapidly down the road to extinction. Those who
thought of the Indian as a noble savage, nature's child, and those
who thought of him as an expendable item in the march of civilization were in agreement on this point. The Indian population
was on the decline and would shortly disappear. We know now
that this belief was incorrect, but to observers of the time the
signs were conclusive. The views expressed in the following extract were typical. Warburton Pike was an Englishman who
explored the north of British Columbia and the Mackenzie River
valley. In 1896, he published a book in which he describes his
experiences. At this point he is in the north of British Columbia
just south of the Yukon border.

Very peculiar individuals were our two Indians, Charley and Two-fingered
Johnny – so named from a malformation of one hand; a couple of good examples of what might have been rather fine characters if they had never come
into contact with the bastard civilization of the mining camp. I don't believe
the red man was ever the noble creature he has often been painted. We can only
suppose that in time past he led a harmless existence, and unconsciously did
his duty in the particular station of life to which he had been called; but, dress
him up in the white man's clothes, feed him on bacon and flour, canned
peaches, and molasses, give him a few drinks of whisky, and be becomes a
despicable brute. He does not like being taken away from all these good things,
and has a profound contempt for the few true Indians who still make a living
in the woods by trapping the precious fur. So it was with Charlie and Johnny.
They were good enough men to track a moose, or work round the camp;
but on all the trips we went with them their hearts were never in the life –
they did everything sulkily, quarrelled with each other, and grumbled because
there was no canned fruit; while their women would on no account go to the
woods to dry meat or cure skins – they were not that sort of women, they
told us, but must dress in the finest that could be bought in the store and sit
through the glorious winter weather by the side of a sheet-iron stove. . . .

We went in every direction – down the Liard, up the Liard, and up the
Dease, but everywhere we found the same abundance of moose tracks. Once
we visited a large lake 20 miles to the westward of the post, and laid in a supply
of whitefish, which we caught in nets under the ice, in great quantities. Here
we found a band of Liard Indians hunting and fishing. Sickness was prevalent
in the camp – very few of the men were well enough to hunt moose, and they
had come to the lake to be sure of making a living. A melancholy spectacle
the camp presented; half a dozen pits in the snow lined with pine brush, a
little more pine brush stuck up as a wind-break, and no other shelter from
the weather. Lying in their blankets were the sick men, some of them evidently
never to get up again – dying among the moose hair and fish guts that were
liberally scattered over everything; and outside the filth of the camp the ice-
bound lake sparkled in the winter sunshine that always seems so full of health
and strength. What was the matter with them all? "Oh! we're always like this,"
the chief explained, "since the white men came to the country. In the old time,

my tribe was powerful, but now many of my people die every winter. Some
children are born, but they are no good – they die soon."

Now in the interests of ethnology, if not of humanity, would it not be worth
somebody's while to send a qualified doctor to patch up as best he might the
remnants of the tribes of the Casca and Liard Indians, and prevent the
spread of contagion? A good deal of money is spent annually by the Dominion
and the various Provincial Governments in doing whatever is done for the
Indians of Canada – surely a little might be spared for this outlying part of the
country; and let the man whose salary it pays be a doctor and not an Indian
agent. No surveys are wanted; no reservations need be staked off; for, if the
present state of affairs continues but a few more years, extinction will put every
Indian beyond the limitation of the agent's reserve.

> Warburton Pike, *Through the Subarctic Forest* (London: Edward
> Arnold, 1896), pp. 86-87, 98-99.

1. What effects of culture contact does Pike observe?
2. "What was the matter with them all?" The chief explained what had
   happened to his people, but did not really explain why. In the light
   of what you have learned so far, write a paragraph giving your
   answer to the question.
3. Pike deplores what has happened to the Indians. What action does
   he propose? Discuss the adequacy of his analysis and his proposals.

---

5.   Industrialization and Urbanization

The Indians of Canada did not have the opportunity to recover
from the effects of the impact of the white man's culture on their
own. While still disorganized by the results of the contact with
fur traders, missionaries, and settlers, they found themselves in a
country that was growing steadily in population while at the same
time rapidly becoming industrialized. The industrialization of
Canada in the twentieth century had tended to keep the Indians
off balance and disoriented. Modern industry has certain essential requirements. Workers must have specialized skills, and these
require special education and training. A modern factory, office,
or other business operation, in order to be successful in a competitive world, has to be efficient; efficiency requires that workers
are on the job regularly, at specific times and for specific periods.
Production schedules have to be achieved and deadlines have to
be met. These requirements are rigorous enough for those reared
in the white culture, but they are specially difficult for the Indians.
For many reasons Indians have not benefited greatly from the
education provided for them. As to the question of time – punctu-

ality and regular attendance – Indians often find it difficult to adjust to the white man's sense of time. Furthermore, they have less tolerance to the boredom of the humdrum routine of the dull, repetitive jobs which are a part of the industrial way of life. Add to this the rapid growth of towns and cities, and one can get some idea of the feelings of confusion and helplessness that assailed the Indians. One of their more eloquent spokesman, Chief Dan George, conveys these feelings in this moving statement.

. . . . Was it only yesterday that men sailed around the moon . . . And is it tomorrow they will stand up on its barren surface? You and I marvel that man should travel so far and so fast. . . . Yet, if they have travelled far then I have travelled farther . . . . and if they have travelled fast, then I faster . . . . for I was born a thousand years ago . . . . born in a culture of bows and arrows. But within the span of half a life I was flung across the ages to the culture of the atom bomb. . . . and from bows and arrows to atom bombs is a distance far beyond a flight to the moon.

I was born in an age that loved the things of nature and gave them beautiful names like Tes-wall-u-wit instead of dried up names like Stanley Park.

I was born when people loved all nature and spoke to it as though it has a soul . . . . I can remember going up Indian River with my father when I was very young . . . . . I can remember him watching the sun light fires of Mount Pay-nay-nay as it rose above its peak. I can remember him singing his thanks to it as he often did . . . . singing the Indian word "thanks . . . ." so very very softly . . .

And then the people came . . . . . more and more people came . . . . like a crushing rushing wave they came . . . . . hurling the years aside!! and suddenly I found myself a young man in the midst of the twentieth century.

I found myself and my people adrift in this new age . . . . but not part of it.

Engulfed by its rushing tide, but only as a captive eddy . . . going round and round . . . . On little reserves, on plots of land we floated in a kind of grey unreality . . . . ashamed of our culture which you ridiculed . . . . unsure of who we were or where we were going . . . . uncertain of our grip on the present . . . . weak in our hope of the future . . . And that is where we pretty well stand today.

I had a glimpse of something better than this. For a few brief years I knew my people when we lived the old life . . . . . I knew them when there was still a dignity in our lives and a feeling of worth in our outlook. I knew them when there was unspoken confidence in the home and a certain knowledge of the path we walked upon. But we were living on the dying energy of a dying culture . . . . that was slowly losing its forward thrust.

I think it was the suddenness of it all that hurt us so. We did not have time to adjust to the startling upheaval around us. We seemed to have lost what we had without a replacement for it. We did not have the time to take your 20th century progress and eat it little by little and digest it. It was forced feeding from the start and our stomach turned sick and we vomited.

Do you know what it is like to be without mooring? Do you know what it is like to live in surroundings that are ugly and everywhere you look you see ugly things . . . . . strange things . . . . . strange and ugly things? It depresses man, for man must be surrounded by the beautiful if his soul is to grow.

What did we see in the new surroundings you brought us? Laughing faces, pitying faces, sneering faces, conniving faces. Faces that ridiculed, faces that stole from us. It is no wonder we turned to the only people who did not steal and who did not sneer, who came with love. They were the missionaries and they came with love and I for one will ever return that love.

Do you know what it is like to feel you are of no value to society and those around you? To know that people came to help you but not to work with you for you knew that they knew you had nothing to offer . . . . ?

Do you know what it is like to have your race belittled and to come to learn that you are only a burden to the country? Maybe we did not have the skills to make a meaningful contribution, but no one would wait for us to catch up. We were shoved aside because we were dumb and could never learn.

What is it like to be without pride in your race, pride in your family, pride and confidence in yourself? What is it like? You don't know for you never tasted its bitterness.

I shall tell you what it is like. It is like not caring about tomorrow for what does tomorrow matter. It is like having a reserve that looks like a junk yard because the beauty in the soul is dead and why should the soul express an external beauty that does not match it? It is like getting drunk and for a few brief moments an escaping from ugly reality and feeling a sense of importance. It is most of all like awaking next morning to the guilt of betrayal. For the alcohol did not fill the emptiness but only dug it deeper.

And now you hold out your hand and you beckon to me to come across the street . . . . come and integrate you say . . . . But how can I come . . . . . I am naked and ashamed. How can I come in dignity? I have no presents . . . I have no gifts. What is there in my culture you value . . . . my poor treasure you can only scorn.

Am I then to come as a beggar and receive all from your omnipotent hand? Somehow I must wait . . . I must delay. I must find myself. I must find my treasure. I must wait until you want something of me . . . . until you need something that is me. Then I can raise my head and say to my wife and family . . . . listen . . . . . they are calling . . . . . they need me . . . . I must go.

Then I can walk across the street and I will hold my head high for I will meet you as an equal. I will not scorn you for your deeming gifts and you will not receive me in pity. Pity I can do without . . . . . . my manhood I cannot do without.

I can only come as Chief Capilano came to Captain Vancouver . . . as one sure of his authority . . . certain of his worth . . . . master of his house . . . . and leader of his people. I shall not come as a cringing object of your pity. I shall come in dignity or I shall not come at all.

You talk big words of integration in the schools. Does it really exist? Can we talk of integration until there is social integration . . . . unless there is integration of hearts and minds you have only a physical presence . . . . and the walls are as high as the mountain range.

Come with me to the playgrounds of an integrated high school . . . . . see how level and flat and ugly the black top is . . . . but look . . . . now it is recess time . . . . . the students pour through the doors . . . . soon over here is a group of white students . . . . and see . . . . . over there near the fence . . . a group of

native students . . . . and look again . . . . . the black is no longer level . . . . . .
mountain ranges rising . . . valleys falling . . . and a great chasm seems to be
opening up between the two groups . . . . yours and mine . . . . but no one
seems capable of crossing over. But wait . . . . . soon the bell will ring and the
students will leave the play yard. Integration has moved indoors. There isn't
much room in a class room to dig chasms so there are only little ones there
. . . . only little ones . . . . . for we won't allow big ones . . . . at least, not right
under our noses . . . . . so we will cover it all over with black top . . . . cold . . . .
black . . . . flat . . . . and full of ugliness in its sameness.

I know you must be saying . . . . tell us what *Do* you want. What do we
want? We want first of all to be respected and to feel we are people of worth.
We want an equal opportunity to succeed in life . . . . but we cannot succeed
on your terms . . . . we cannot raise ourselves on your norms. We need specialized help in education . . specialized help in the formative years . . . . . special
courses in English. We need guidance counselling . . . . we need equal job
opportunities for our graduates, otherwise our students will lose courage and
ask what is the use of it all.

Let no one forget it . . . . we are a people with special right guaranteed to
us by promises and treaties. We do not beg for these rights, nor do we thank
you . . . we do not thank you for them because we paid for them . . . . and God
help us the price we paid was exorbitant! We paid for them with our culture,
our dignity and self-respect. We paid and paid and paid until we became a
beaten race, poverty-stricken and conquered.

But you have been kind to listen to me and I know that in your heart you
wished you could help. I wonder if there is much you can do and yet there is a
lot you can do . . . when you meet my children in your classroom respect each
one for what he is . . . a child of our Father in heaven, and your brother. Maybe
it all boils down to just that.

> The difficulties faced by Indians in adjusting to the requirements
> of a rapidly-changing industrial society have been studied by
> anthropologists. The two tables which follow are summaries of
> the cultural beliefs and preferences of Indians before contact
> with Whites and after prolonged exposure to the White Man's
> culture. They should help us to see what changes have occurred
> and how the changes have not helped Indians to cope with modern
> Canadian society.

1. If ambition to succeed through competition and striving to achieve
   one's own ends is important in our society, how would an Indian
   who believed in the traditional values get on in our society?

2. A white person judging an Indian in terms of the White value orientation might easily come to the conclusion that he is lazy, careless
   about the future, and unambitious. How might an Indian judge an
   average White person in terms of traditional Indian values?

3. What signs do you see in our society of groups of White people
   adopting values similar to the traditional Indian values?

Table H.   Dominant Value Orientation prior to White Dominance

White	Indian-Eskimo
Human nature is evil but perfectable	
Man dominates, exploits and controls nature	In harmony with nature
Future-oriented	Past and present oriented
Doing and activity oriented	Being-in-becoming
Individualistic	Collaborative (tribal)
Capitalistic (commercial)	Communistic in the non-political sense (sharing)
Nationalistic	Communal

C. Hendry, *Beyond Traplines* (Toronto: The Anglican Church of Canada, 1969), p. 32.

1. What is the traditional attitude towards time? How does it differ from that of Whites? What would be the Indian attitude towards such things as long-range planning, meeting future deadlines, etc.?

2. If you were managing an industrial undertaking e.g. a factory or a logging operation, would you tend to prefer to employ a person with the White orientation or the traditional Indian value orientation? Explain and defend your decision.

Table I.   Indian Accommodation and/or lack of Accommodation to the Dominant White Culture

Before	After Sustained Exposures to Whites
In harmony with nature, a sense of wholeness	Loss of integrated whole and personal integrity
Community concept of possession	Cumulative concept applied to the individual
Collaborative relations (collateral)	Individualistic relations
Friendliness and trust	Hostility, contempt, suspicion
Concrete behavior governed by moral codes	Increased license due to cultural breakdown
Interdependence	Ecologically trapped in poverty, dependent on subsidies, and uneconomic occupational activities

Ibid., p. 35.

1. What are the attitudes towards White society which have been generated in Indians by prolonged exposure to White culture? How would these attitudes make it difficult for Indians to adjust to an environment predominantly White? (e.g. an industrial plant in which most of the workers were white, a modern Canadian town or city, etc.)

2. What would probably be the attitudes of Indians who remained in an impoverished reservation environment towards those Indians who "made it" in the white man's world?

3. How have the effects of culture contact made the Indians susceptible to alcoholic excess? How does excessive drinking make their adaptation to modern society more difficult?

4. Generally speaking, how would you describe the effects of culture contact on Indian personality? Do these effects contribute to the Indians' ability to adapt successfully to an urban-industrial way of life?

Despite the difficulties facing them in the urban and industrial world, there has been a significant movement of Indians off the reserves. The figures for British Columbia may be taken as typical of nation wide trends during the ten year period 1960–1970.

	On Reserve	Off Reserve	Total
1960	32,210 (83.2%)	6,520 (16.8%)	38,730
1970	32,935 (66.3%)	16,716 (33.7%)	49,651

This is not to suggest that the traffic is all one way – off the reserve. Many Indians who leave the reserve find that they cannot make a satisfactory adjustment to life off the reserve, so they return. But the trend is definitely there. Life on many reserves means poverty and dependence. The young in particular are attracted by the apparent opportunities in the larger society. Some make a successful, or at least a satisfactory, adjustment. Many more, however, have been attracted to towns and cities, but do not have the skills they need in order to succeed. Unable to secure employment, they find themselves on the welfare rolls and living in poor accommodation on the fringes of the community. Unfortunately in this condition, they render themselves liable to prejudice and discrimination. Too easily they are labelled lazy, drunken, and irresponsible. These people are in a kind of no-man's land. They do not have the psychological support that life on the reserve could provide, nor have they found acceptance in the larger society. At best, this is a marginal existence of psychological and material deprivation; at worst, it leads through loneliness to tragedy. This poem, written by a young Indian man about the Skid Row area of Vancouver, tells of the route travelled by many young Indians, men and women alike.

Hardened Artery

Vancouver, a sprawling city, a brawling city, a knocked-down-dragged-out kind of city.
This is the city of bright sounds, the fight sounds and the thirty-cents-short-to-get-tight sounds.

Listen Jack . . . do you hear that beat? Do you hear the rustling of restless feet . . . and muffled shuffle of night, flowing down on a down, down street of a down, down town?
You're at Hasting and Columbia Jack, the end of the track and there's no turning back, because this is the corner!

This is the Corner man! and this is the East End of Town.
The East End of Town, and some people say its the best end of town, and you're standing on wasting street, a bitter tasting street, a foot-sore drag called Hasting Street . . .
You want to see this street for real?
Be a lamp post.

This is a bruised street, a used street, a very much accused street.
It's a sometime street, a funtimes street, but mostly it's a you're-just-about-through street!
A tired street, a liared street, and when you're with it and having it rough, it's a "God it's hell to-be-wired street."
This is an odd sort of street, a people who forgot-God-sort-of street.

A drab buildinged homely street, a sure-as-hell lonely street. It's a great street, full of bad ones, a street full of sad ones, slouching and staring, their pale faces wearing a look of indifference and their slumped shoulders bent from the weight of the monkey.
These are the night people, the living-in-fright people.
These are the face hardened, these are the case hardened.
These are the tough ones, the always-got-stuff ones.
The quick ones, the slick ones, and the five o'clock bile-throated sick ones.

This is the corner man, and down here is really down. Take a good look around. Take a good look! A GOOD LOOK!

BE A LAMP POST . . . .

The First Citizen, No. 1, November 1969, p. 2.

One institution which has come into being in response to this problem is the Friendship Centre. Many Friendship Centres have sprung up. Rural centres serve as "drop in" places where people of Indian ancestry can meet and get information about what they may expect when they move from the reserves or remote areas to towns and cities. Those in the urban centres refer Indians to community services and agencies which can provide them with assistance, find jobs and housing, secure legal aid, provide loans

from emergency funds, offer recreational and group activity programs and numerous other services.

Some figures may convey an idea of the extent of the work:

In the year ending March 31, 1966, the Canadian Indian
Centre of Toronto saw 15,338 persons participate in their programs, with an average monthly attendance of 1,728 during the
period.

Between May, 1965 and August, 1966, the Winnipeg Centre
sponsored an Alcoholics Anonymous group, referred 32 people
to legal aid, 5 to the National Parole Board, 286 to the Indian
Affairs Branch, made 326 job placements, and operated a home-
finding service.

During 1966, the Calgary Indian Friendship Society placed
1,450 men and women in jobs, referred 250 to other services and
agencies, gave legal advice to 175, found housing for 125, provided special tutoring for 32 students and made loans to 135
people.

Clearly the work being done by these centres across the
country is valuable, although they are all working with inadequate
budgets and underpaid staff. A study sponsored by the Department of Indian Affairs and Northern Development states:

> The number of Indian people moving into the cities
> and towns of our country is already large and will
> undoubtedly increase substantially as over-popula-
> tion of the reserves forces Indian people to move
> elsewhere. The problem is already serious and gov-
> ernments have been slow to recognize a trend that
> cannot fail to create serious problems in the very
> near future.

Indians and the Law (Ottawa: Department of Indian Affairs and
Northern Development, 1967), p. 54.

It recommends that the work of Friendship Centres be encouraged by substantial increases in federal, provincial and municipal
grants; and that the Citizenship Branch of the federal government
study ways of assisting the centres to develop sound programs
for Indian people coming into the cities and towns.

The chairman of the group making this study, Dr. Gilbert
Monture, summarizes the problem in his preface to the report:

> The transition from the relatively happy and secure
> life of the reserve to the highly competitive urban-
> ized life of our cities and towns has been made
> necessary by overwhelming economic pressures.
> However, it often inflicts too severe a strain on a
> people ill-equipped by tradition, temperament, edu-
> cation, and economic attitudes to withstand. (Many

non-Indians are also breaking under this strain and are indulging in dangerous forms of escape from the realities of life.) Add to this the latent non-acceptance of the Indian by much of the non-Indian society and the difficulty of adjustment to the white man's standards of moral and social conduct becomes compounded. Small wonder that many Indians seek to withdraw and exhibit a disregard for the concepts and the values of the dominant society. I am of the opinion that just as the blame for the present unhappy condition does not rest solely on the shoulders of any one of the parties involved, the ultimate solution can be found only by joint and sincere action.

Ibid., pp. 7-8.

1. The choice available to Indians seems to be either to remain on the reserve or to enter urbanized life. What are the implications of each choice?
2. What are the special difficulties Indians have to cope with if they are to make a successful adjustment to urbanized life? In what ways are non-Indians better prepared for this way of life?
3. Give one or two examples of "the latent non-acceptance" of the Indian mentioned by Dr. Monture. Explain how these would make successful adjustment difficult.
4. Dr. Monture mentions that some non-Indians are cracking under the pressure of modern urban-industrial living and are indulging in dangerous forms of escapism. Give examples of these. Are changes in our way of life needed to reduce stress? If so, what changes you suggest?

Despite the difficulties, some Indians have made a successful adjustment to the urban-industrial way of life. Many have competed successfully with white men in business. There are individual Indians, for example, who own fishing boats and equipment worth hundreds of thousands of dollars, and who make incomes in the five figure bracket. Indians have distinguished themselves in many aspects of Canadian life. You may be able to add to this list of some who are active at the present time:

Dr. Gilbert Monture, internationally-known engineer and world expert on mineral economics.
Ethel Brant Monture, noted authority on Indian culture and traditions
Senator James Gladstone
Len Marchand, Member of Parliament
George Clutesi and Gerald Tail Feather, painters of renown
Dr. Howard Adams, a spokesman for Indians and Métis in Saskatchewan
Harold Cardinal, author of *The Unjust Society*

Chief Dan George, actor in plays and films
Jean Paul Nolet, a prominent radio announcer
Buffy Ste. Marie and Alanis Obomsawin, folk singers
Dr. A. Spence and Dr. Peter Kelly, Anglican and United Church
ministers.

Questions for Discussion

1. It is often argued by Indian critics that the history taught to Canadian students is biased and unfair in that it conveys misconceptions about Indians and their role in Canadian history. To what extent do you think this criticism is justified?

2. Discuss the ideas expressed in these statements taken from school textbooks:

   a) Who calls, the Redman poor and sick,
   he calls.
   Who comes, the white man rich and strong,
   he comes.
   Who watches to see that pity reigns,
   God watches.

   b) "They fought more ferociously than any other Indians that we encountered in our westward movement."

   c) "The white man from Europe brought with him knowledge and skill far greater than that of the wisest Indian."

   d) "Indians were doomed by the coming of the white man. The number of Indians was small because they didn't know how to develop America's natural resources, that is the soil, the minerals, the water power and the other natural riches of the land."

   e) "The missionaries regarded the Indians primarily as souls to be saved. They taught the Indians agriculture and handicrafts."

   f) "It is probable that the North American tribes, in the course of their wanderings, lived for generations in the frozen waste of Alaska. This experience deadened their minds and killed their imagination and initiative."

   g) "How, for instance, could the missionaries express the idea of a loving father to natives whose conception was that of cruel and evil spirits?"

   h) "After the laws were passed [legalizing the treaties with the Indians], the condition of the Indian improved somewhat. Thousands of Indians continued to live in squalor on their reservations, but other thousands took their place as citizens."

3. The Indians were not the only people who came under the impact of European culture. India, China and Japan were influenced by Europeans. But whereas Indian cultures were shattered by the contact, those of the countries mentioned were changed but not to such a great degree. How do you account for the difference?

4. It may be argued that, without the co-operation of the Indians and without the benefit of the technology that they had developed to enable them to cope with their environment, white men could not succeeded in establishing themselves in Canada.

a) Consider these extracts from the journal of Simon Fraser in which he recorded his journey down the Fraser River in 1808. List the evidence you can find in this document to support the hypothesis stated above.

Saturday, May 22 [28], 1808.   Having made every necessary preparation for a long voyage, we embarked at 5 o'clock, A.M. in four canoes, at Fraser's River [i.e., at the mouth of the Nechako River]. Our crew consisted of nineteen men, two Indians, Mr. Stewa:d [Stuart], Mr. Quesnil [Quesnel], and myself; in all twenty four. At this place [the] Columbia [i.e., the Fraser River] is about 300 yards wide. It overflows its banks, and has a very strong current.

Monday, May 30.   In the afternoon, some Toohowtins [Tautens] and Atnaughs [Atnahs] arrived on horse back. They seemed peaceably inclined, and appeared happy to see us, and observed that having heard by their neighbours that white people were to visit their country this season, they had remained near the route on purpose to receive us.

Tuesday, May 31.   ... we embarked at 5, accompanied by one of the Toohow-tin [Tauten] Indians as an interpreter for the Atnah language.
  The Chief and the Indians, recommended to our attention yesterday, who were encamped on a hill to the left, soon joined us, and presented us with dried salmon and different kind[s] of roots.
  The Chief who had been an advocate in our cause spoke much in favour to his own people, and assured us that the next nation were good Indians and would be kind to white strangers. Having given to our new friend a hint that trading posts should be established in his country within a short period, he immediately offered to accompany us all the way, remarking at the same time that he was well known, and that his experience and influence would be of great consequences to security of our success. Then his brother presented me with a fine beaver skin, and a well dressed deer skin, and then recommended the Chief to our particular protection.

Wednesday, June 1.   Numbers of the Natives came to see us in [the] course of the day and remained. They all assured us that the navigation for a certain distance below was impractible [impracticable], and advised us to leave our canoes in their charge and proceed on our journey by land to a great river [the Thompson] that flows from the left into this communication.
  The Indians seemed pleased in our Company. They carry no

arms, and this confidence I suppose was meant as a testimony of their friendship.

Sunday [Saturday], June 4.   One of the Indians brought us a Pistol which Mr. Quesnel lost yesterday when he was on horse back. This was a piece of honesty we did not expect. Yet all the time we have been at this place though many things were left loose, and scattered in such a manner as to afford the natives plenty of opportunities, nothing went astray.

Friday [Thursday], June 9.   I prevailed upon another Indian to embark with us as pilot. We then continued our course until late in the evening when our pilot ordered us ashore for the night.

Wednesday [Tuesday], June 14.   Last night some of the natives having remarked that we were not white men but enemies in disguise, displeased our Old Chief and a serious altercation took place in consequence. They stated that his tribe were their natural enemies, and that some of his young men had made war upon them in the spring. This he readily admitted, but affirmed that these were foolish young men who had escaped without his knowledge. Seeing the debate getting high, we interposed and the argument immediately ended amicably. Then the Old Chief sent couriers, to inform the natives ahead that we were not enemies, [and to tell them] not to be alarmed at our appearance, and to meet us without arms. At the same time he strongly recommended to us to be on our guard.

The Indians brought us plenty of fish, roots, and berries.

Thursday [Wednesday], June 15.   With difficulty we procured a canoe. The Indians after bargaining a long while consented to accept of a file, and a kettle in exchange. But of provisions we could only procure thirty dried salmon.

Friday [Thursday], June 16.   This morning the men joined us. Of the two canoes which the Indians had, we could obtain but one. It belonged to a sick man, who accepted of medicines in payment.

Here we met some of a neighbouring nation called Haka-maugh [the Thompson Indians] – with these were two of another Tribe called *Suihonie* [Shoshone?]; all were exceedingly well dressed in leather, and were on horseback. . . . They were kind to us, and assisted us at the carrying place with their horses.

An Indian, who had been out a hunting, returned with a deer he had killed. We applied for a share of the meat; but he would not part with any. The chief invited us to his quarters; his son, by his orders, served us upon a handsome mat, and regaled us with salmon and roots. Our men had some also, and they procured, besides, several Dogs which is always a favourite dish with the Canadian voyagers.

Sunday [Saturday], June 18.   At 3 P.M. we passed a camp of the natives. These were poor, but generous, for they assisted us.

Monday [Sunday], June 19.   The Hakamaugh nation are different both in language and manners from their neighbours the Askettels [Askettihs; Lillooets]. They have many chiefs and great men, appear to be good orators, for their manner of delivery is extremely handsome. We had every reason to be thankful for our reception at this place; the Indians shewed us every possible attention and supplied our wants as much as they could. We had salmon, berries, oil and roots in abundance, and our men had six dogs. Our tent was pitched near the camp, and we enjoyed peace and security during our stay.

Thursday [Monday], June 20.   The Indians sung and danced all night. Some of our men, who went to see them, were much amused. With some difficulty we obtained two wooden canoes; the Indians, however, made no price, but accepted of our offers.

Two Indians from our last encampment overtook us with a piece of Iron which we had forgotten there. We considered this as an extraordinary degree of honesty and attention, particularly in this part of the world.

Thursday [Wednesday], June 22.   Our guides returned as they had promised. Four men were employed in bringing down the canoes by water. They make several portages in course of this undertaking. The rest of the men carried the baggage by land. When this troublesome and fatiguing business was over, we crossed over to the village, where we were received with loud acclamations and generously entertained.

Saturday [Friday], June 24.   . . . about the middle of the rapids two of them struck against one another, by which accident one of them lost a piece of its stern, and the steersman his paddle: the canoe in consequence took in much water.

After repairing the damages we continued, and in the evening arrived at an Indian village. The Natives flocked about us, and invited us to pass the night with them. Accepting their invitation we were led to the camp which was at some distance up the hill. . . . We were well treated, they gave us fresh salmon, hazle nuts, and some other nuts of an excellent quality. The small pox was in the camp, and several of the Natives were marked with it.

Sunday [Saturday], June 25. . . . we continued our course up and down, among hills and rocks, and along the steep declivities of mountains, where hanging rocks, and projecting cliffs at the edge of the bank made the passage so small as to render it difficult even for one person to pass sideways at times.

Many of the natives from the last camp, having accompanied us, were of the greatest service to us on these intricate and dangerous occasions. In places where we were obliged to hand our guns from one to another, and where the greatest precaution was required to pass even singly, the Indians went through boldly with loads.

Tuesday [Monday], June 27. We came to a small camp of Indians consisting [of] about 60 persons. The name of the place is Spazum [Spuzzum]. . . . Here as usual we were hospitably entertained, with fresh Salmon boiled and roasted, green and dried berries, oil and onions.

W. Kaye Lamb, ed., *The Letters and Journals of Simon Fraser 1806-1808* (Toronto: The Macmillan Company of Canada, 1960), pp. 61-97 *passim.*

 b) Examine the journals of other explorers for similar evidence.
 c) What aspects of Indian technology were used by explorers and fur traders to ensure their survival and to enable them to carry on their work?
 d) In what other ways did Indians help white men to establish themselves in Canada?
5. It is not uncommon for white Canadians to lay the blame for the problems of Indians on the Indians themselves. Using your knowledge of the history of White-Indian relations in Canada, prepare an essay to rebut this argument.

THREE

Solving the Problem

In Parts One and Two we have looked at the problem of Indians in Canadian society and we have traced the historical development underlying the problem. We have seen that Indians are poor compared to the majority of other Canadians and that they are becoming relatively poorer. With a few exceptions they work at the poorest paid jobs and suffer a high level of unemployment. Many are dependent on some kind of welfare payment. Generally speaking they have benefited little from the kind of education that has been provided for them. We have seen, too, that they are subjected to many forms of discrimination.

The historical study has shown that the Indians of Canada are a people who have been disinherited both territorially and culturally. Today they are a people who live uncertainly between two cultural worlds – the one consisting of the remnants of a traditional culture, shattered by that of the White Man, and the other the world of the White Man's culture. They are unable to return to the past. The march of historical events has made that impossible. Hitherto they have not been able to make a satisfactory adjustment to a world dominated by Whites. A few have entered the world of the White Man and have been successful in it, usually at the price of assimilation. Many do not wish to enter this world, especially if the price of admission is the sacrifice of their identity as Indians. Meanwhile, they remain second-class citizens.

But things are stirring. An increasing number of Indians are voicing dissatisfaction with their poverty, inferior social status, and the general hopelessness of their lives. They are becoming increasingly aware of what has happened to them in the past and how this has affected what they are today. The number who are angry and impatient is growing. They want a new deal and they want it soon. The demands for action will grow, as the rapidly growing Indian population intensifies pressure on the resources of the reserves.

The problem facing Canada is how to make it possible for Indians to live a full and satisfying life within Canadian society. It is a difficult problem. Whether it is fairly met and dealt with will be a test of Canada's claim to be a truly just and democratic society. In Part Three we shall look more closely at the problem, what proposals are being offered for its solution, and how and why proposed solutions differ. This book will offer no final conclusions. It will be up to you, on the basis of your study of the problem, to arrive at your own conclusions as to what should be done to resolve it.

1.   Possible Solutions

What then are the possible answers to the question of the future role of Indians in Canadian society? It seems that there are three: assimilation, separation, and integration.

Assimilation

The dictionary definition of assimilate is "to make or become like: to digest." If a cat eats a canary, it assimilates it. The canary becomes, in some way, a part of the cat. It is absorbed by the cat.

For the Indians, assimilation would mean that they would be absorbed into the larger society. They would no longer be identifiable as different from other Canadians. Eventually, if assimilation were complete, they would inter-marry with other Canadians and disappear as a separate, identifiable part of the population. There would, in effect, be no more Indians as such, but merely Canadians of Indian or partially Indian ancestry.

Separation

This would mean that the Indians would exist as a separate and distinct group. Those who are in favour of this arrangement hold a view which is similar to that held by the separatists in Quebec, or those black people in the United States who want a separate black community.

While remaining within the territory now know as Canada, they would be independent of and separate from Canadian society. They would have a separate Indian society, organized by Indians, governed by Indians, and presumably operating according to Indian ideas and values. This philosophy rejects or considers impossible the integration of Indians into Canadian society. Those who believe in it view with alarm the idea of assimilation. They wish, above all, to preserve an Indian way of life.

Integration

Somewhere between the two schools of thought advocating assimilation and separation, are those who believe that the future of the Indians lies in some form of integration into Canadian society. Basic to this philosophy is the belief that, within the framework of Canadian society, Indians should be assisted, through financial aid, education, and expert technical advice where required, to break out of their present depressed social and economic conditions, and to live full and satisfying lives. This would mean putting an end to poverty, dependency and discrimination. It would require that Indians take over the responsibility for making the important decisions in matters affecting their lives. They would decide for example, how to implement the kind of education program that will best serve their needs, the way they should organize their government, how to plan for the best use of their resources, etc.

All this should take place within, and with the assistance and co-operation of, Canadian society. Integration differs from assimilation in that the choice would be left to individual Indians to decide for themselves whether they wish to be assimilated into Canadian society or to retain their Indian identity. It differs from co-existence in that a working relationship would be maintained between the Indians and the larger Canadian society. Indians would still be a part of Canadian society, not distinct and separate from it.

Before considering the merits of these different points of view and examining what is being proposed at the present time, we shall look at the way things now stand. We have already studied some of the components of the problem, but we have yet to look at some of the questions raised by it. How, for example, is an Indian defined in law? What is the Indian Act and how does it affect Indians? What relations exist between the Indians and the various levels of government – federal, provincial and local? It is necessary to know something about these matters in order to understand the implications of the proposals, to understand the attitudes of Indian and non-Indian spokesmen, and to appreciate the complex nature of the problem and the difficulties in the way of achieving change satisfactory to everyone concerned.

2.   What is an Indian?

The Indian Act defines an Indian as "a person who pursuant to this Act is registered as an Indian or is entitled to be registered as an Indian." If you are legally an Indian, you can live on reserves and are entitled to certain rights. However, a person may be a full-blooded Indian and yet may not be an Indian according to the law, in which case he does not have a right to membership on a reserve or any title to resources or reserve land.

How, then, does one come to be defined as an Indian by this law? Normally, children of registered Indians are Indian. A woman, whether Indian or non-Indian, who marries a treaty or registered Indian automatically becomes a legal Indian.

However, Indian status can be lost. That is, a legal Indian can become, in the eyes of the law, a non-Indian. For example, if an Indian woman marries a non-Indian man, she automatically loses her Indian status. Also, an Indian may choose to give up his Indian status by applying to Ottawa for enfranchisement. Thus he gains full citizenship rights and becomes, in effect, a Canadian like anyone else. In doing so he renounces his treaty or aboriginal rights, gives up forever his right to membership on a reserve and all title to his share of resources or reserve land, and cannot return to the reserve to take up residence. Thus he may cut himself off from the rest of his family and his friends. By the same act he prevents his descendants from establishing a legal Indian identity should they wish to do so. There are many people of Indian descent in Canada today who might wish to be recognized legally as Indians but are unable to do so because an ancestor decided to renounce his legal claims to being Indian.

Even within the legal definition there are differences and distinctions, such as those between treaty Indians and registered Indians. Treaty Indians are those whose ancestors signed treaties with the crown whereby they ceded land in return for specified rights. Registered Indians are those whose ancestors did not sign treaties (in the Maritimes, Quebec, parts of the Northwest Territories, and in most of British Columbia), but who chose under the Indian Act to be regarded as legal or registered Indians. These differences are divisive. Many non-treaty Indians are afraid that association with treaty Indians will weaken their position with regard to aboriginal claims. On the other hand, many treaty Indians believe that association with non-treaty Indians will endanger their treaty rights.

There is a growing impatience, particularly among the younger people, with the anomalies and divisions created by this legal definition. They are seeking a definition of themselves which is satisfying and meaningful because it expresses their true identity, their "Indianness."

It is self-definition, not this network of inhuman legalities or the recently proposed alternative of assimilation, that will foster Indian unity. All the legal definitions fail to accomplish one thing – they fail to solve the real, human problem of identity. . . .

Our identity, who we are; this is a basic question that must be settled if we are to progress. A native person in Canada cannot describe himself without basically talking about himself as a Canadian. Being Canadian is implied and understood. To an Indian, being Indian in Canada simultaneously and automatically means being Canadian. The German Canadian has a homeland called Germany; the Ukrainian has a homeland; even the French Canadian, although he may have ancestors going back three hundred years in Canadian history, has a homeland called France. The Indian's homeland is called Canada.

The challenge to Indians today is to redefine that identity in contemporary terminology. The challenge to the non-Indian society is to accept such an updated definition.

If I were to accept the bothersome term *Indian problem*, I would have to accept it in light of the fact that our most basic problem is gaining respect, respect on an individual basis that would make possible acceptance for us as an ethnic group. Before this is possible, the dignity, confidence and pride of the Indian people must be restored. No genuine Indian participation in the white world can be expected until the Indian is accepted by himself and by the non-Indian as an Indian person, with an Indian identity.

As long as Indian people are expected to become what they are not – white men – there does not and there will not exist a basis upon which they can participate in Canadian society.

Before we can demand acceptance by the white man, we must earn his respect. Before we can take our place in a larger society, we must regain our own confidence and self-respect. To do this we must be allowed to rebuild our own social institutions, torn down by their white counterparts. We must re-build our structures of social and political leadership, demoralized and under-mined for a hundred years by the Department of Indian Affairs; we must restore our family unit, shaken and shattered by the residential school system; we must rebuild communications between the younger and older generations of our people. We must recognize that the negative images of Indianness are false; the Canadian government must recognize that assimilation, no matter what they call it, will never work. Both Indian and non-Indian must realize that there is a valid, lasting Indian identity.

Cardinal, *op. cit.*, *pp.* 21, 24-25.

1. For what reasons does the writer consider it essential for Indians to define their own identity?
2. Why is he opposed to a policy of assimilation? Do you agree with him?
3. Give examples of what you think he means by "negative images of Indianness." Why must both Indians and Whites recognize them as false?
4. In the last sentence, Cardinal asserts that there is a "valid, lasting identity." He also uses the term "Indianness." What is the meaning of this term that differentiates Indians from non-Indians in their beliefs, feelings, attitudes and general style of life? We already have some clues in the statement by Chief Dan George (p. 109) and Table H (p. 112). Here are four more statements, two by Indians, two by a non-Indian, which provide further clues. After reading these statements and any others you can find, write your own definition of "Indianness."

Sheila Burnford: a non-Indian writer

Then there was Tommy – one of three workmen on a tree-planting project of mine. One of the three was of solid Dutch stock, whose talk was mostly of a grumbling personal nature, and whose eyes brightened only at the sight of a bottle of beer; one was a gigantic Finn who said nothing at all and worked like a bulldozer — I doubt if his vision took in anything beyond the end of pick or shovel. The third was Tommy, small and slight, half Cree, half Ojib, who, as a labourer was probably not as worthy of his hire as the other two, but immeasurably worthier to me in other respects. Despite the loss of several fingers on one hand he tied strange magical flies (which he varied from day to hour it seemed according to the portents) from almost anything he happened to have or pick up — a piece of fur, a feather, a rubber band or a snip of pink plastic. He could take his knife to a piece of soft wood, whittling here, slicing there, until suddenly he gently slid the slices open and there would be intricately carved fan. And he was a mine of information to me on everything that flew, walked or swam. His hands might be digging a hole but his eyes were everywhere. "Eagle," he once said, when I asked him what he was watching, and he pointed it out over the lake. But it must have been half a minute before the black dot materialized for me, and by that time he had already seen the identifying white feathers of a bald eagle on its head — and probably the fish in the beak of the osprey it was harrying. Yet I thought I had good sight.

The three were quite a study in contrasts. When they stopped for lunch and the other two had finished eating and drinking, they stretched out and had a little nap. Tommy, whose lunch had consisted of a piece of bannock fished out of his pocket and a drink of water from the lake, invariably vanished into the bush with my fishing rod and today's lethal lure. If he did not return — usually late, to the tight-lipped indignation of the other two — with a nice cleaned trout for my supper, it was always with news of something interesting going on in the bush, evidence of a bear or deer, or a hatch of partridge chicks. When it was time to down tools and go the others did so with promptitude, and left in the shortest possible line between (a) the site and (b) their car. Tommy was far more likely to walk around by the shoreline so that he could show me where the mergansers were nesting on the way. The other two were hardworking and ambitious, and would undoubtedly get on in the New World; they were only doing odd jobs at the moment because they were temporarily laid off at one of the mills. But I always thought they only existed whereas Tommy lived.

Sheila Burnford, *Without Reserve* (Toronto: McClelland and Stewart Ltd., 1969), pp. 31-33.

In the meantime, there were the other children to think about, those who had made it "outside" and were theoretically on the way to a successful integration between both worlds. It will not be easy for them, and much of the difficulty will lie in the demands of their own people upon them. The criterion of success in the white world is financial — the individual acquisition of property or dollars; but should an Indian too close to his own people achieve such success through a good job, he will be lucky if he can hang on to it. As I learned one day from Johnny Anishanabe, there is sometimes another side to their frequently quoted reputation for not sticking to a job. Anishanabe means "human being," but is usually translated by us as "Indian," and Johnny was the popular white conception of the shiftless Indian; he lived in a shabby log shack with innumerable outbuildings leaning every which way and weeds pushing up through scattered trash, with many children and a slatternly wife whom I had at first taken for his mother; and he could never be relied on to stay at anything lucrative for long, doing odd jobs when the fancy apparently took him and collecting welfare the rest of the time. He was a most bright, intelligent and cheerful man, his children among the happiest I have ever met. One day I asked him during one of those jobless times, why he didn't sign up for one of the government manpower training schemes, where he would be paid while being trained; he had the requisite schooling to be trained as a heavy equipment operator. His answer was very revealing, and unexpectedly straightforward for an Indian: if he *did* earn good money, most of his wife's relatives, and a good many of his own, would immediately move in to help him spend it. In which case he wouldn't want to be the only one leaving for work each day while everyone was partying at his home, just so that they could stay to go on partying. . . . But why on earth wouldn't he just tell them to shove off and party elsewhere, I asked. He was quite shocked at this; apparently it would be a very improper suggestion among relatives: they expected to share, and they would have expected him to do the same had the position been reversed.

It was obvious that the once necessary tradition, that all should share in the kill so that the band could survive, was dying hard. This translation into modern parasitism must have a killing effect on ambition; for the first time I appreciated the double difficulties of forging ahead too quickly.

The Indian returning to his reserve in any public capacity has a hard time too. Or if he is ambitious, and is taken on, perhaps, as a clerk in the Hudson's Bay post, his friends and relatives will then assume that they are entitled to unlimited tick. Should he refuse them this, as he must, he will be slighted and maligned, and it will be a lonely life – neither fish nor flesh nor good red herring – that he will lead if he continues in his job.

> *Ibid.*, pp. 234-236.

George Clutesi: a Nootka Indian

My father taught that all people, no matter what their station, were to be treated alike. He would say: "My son, when a man passes in his canoe, if you are too poor to offer him bread, call him in anyway to rest, and to share the warmth of your fire." How much more beautiful can life be?

It is that belief which has been lost; that life is to share – not to acquire.

As we shared, so people respected us.

You. The more you have, the more you take, in order to show in worldly possessions what you command.

He turns to the gleaming river: Look down there. If you lived here, you'd tear up nature and plant a beautiful lawn. You'd spend a fortune raising that lawn. And the winter freshet would come and wash it away. Next year, you'd do it over again and put down a big levy to protect it and to tame the freshet.

Why?

Because you do not want nature. You want *something that belongs to you*. I put it there; you can't have it.

And the white man accuses the Indian of living for the day! No. We did not, not ever. We live for centuries ahead.

You are the people who live for the day, destroying wherever you go. You do not worry about your grandchildren and how they will live.

We think every day of our grandchildren. I plant a patch of strawberries. The children come. "Grandpa, may I have some strawberries?" Of course you can, it's yours.

And because they know it's theirs they're going to care for it. They're going to take what they want, and then: "Oh, I've got too many now. I'll give them to Grandma."

That is the beginning of generosity.

We do not preach: "Be generous." We give them the actual experience.

Somehow you must get back to this teaching, if you're going to survive as a human race. You are now a super-race. But you're drawing further and further away from humanity. You're going to have. You took two million dollars last year, so it has to be three this year and to hell with what's left over. You'll get that the next year – as long as you get it and nobody else does.

The white world is producing very smart, stereotyped non-humans who have lost their feeling, not just for other humans, but for all living things. Your whole life meaning is to be on top of the other person.

>*Don't you think that many people today, especially the young, are seeking for something very close to Indian values?*

Yes. And all their trial and error does not matter. Their mistakes are worth making if, sooner or later, they come into our own sphere of life. If they are in earnest, they will find the way so dear to the Indian and which saved him from extinction.

>*Faith?*

What is that? The Indian says: "Nature. God."

And even now, we do not really understand what this Christianity is all about, that teaches us to get down on our knees and hide our faces and grovel in the dust!

We worshipped joyfully, with face towards the sky; even the headband we wore was to keep the hair from coming between our face and that of God. We do not need to shout for mercy in front of 300 people. We ask silently. He knows what is needed; and He will give it, if we prove our merit.

>*Are you not alarmed by the current money deluge being poured out to Indians? And your own young people are impatient.*

If we do not return to those values, we will fall for this gimmick, for that is what the whole Indian nation is being groomed to fit into. To build, and own, and consume.

The great problem now is that either your society relents and understands, or we go in and join your society and become grabbing people too. Because of this conflict, we'll never get together.

Have you no hope that new and great leaders may come from Indian and white together? There are already signs that the white is turning to the Indian.

For comfort, perhaps. But while we can give comfort, I do not know that we can give counsel, for we have learned that the so-called Western Man can only condescend; he cannot accept.

Now, I will not send one of my own girls from my own eyesight, because I know your society will molest her. Every day, no matter where or when, there are accounts of dastardly deeds in white society. Your people turn even on their own kind. Everywhere is rape and violence. You are going downhill. Your own technology will destroy you unless you come back and make amends with nature!

> George Clutesi, painter, author, and philosopher, interviewed by Hilda Mortimer in *The Montreal Star*, August 9, 1969.

Boyce Richardson: associate editor of the Montreal Star

The tragedy of relations between Indians and non-Indians began at the moment when white people set foot in North America, and has never really abated until this day.

Europe was a feudal society, owned by feudal authorities, at the moment of the discovery of America. But at that time not an acre of America was owned by anyone, and no man worked for another. Far from having a mania for ownership, the Indians regarded themselves as being possessed by the land.

The European Christians came from the paranoia of the Inquisition. The Protestants, when they arrived, were no better, but came laden with feelings of guilt which were unknown to the men who roamed the American continent, maintaining themselves in perfect ecological balance with their environment.

And how did the Europeans find these people? Christopher Columbus himself described them well in a letter to Philip of Spain:

"They are artless and generous with what they have, to such a degree as no one would believe but him who had seen it. Of anything they have, if it he asked for, they never say no, but do rather invite the person to accept it and show as much lovingness as though they would give their hearts . . . and they know no sect, nor idolatry; save that they all believe that power and goodness are in the sky . . .

"They are not ignorant; on the contrary, they are men of very subtle wit, who navigate all these seas, and who give a marvellous good account of everything."

Nevertheless, Columbus reported, Christian-like, that they would make excellent slaves, "as many as you shall order to be shipped."

And that about explains the history of relations between the two peoples. The Indians moved over – there was plenty of land – and made way for the newcomers, who put a gun to their heads and stole the continent from them.

The elements of "Indian thinking" which one is constantly running into as one moves among Indian communities today were already well described by Columbus.

To this day the Indian value-system has never been destroyed or assimilated in the white man's ways. As one soon discovers in moving among Indian communities, Indians today still judge a man who comes among them not by his clothes, or his manners, not by his appearance or position, but by his behavior, by his totality.

The traditional Indian emphasis was on living, on knowing how to live, on being; and still, today they place greater store by these values than by the white man's mania for acquisition.

Thus Indians may be considered by us to be lazy or indolent, but all that means is they are not activated by personal incentives. They have little sense of collecting and acquiring wealth.

Generosity and hospitality remain for them prime virtues. Indians living in Toronto, for example, are constantly being approached by travelling Indians who get in touch and without even asking directly feel out the possibility of staying with them.

"We just take them in," one Indian woman told me. "It does not occur to us to turn them away. We just cannot do that."

But if, for some reason, they are turned away, they do not take umbrage or sulk. "They will then accept that; they will say to themselves that the person must have some good reason for refusing them, and accept that.

"For the Indian way is that you worry more about the other person; they will think first of the person who is doing the refusing and what her reason may be, and only secondly about their own problem of finding somewhere to stay. That is Indian thinking."

This "Indian thinking" permeates the upbringing of children in Indian communities. They are left to grow and explore the world for themselves. Their parents do not interfere with their play, they are seldom cautioned and directed about what to do or not to do, but their curiosity is given full scope.

Indian manners are different, too. Much is achieved by silence. Indians learn early to react to difficulties with "motionless alertness." They do not react on the surface while they are considering their answer.

Among Indians nothing ever happens quickly. When you meet them you can spend a long time just sitting until they feel you out. They are embarrassed by questions thrown at them too quickly.

Many Indians today say that they have much to offer to Canadian society. Faced with the increasing size and monolithic nature of modern society, white people are finding that they must turn back to more fundamental human values, which, the Indians say, they have not entirely lost, in spite of the many assaults mounted on their values by Canadian society.

That these "Indian values" are real, and not just romantically imagined, is shown by the unanimity with which Indians today are rejecting assimilation, and even integration.

As the Indian future comes under intensive public discussion, the Indians are not basing their case so much on their need for education, jobs and equal chances, as on their treaty rights and the need – as a matter of principle – for the white world to fulfil its obligation to the Indian people.

The Montreal Star, August 9, 1969.

A United States Indian

This writer can only offer an opinion as to names and types, define their characteristics, and offer a possible alternative; notice alternative – not a definite solution. All this writer is merely saying is he does not like Indian youth being turned into something that is not real, and that somebody needs to offer a better alternative:

Type A – Slob or Hood.   This is the individual who receives his definition of self from the dominant society, and unfortunately, sees this kind in his daily relationships and associations with his own kind. Thus, he becomes this type by dropping out of school, becomes a wino, steals, eventually becomes a court case, and is usually sent off. If lucky, he marries, mistreats his family, and becomes a real pain to his tribal community as he attempts to cram that definition [of himself] down the society's throat. In doing this, he becomes a Super-Slob. Another Indian hits the dust through no fault of his own.

Type B – Joker.   This type has defined himself that to be an Indian is a joke. An Indian does stupid, funny things. After defining himself, from cues society gave him, he proceeds to act as such. Sometimes he accidentally goofs-up, sometimes unconsciously on purpose, after which he laughs, and usually say, "Well, that's Indian." And he goes through life a bungling clown.

Type C – Redskin "White-noser" or The Sell-out.   This type has accepted and sold out to the dominant society. He has accepted that definition that anything Indian is dumb, usually filthy, and immoral, and to avoid this is to become a "LITTLE BROWN AMERICAN" by associating with everything that is white. He may mingle with Indians, but only when it is to his advantage, and not a second longer than is necessary. Thus, society has created the fink of finks.

Type D – Ultra-pseudo-Indian.   This type is proud that he is Indian, but for some reason does not know how one acts. Therefore he takes his cues from non-Indian sources, books, shows, etc., and proceeds to act "Indian." With each action, which is phony, we have a person becoming unconsciously phonier and phonier. Hence, we have a proud, phony Indian.

Type E – Angry Nationalist.   Although abstract and ideological, this type is generally closer to true Indianness than the other types, and he resents the others for being ashamed of their own kind. Also, this type tends to dislike the older generation for being "Uncle Tomahawks" and "yes men" to the Bureau of Indian Affairs and whites in general. The "Angry Nationalist" wants to stop the current trend toward personality disappearance, and institute changes that will bring Indians into contemporary society as real human beings; but he views this, and other problems, with bitter abstract and ideological thinking. For thinking this [he] is termed radical, and [he] tends to alienate himself from the general masses of Indians, for speaking what appears, to him, to be truths.

None of these types is the ideal Indian. . . .

It appears that what is needed is genuine contemporary creative thinking, democratic leadership to set guidelines, cues and goals for the average Indian. The guidelines and cues have to be *based on true Indian philosophy geared to modern times.* This will not come about without nationalistic pride in one's self and one's own kind.

This group can evolve only from today's college youth. Not from those who are ashamed, or those who have sold out, or those who do not understand true Indianism. Only from those with pride and love and understanding of the People and the People's ways from which they come can this evolve. And this appears to be the major task of the National Indian Youth Council – for without a people, how can one have a cause?

This writer says this because he is fed up with religious workers and educationalists incapable of understanding, and pseudo-social scientists who are consciously creating social and cultural genocide among American Indian youth.

I am fed up with bureaucrats who try to pass off "rules and regulations" for organizational programs that will bring progress.

I am sick and tired of seeing my elders stripped of dignity and low-rated in the eyes of their young.

I am disturbed to the point of screaming when I see American Indian youth accepting the horror of "American conformity," as being the only way for Indian progress. While those who do not join the great American mainstream of personalityless neurotics are regarded as "incompetents and problems."

The National Indian Youth Council must introduce to this sick room of stench and anonymity some fresh air of new Indianness. A fresh air of new honesty, and integrity, a fresh air of new Indian idealism, a fresh air of a new Greater Indian America.

How about it? Let's raise some hell!

> Stan Steiner, *The New Indians* (New York: Harper and Row Inc., 1968), pp. 306-307.

3. The Indian Act and the Department of Indian Affairs

Everything in the Indian's life is governed by the Indian Act – his status, his reserve, his rights and privileges, and his local government. For the Indians have two kinds of government, local and federal. There is the local band council and the Federal Government in Ottawa. The Federal Government, through the Indian Act, exerts a good deal of control over the local government.

In theory, everything concerning the administration of the affairs of the band and the reserve is decided by the chief and council. By-laws are made, grievances heard, and disputes settled. If it has funds, the band may set up welfare and road-building funds. But the assets of the band are held by the Federal Government. Two funds are held for each band – a capital fund derived from the sale of assets such as reserve land, and a revenue fund derived from interest on the capital fund, rents from leased land, returns from the sale of timber, income from gas and oil wells, etc. If the band wishes to administer the revenue fund itself, the council draws up a budget of proposed expenditures. If this is approved by Ottawa, the band will be credited with the amount proposed in the budget, and the council can issue its own cheques for the approved expenditures.

In other words, the Indians have only a limited amount of control over their own assets. The intention behind these restrictions was, no doubt, to protect the Indians' interests against their own inexperience in these matters and against those who might take advantages of them. There are still many Indians who believe that they are not yet ready to take over the responsibility, that they do not have the necessary experience, knowledge and skill. But there are others, usually younger ones, who are impatient with the controls and restrictions that the Indian Act imposes on this and other aspects of their lives. They resent the paternalistic attitudes towards Indians which are reflected in the Act, and see the Act as a barrier to the growth towards autonomy which they consider necessary if Indians are going to make progress.

In the following extract Harold Cardinal, a young Indian leader from Alberta, reviews and criticizes the Indian Act.

The *Indian Act*, instead of implementing the treaties and offering much-needed protection to Indian rights, subjugated to colonial rule the very people whose rights it was supposed to protect.

For example, all lands on the reserves are held by the queen for the use and benefit of the Indian bands for whom the reserves were set apart. Accordingly, section 18 of the act gives the minister responsible a discretionary power to authorize the use of reserve land for schools, hospitals and various other projects which the minister may desire to initiate once the consent of the band has been obtained. An individual Indian living on the reserve can't work up much interest in improving or even maintaining his home because he cannot by law even acquire title to the land on which he resides. If he makes improvements to the land, he does so at the risk of later being removed from it by the minister or one of his agents without receiving one iota of compensation for the improvements.

Local government of the reserve lies largely in the hands of the Department of Indian Affairs and Northern Development. Under section 72 of the *Indian Act*, the governor in council is invested with discretionary power to make regulations for such matters as medical treatment, hospitalization and health services on the reserves. In addition, he may provide for the inspection of dwellings and make regulations concerning sanitary conditions in both public and private premises.

Section 73 of the act allows the minister, when he deems it necessary for the good government of the reserve, to declare that a band council may be elected by all persons of twenty-one years of age on the reserve. The council consists of one chief and one councillor for every hundred members of the band provided that there shall never be more than twelve nor less than two councillors. Under section 80 the band council is authorized to make bylaws for such matters as the health of band members, regulation of reserve traffic, construction and maintenance of roads, ditches and fences and the use of all public facilities. This, of course, is power of a sort, self-government of a sort, except that any bylaws enacted by the band may be disallowed by the minister or his agent and must not contravene any regulations made under the *Indian Act*.

The finances of the reserves are almost exclusively under the control of the Department of Indian Affairs acting through the powers of the minister. Both the capital and revenue monies of the band are held by the government in a consolidated revenue fund. (Capital monies are defined as those derived primarily from the sale of surrendered lands or capital assets while revenue monies are obtained primarily from the sale of the jointly-owned produce of the band.) Together these monies constitute the entire band fund, comprising all financial assets of the band. Under section 64 the minister may, with the consent of the band council, direct the expenditure of these monies for various public works and/or welfare projects. The band council, however, is powerless to make such expenditures without the consent of the minister.

Except possibly for the slight ameliorating effect of sections 86-89, the *Indian Act*, that piece of colonial legislation, enslaved and bound the Indian to a life under a tyranny often as cruel and harsh as that of any totalitarian state. The only recourse allowed victims of the act is enfranchisement, whereby the Indian is expected to deny his birthright, declare himself no longer an Indian and leave the reserve, divesting himself of all his interest in his land and people. This course of action is one that any human being would hesitate to take. To the Indian it means that he must leave his home, the community of his family, to which neither he nor his wife nor his children may ever return. All this to enter a society which he generally finds prejudiced against him.

> Cardinal, *op. cit.*, pp. 44-45.

> The task of administering the Act is the responsibility of the Department of Indian Affairs. The Department is divided into agencies each of which is responsible for one of the following aspects of Indian affairs; reserves and trusts, which look after Indian lands and funds; education; economic development; training; job placement; wild life; and welfare. To most Indians, the most important part of the government is the Indian superintendent, the government representative on the spot.

> Within his unit or agency the superintendent is responsible for three thousand Indians or more. He is responsible for seeing that the children receive an education, and for job placement. He helps to organize and run band councils, supervise elections, plan housing developments and arrange for social welfare assistance where required. He explains the Indian Act and advises on matters relating to it. He may be called upon to give advice on matters relative to the industries in which the Indians make their

living – agriculture, fishing, forestry, mining and so on. It is a difficult and exacting job. Superintendents are subject to many pressures – from the Indians, from their superiors in the Department, and from members of the public – in working towards their objective which is to raise the social, economic, and educational standards of the Indians to the general level of the Canadian population.

Indian attitudes towards the superintendents and the system vary greatly as can be appreciated from some actual comments made by Indians in a discussion on a CBC radio program.

CHIEF CHARLES FRANCIS   My objections to the government in picking out Indian agents – I don't know whether they do it on a political basis, or on the education basis, or how they do it. But we've had a former school teacher, we've had a miner, we've had a man just out of the Army and, let's see, we've had another fellow just out of the Air Force. And these fellows have no knowledge of the Indians' problems and they have no way of dealing with the Indian population. You see, they come here and start off at scratch.

CHIEF JOHN ALBANY   Most of the superintendents I've met have been really fine men. Dedicated to helping the Indian in every way. But there are some just like Chief Charles Francis mentioned – men with no manners, who'll send for you and keep you waiting all day. Men who haven't got time to see the Indian who wants advice on a problem. Men who shout at you as if you were children, or talk about you as if you aren't there.

ED ANDERSON   We have men more capable than they are right here on this reservation to handle those affairs.

ROY WHITNEY   I feel that the Indian could do it, provided the government was actually going to screen all the Indians and take just the ones that were capable of being the head, as superintendents.

BURTON KEWAYOSH   I sort of favour a white superintendent on a reserve. I would think if an Indian were superintendent on the reserve some of the Indians would be a little bit prejudiced against him being over them, as he's the same colour. You see, a bunch of Indians can run down a white superintendent, and it's no skin off anybody's nose. But a bunch of Indians will run down another Indian; well, they don't stop at running him down. I don't know, they don't want to see another Indian just a shade better than them.

ANNOUNCER   It's easy enough to criticize, and a great many Indians and a great many non-Indians indulge in that luxury. But there are valid criticisms.

WEBSTER WHITE   Say that particular house over there was mine. It was my lot and my property. If I wanted to rent that to you, I'd have to get the o.k. from the Federal Government. If it was o.k.'d by the Federal Government then I could rent it to you and make a profit of it. But sometimes that takes quite a bit of time. So in other words we are still governed as if we were incapable of managing our own affairs. And that goes all the way down the line.

The Way of the Indian, p. 32.

These are moderate views. Increasingly, however, statements are being made by the younger, better educated Indians which are sharply critical of the system – the Indian Act, the Department of Indian Affairs – which dictates their way of life. They point to the lack of progress in raising economic and educational standards. In their opinion, the system is a means of keeping Indians in poverty and dependency, preventing them from developing initiative, self-confidence and a worthy image of themselves, and generally denying them the rights enjoyed by other Canadians. Harold Cardinal presents this point of view forcefully in his book, *The Unjust Society*.

As an Indian writing about a situation I am living and experiencing in common with thousands of our people it is my hope that this book will open the eyes of the Canadian public to its shame. In these pages I hope to cut through bureaucratic doubletalk to document the betrayals of our trust, to show step by step how a dictatorial bureaucracy has eroded our rights, atrophied our culture and robbed us of simple human dignity. I will expose the ignorance and bigotry that has impeded our progress, the eighty years of educational neglect that have hobbled our young people for generations, the gutless politicians who have knowingly watched us sink in the quicksands of apathy and despair and have failed to extend a hand.

The facts are available, dutifully compiled and clucked over by a handful of government civil servants year after year. Over half the Indians of Canada are jobless year after year. Thousands upon thousands of native people live in housing which would be condemned in any advanced society on the globe. Much of the housing has no inside plumbing, no running water, no electricity. A high percentage of the native peoples of Canada never get off welfare. This is the way it is, not in Asia or Africa but here in Canada. The facts are available; a Sunday drive to the nearest reserve will confirm them as a shocking reality.

The white man's government has allowed (worse, urged) its representative to usurp from Indian peoples our right to make our own decisions and our authority to implement the goals we have set for ourselves. In fact, the real power, the decision-making process and the policy-implementing group, has always resided in Ottawa, in the Department of Indian Affairs and Northern Development. To ensure the complete disorganization of native peoples, Indian leadership over the past years and yet today has been discredited and destroyed. Where this has not been possible, the bureaucrats have maintained the upper hand by subjecting durable native leaders to endless exercises in futility, to repeated, pointless reorganizations, to endless barrages of verbal diarrhoea promising never-coming changes.

These faceless people in Ottawa, a comparatively small group, perpetually virtually unknown, have sat at their desks eight hours a day, five days a week, for over a century, and decided just about everything that will ever happen to a Canadian Indian. They have laid down the policy, the rules, the regulations on all matters affecting native peoples. They have decided where our sons will go to school, near home or hopelessly far from home; they have decided what houses will be built on what reserves for what Indians and whether they may have inside or outside toilets; they have decided what types of social or economic development will take place and where and how it will be controlled. If you are a treaty Indian, you've never made a move without these guys, these bureaucrats, these civil servants at their desks in their new office tower in Ottawa saying "yes" – or "no".

And, you know something? It would almost be funny if it weren't so pathetic. In the latter part of 1968, a government official in Ottawa suggested publicly that the mandarins in Ottawa would probably not even recognize an Indian if they met one in the street.

These are the people who make the decisions, the policies, the plans and programmes by which we live, decisions made in almost total isolation from the Indians in Canada. Their ignorance of the people whose lives and destinies they so routinely control perpetuates the stereotype image they have developed of the native people.

Through generations of justifying their positions to the Canadian public and to Canada's political leaders, the bureaucrats within the department have come to believe their own propaganda. They have fostered an image of Indians as a helpless people, an incompetent people and an apathetic people in order to increase their own importance and to stress the need for their own continued presence.

> Cardinal, *op. cit.*, pp. 2-3, 8-9.

> Gerry Gambill is a non-Indian. Dismissed by the Department of Indian Affairs as Community Development Officer on the St. Regis Reserve in Cornwall, Ontario, he remained on the reserve at the request of the people. Here are extracts from a talk given by him at the New Brunswick Conference on Human Rights at the Tobique Reserve in August, 1968.

The art of denying Indians their human rights has been refined to a science. The following list of commonly used techniques will be helpful in burglar-proofing your reserves (and rights):

GAIN THE INDIANS' COOPERATION.   It is much easier to steal someone's human rights if you can do it with his own cooperation.

so —1. Make him a non-person. Human rights are for people. Convince Indians their ancestors were savages, that they were pagan, that Indians are drunkards. Make them wards of the government. Make a legal distinction, as in the Indian Act, between Indians and persons. Write history books that tell half the story.

2. Convince the Indian that he should be patient, that these things take time. Tell him that we are making progress, and that progress takes time.

3. Make him believe that things are being done for his good. Tell him that you're sure that after he has experienced your laws and actions that he will realise how good they have been. Tell the Indian he has to take a little of the bad in order to enjoy the benefits you are conferring on him.

4. Get some Indian people to do the dirty work. There are always those

who will act for you to the disadvantage of their own people. Just give them a little honour and praise. This is generally the function of band councils, chiefs and advisory councils: they have little legal power, but can handle the tough decisions such as welfare, allocation of housing etc.

5. Consult the Indian, but do not act on the basis of what you hear. Tell the Indian he has a voice and go through the motions of listening. Then interpret what you have heard to suit your own needs.

6. Insist that the Indian "goes through the proper channels." Make the channels and the procedures so difficult that he won't bother to do anything. When he discovers what the proper channels are and becomes proficient at the procedures, change them.

7. Make the Indian believe that you are working hard for him, putting in much overtime and at a great sacrifice, and imply that he should be appreciative. This is the ultimate in skills in stealing human rights: when you obtain the thanks of your victim.

8. Allow a few individuals to "make the grade" and then point to them as examples. Say that the "hardworkers" and the "good" Indians have made it, and that therefore it is a person's own fault if he doesn't succeed.

9. Appeal to the Indian's sense of fairness, and tell him that even though things are pretty bad it is not right for him to make strong protests. Keep the argument going on his form of protest and avoid talking about the real issue. Refuse to deal with him while he is protesting. Take all the fire out of his efforts.

10. Encourage the Indian to take his case to court. This is very expensive, take lots of time and energy and is very safe because the laws are stacked against him. The court's ruling will defeat the Indian's cause, but makes him think he has obtained justice.

11. Make the Indian believe that things could be worse, and that instead of complaining about the loss of human rights, to be grateful for the human rights we do have. In fact, convince him that to attempt to regain a right he has lost is likely to jeopardize the rights that he still has.

12. Set yourself up as the protector of the Indian's human rights, and then you can choose to act on only those violations you wish to act upon. By getting successful action on a few minor violations of human rights, you can point to these successes as examples of your devotion to his cause. The burglar who is also the doorman is the perfect combination.

13. Pretend that the reason for the loss of human rights is for some other reason than that the person is an Indian. Tell him some of your best friends are Indians, and that his loss of rights is because of his housekeeping, his drinking, his clothing. If he improves in these areas, it will be necessary for you to adopt another technique of stealing his rights.

14. Make the situation more complicated than is necessary. Tell the Indian you will have to take a survey to find out just how many other Indians are being discriminated against. Hire a group of professors to make a year-long research project.

15. Insist on unanimity. Let the Indian know that when all the Indians in Canada can make up their minds about just what they want as a group, then you will act. Play one group's special situation against another group's wishes.

16. Select very limited alternatives, neither of which has much merit, and then tell the Indian that he indeed has a choice. Ask for instance, if he would rather have council elections in June or December, instead of asking if he wants them at all.

17. Convince the Indian that the leaders who are the most beneficial and powerful are dangerous and not to be trusted. Or simply lock them up on some charge like driving with no lights. Or refuse to listen to the real leaders and spend much time with the weak ones. Keep the people split from their leaders by sowing rumour. Attempt to get the best leaders into high-paying jobs where they have to keep quiet to keep their paycheck coming in.

18. Speak of the common good. Tell the Indian that you can't consider yourselves when there is the whole nation to think of. Tell him that he can't think only of himself. For instance, in regard to hunting rights, tell him we have to think of all of the hunters, or the sporting goods industry.

19. Remove rights so gradually that people don't realise what has happened until it is too late. Again, in regard to hunting rights, first restrict the geographical area where hunting is permitted, then cut the season to certain times of the year, then cut the limits down gradually, then insist on licensing, and then Indians will be on the same grounds as white sportsmen.

Cover illustration from
The Unjust Society.

20. Rely on reason and logic (your reason and logic) instead of rightness and morality. Give thousands of reasons for things, but do not be trapped into arguments about what is right.

21. Hold a conference on Human Rights, have everyone blow off steam and tension, and go home feeling that things are well in hand.

1. What is the central idea of the cartoon shown on page 140?

2. In what ways are the ideas expressed similar to those expressed by (a) Cardinal, (b) Gambill?

3. On the basis of the knowledge you have acquired so far, do you consider that the cartoon represents the truth about Indians and their relationship to the government, the law and the church?

© King Features Syndicate.

1. What idea is this cartoon trying to get across?

2. If Indians do, in fact, generally mistrust white men, what is likely to be their reaction to proposals for change which originate from them?

3. Do these criticisms reflect only the views of a minority of radical individuals who are speaking only for themselves? Or do they express the attitudes of a significant number of Indians? You may be able to answer this by reading the following statement, part of a presentation made in 1969 by the Manitoba Indian Brotherhood to a conference on human rights in Brandon, Manitoba. What view is expressed of the past work of the Federal Government and the Department of Indian Affairs? What similarity does it bear to Cardinal's statement?

The Past certainly is a catalogue of inaction and error. Whatever the society as a whole has effected or accomplished, nothing has been done to enable the Indian people to control any aspect of their own destiny. The Indian has never been asked for an opinion concerning his own well-being.

A federal bureaucracy has not been effective in dealing with Indian problems. Government bureaucracy begins with great energy and excitement and then metamorphoses into vast organisms entirely oblivious to the purpose for which they were founded.

The Federal Government is best at collecting revenues but rather bad at disbursing services. The only logical conclusion is that the Federal Government must finance programs entirely administered at the local level.

The first step is to face harsh facts which are indicative of the truth that past policies were in error or at best not effective.

The fact is that in 1961 all ethnic groups except Indians and Eskimos were more than half urban. Yet, even in the urban areas no solution has been found by society as to how to ameliorate the lot of 1000's of citizens against whom there are innumerable irrational prejudices not susceptible to legislation.

The fact is that in the professional and financial occupations the native Indian follows both East-Europeans and Asians in last place as the most underrepresented group relative to population.

In the unskilled category the Indian leads among those groups over-represented, by a wide margin.

In clerical occupations the Indian is in last place following far behind the Japanese.

Since 1951 the position of the Indian as measured by representation per capita in the economic life of Canada has deteriorated. This deterioration actually accelerated between 1951 and 1961!

Coupled with this fact is the incredible and disgraceful statistic that representation by the Indians on a per capita basis in schools also deteriorated between 1951 and 1961 compared to all other groups.

Trends must not only be changed, but actually reversed.

Today 40 per cent of Canada's Indians live on welfare. 47 per cent of Indian families earn less than $1000 per year.

The infant mortality rate is twice the national average. The life expectancy of Indians is 34 years compared to the national average of 62 years.

Only 9 per cent of Indian families have indoor toilets, and 44 per cent have electricity.

In education these statistics are even more alarming. About 40 per cent of Indian children enter school unable to speak or understand either English or French.

61 per cent of Indian children fail to reach Grade 8, and 97 per cent fail to reach Grade 12.

The goals – at least those of a basic nature – become evident by analysis of readily available factual data.

The programs, however, must work in actuality, not only in theory. The gap between theory and fact to date is that Indian programs have been for Indians but that they have not been *by* Indians.

> Submission of the Manitoba Indian Brotherhood to the Brandon Conference on Human Rights, February, 1969, pp. 3-4, 6-7.

The Federal Government has not been unaware of the feelings of the Indians. Its response came in 1969 when the Hon. Jean Chrétien, Minister of Indian Affairs and Northern Development in the government led by Prime Minister Trudeau, presented to Parliament a *Statement of the Government of Canada on Indian Policy.* More usually referred to as *The White Paper on Indian Affairs,* this document is extremely important. It contains far-reaching proposals which, if implemented, will shape the future of Indians in Canada. Before examining the proposals, it might be advisable to read the opening statement which gives the historical background to the problem.

The weight of history affects us all, but it presses most heavily on the Indian people. Because of history, Indians today are the subject of legal discrimination; they have grievances because of past undertakings that have been broken or misunderstood; they do not have full control of their lands; and a higher proportion of Indians than other Canadians suffer poverty in all its debilitating forms. Because of history too, Indians look to a special department of the Federal Government for many of the services that other Canadians get from provincial or local governments.

This burden of separation has its origin deep in Canada's past and in early French and British colonial policy. The elements which grew to weigh so heavily were deeply entrenched at the time of Confederation.

Before that time there had evolved a policy of entering into agreements with the Indians, of encouraging them to settle on reserves held by the Crown for their use and benefit, and of dealing with Indian lands through a separate organization — a policy of treating Indian people as a race apart.

After Confederation, these well-established precedents were followed and expanded. Exclusive legislative authority was given the Parliament of Canada in relation to "Indians, and Lands reserved for the Indians" under Head 24 of Section 91 of the British North America Act. Special legislation — an Indian Act — was passed, new treaties were entered into, and a network of administrative offices spread across the country either in advance of or along with the tide of settlement.

This system — special legislation, a special land system and separate administration for the Indian people — continues to be the basis of present Indian policy. It has saved for the Indian people places they can call home, but has carried with it serious human and physical as well as administrative disabilities.

Because the system was in the hands of the Federal Government, the Indians did not participate in the growth of provincial and local services. They were not required to participate in the development of their own communities which were tax exempt. The result was that the Indians, persuaded that property taxes were an unnecessary element in their lives, did not develop services for themselves. For many years such simple and limited services as were required to sustain life were provided through a network of Indian agencies reflecting the authoritarian tradition of a colonial administration, and until recently these agencies had staff and funds to do little more than meet the most severe cases of hardship and distress.

The tradition of federal responsibility for Indian matters inhibited the development of a proper relationship between the provinces and the Indian people as citizens. Most provinces, faced with their own problems of growth and change, left responsibility for their Indian residents to the Federal Government. Indeed, successive Federal Governments did little to change the pattern. The result was that Indians were the almost exclusive concern of one agency of the Federal Government for nearly a century.

For a long time the problems of physical, legal and administrative separation attracted little attention. The Indian people were scattered in small groups across the country, often in remote areas. When they were in contact with the new settlers, there was little difference between the living standards of the two groups.

Initially, settlers as well as Indians depended on game, fish and fur. The settlers, however, were more concerned with clearing land and establishing themselves and differences soon began to appear.

With the technological change of the twentieth century, society became increasingly industrial and complex, and the separateness of the Indian people became more evident. Most Canadians moved to the growing cities, but the Indians remained largely a rural people, lacking both education and opportunity. The land was being developed rapidly, but many reserves were located in places where little development was possible. Reserves were usually excluded from development and many began to stand out as islands of poverty. The policy of separation had become a burden.

The legal and administrative discrimination in the treatment of Indian people has not given them an equal chance of success. It has exposed them to discrimination in the broadest and worst sense of the term – a discrimination that has profoundly affected their confidence that success can be theirs. Discrimination breeds discrimination by example, and the separateness of Indian people has affected the attitudes of other Canadians towards them.

The system of separate legislation and administration has also separated people of Indian ancestry into three groups – registered Indians, who are further divided into those who are under treaty and those who are not; enfranchised Indians who lost, or voluntarily relinquished, their legal status as Indians; and the Métis, who are of Indian ancestry but never had the status of registered Indians.

> *Statement of the Government of Canada on Indian Policy* (Ottawa: Queen's Printer, 1969), pp. 7-8.

1. What evidence is there in this part of the White Paper that the Federal Government realizes that past policies have been unsuccessful in helping Indians to achieve equality with other Canadians?

2. According to this statement, what have been the ill effects of the system established by the Indian Act?

3. In view of the analysis in this statement, what proposals might you reasonably expect to find in the White Paper?

4.   Assimilation? Separation? Integration?

It is obvious that there are going to be changes in the affairs of the Indians of this country. We have already seen that there are three possible solutions to the problem – assimilation, separation, or some form of integration.

Separation

Since separation seems to be the solution least likely to be adopted, we will discuss it first. There are some young Indian thinkers who believe that separation is inevitable. One of these is Lloyd Caibaiosai, an Ojibway from Spanish River, Ontario. Here is part of a speech he made at Glendon College, York University, Toronto:

The white middle-class view, compounded of self-righteousness and paternalism, leads naturally enough to the unbreakable habit of talking about "them" and "us." Thus whites glide smoothly to the conclusion that "we" will somehow rule "them." Right, Great White Father?

This brings me to a proposition which is the key to my understanding of the situation. I offer it tentatively even though I am convinced it is valid. If it is, it makes all of our present difficulties trifling and we have before us a problem of statecraft whose dimensions cannot now be imagined.

The proposition is that racial integration in Canada is impossible.

I set forth this proposition without qualification. There are no hidden unlesses, buts, or ifs in it. I shall not deny that in some remote future integration may come about. But I do not see it resulting from the actual present trends and attitudes in Canadian society. It can only be produced by some event overturning these trends. There is no denial in this proposition that there will be a steady betterment in the material situation of Indians.

My proposition is sad. My proposition, in short, smashes the liberal dream. It eliminates the democratic optimistic claim that we are finding our way to a harmonious blending of the races. It changes the words of the marching song to "We Shall Not Overcome," or was that "Overrun"?; for what was eventually to be overcome was hostility and non-fraternity, between Indian and White. My proposition dynamites the foundations of the Indian-Eskimo Association, and similar organizations. It asserts that 'Indian Reserve, Canada', and 'Whitetown, Canada' for all practical purposes and with unimportant exceptions, will remain separate social communities.

I am not sure, but it may also mean Indiantown will become a separate political community.

The proposition would seem to place me in the camp of the bigots and locate me with the hopeless, also probably the racists. It puts at ultimate zero the efforts of the tough and high-minded who are giving their lives to the dream of equality among men.

Yet I am convinced that integration in Canada is a sentimental not a doctrinal, idea. We came to the idea late in Canadian history, and it disappears readily from the rhetoric of politics – though not from the list of sacred democratic aims – at the first sign of indocility. The vast fuss of improvement in Indian communities is not aimed at integration. Few are afflicting us any longer with such a tiresome lie. All these measures are primarily aimed at the prevention of civic commotions, secondarily at assuaging the conscience of Whitetown, and finally helping the Indians tell the story.

The country of Canada is a white man's country conducted according to White customs, and White laws for White purposes. I would not even argue that Whites should not run the country for their own interests, but they can't see that racial integration is one of these interests, except in perilous self-deceit. Whites *like* Indians so long as they themselves are not disturbed by Indians. Whites have no objection to bettering the Indians' lives so long as it does not cost much, and as long as it leads to the continuance of Indian Reserve and so does not present the threat of genuine integration at any level. The White condition for Indian betterment is, to put it simply, separation.

Why is it so hard for Whites to say clearly that they do not want Indians or Blacks living among them and sharing their world? There must be dozens of reasons playing on one another. One, I suppose, is that they are ashamed to admit they do not subscribe, after all, to a glorious myth. Another is the Christian message that binds them to brotherhood. But as something in their understanding of Christianity made possible the acceptance of slavery, it continues to make possible the shunning of Indians as less worthy than themselves. Often enough this is accompanied by an aching conscience.

Another reason, I suppose, is that after 476 years Indians are still strangers to Whites. It is a rare white man who is really acquainted with an Indian. Almost as though arranged by Whites.

A commanding reason, I would guess, is to be found in the mystique of progress, in the belief that by nature everything must somehow improve all the time. Thus the present degradation of Indians can be waved aside by referring to better things to come, as come they must to the deserving, perhaps in another century or two or three.

In giving up on integration I am not giving up on the Indians but on the Whites. White attitudes are the problem. Sadly enough, there is only one place where we have registered even a mild success: we have more or less integrated poverty. The liberal view is that patience and persistence will in the end perform the miracle. The enemy is ignorant. Whitetown's resistance, accordingly, is temporary-stubborn perhaps but penetrable by knowledge and association.

Let me put forward the more general testimony in support of my proposition, the race situation is marked by growing expression of distrust, hate, and fear on the part of both Indians and Whites; growing disillusionment throughout all the reserves; increasing belligerency of young Indians and their leaders; increasing impatience of our Dad – Whitey; growing isolation of the Indian middle class who have made it; growing uselessness of treaties between Indians and Whites as Indian demands become more basic and White resistance more determined.

The outside agitator is Whitetown itself. It is more important to recognize that separation-not-integration is the way it has always been. The fostering of the illusion that integration is an achievable goal is bad enough in its effects on Indians, some of whom may still entertain a vision of their children fore-gathering in total equality under the White yum-yum tree. But the illusion is sinister in its likely consequence for Whites. By engaging in it they are leaving themselves unprepared for the grand finale.

What is necessary is the development of a Canadian democratic system which, in itself, allows men to be equal and live in peaceful coexistence, but maintains the existence of two or three viable separate societies.

> Gooderham, *op. cit.*, pp. 101-103.

1. Mr. Caibaiosai believes that "racial integration in Canada is impos-sible." What reasons does he have for believing this? Do you share his belief? Do you accept his reasons?

2. He believes that in Canada we already have separation, a kind of apartheid, as in the Union of South Africa. What similarities or differences do you see between the Canadian and South African situations?

3. Do you believe that Whites "do not want Indians or Blacks living among them and sharing their world"? If so, do you think that this attitude (a) can be changed, (b) should be changed?

4. What is Mr. Caibaiosai's long-term answer to the problem of White-Indian relations in Canada? List the conditions which would be necessary for the "peaceful co-existence . . . of two or three viable separate societies." (Consider such questions as: Would the majority of Canadians agree to this form of Canadian society? Would diversity of language, culture, and present lack of economic resources and technical expertise lead to even greater problems in a separate Indian community?

5. Mr. Caibaiosai points to the increasing belligerency of young Indians. If they reject assimilation, and are convinced, as he is, that integration is an impossible dream, they are left with the alternative of separatism. A few believe that this is the only way. Assuming that they are not prepared to wait for the long-term solution of "viable separate so-cieties," what chances do you think they have of achieving separatism in a comparatively short time?

   Here are a few facts to take into consideration:

   a) Indians represent about 1 per cent of the Canadian population.
   b) They are dispersed throughout Canada, both from east to west, and from north to south.
   c) Some live near urban centres; others have never seen a city.
   d) They have many different languages; not all speak English.
   e) They suffer from poverty and generally low educational standards.

Another approach to separatism might be to achieve it on a local rather than a national scale. By this method, a tribe or a number of bands might become independent, maintaining close relations with, but not belonging to, Canada. The following is a discussion with leaders from the Six Nations Reserve near Brantford, On-tario. Do you think it is likely that they will achieve their wishes? Give reasons for your opinion.

Have you wondered what Red Power is all about? What do Canada's Indians really want?

Well, some say that they want nothing less than to turn their reservations into a sovereign state, a separate nation of their own. They propose to achieve this not by staging a replay of Custer's last stand with the losers winning but by a pow-wow with the Great White Father in Ottawa.

"For us," said Joseph Logan, one of the hereditary chiefs of the Six Nations near Brantford, "integration into Canadian life, as Ottawa wants, would mean creeping genocide.

"We don't want our traditional way of life wiped out. We happen to like it."

"Yes, we prefer out own social structure and religion to the white man's," added Emerson Hill, another hereditary chief who acts as faith-keeper or priest of the ancient Longhouse religion, (he doubles as a medicine man dispensing remedies for everything from colic to cancer).

Of the estimated 9,000 Indians on the Six Nations reserve "at least three-quarters want an independent state," declared Chief Logan.

A pipe dream? Presumably. But then the Jews got Israel back after 2,000 years.

"Look at our side as we see it," suggested Logan, an articulate, persuasive man in his 50's who wore a sports shirt and an Indian-head pendant around his neck.

"To start with, we don't call ourselves Indians. That was Columbus' mistake, remember? We are ongwehwaweh – the original people.

"Our ancestors were a mighty nation long before the white man came to this continent. We had our own version of the UN, a confederacy or peace league of five tribes. Later another tribe joined and we became the Six Nations.

"Our ancestors were farmers, not bloodthirsty savages. Sure, they killed the Jesuit martyrs near what's now Midland, but why? In retaliation for the murder of six of our braves by Hurons who were the allies of the French.

"Our confederacy was a democracy and a matriarchal society in which the woman had superior status to the man, unlike the white man's world. The hereditary chiefs were elected by the klan mothers, leaders of family groups within the tribes, and could be deposed by them.

"In 1664 our people made a treaty with the Dutch, the first white men in what is today New York state. When the British displaced the Dutch we made the same treaty with them.

"This treaty was called the Two Row Wampum. Its symbol was a white belt with two parallel black stripes. This meant that the white man's boat and the red man's boat were to travel side by side in peace but they must never interfere with one another.

"That treaty, and others like it, were never revoked. According to international law the only way a sovereign nation can lose its sovereignty is by voluntarily surrendering it or being defeated in war. Neither is true of us. Therefore we are legally still a sovereign nation."

Well, an Indian version of such vest pocket principalities as Andorra and San Marino might be a tourist attraction but could it really work?

"Yes," said Logan gravely. "As an independent state we would maintain close relations with Canada but run our own internal affairs."

How could such an Indian nation be brought into being at this late date?

"We've been advised to take our case to the world court in the Hague," said Logan with a faint smile. "If we did we probably would sue for the return of Vermont while we were at it since by treaty it still belongs to us.

"But what good would it do? If the court decided in our favor, who would enforce its ruling?"

Chief Hill, who as faith-keeper presides over weddings, funerals, name-giving ceremonies and other seasonal festivals of the Longhouse religion, said the Indians' traditional God is not dead or even ailing.

"We worship the Great Spirit in our dances and offer him thanksgiving for the good things of life," he said. "We have high moral standards. There's no divorce in our religion."

Before the Apollo II moon mission Chief Logan warned that the Great Spirit was unhappy about man trespassing on the moon and predicted dire sickness on earth as a result.

"I still see sickness," he maintained, "but maybe economic sickness."

Chief Logan's parting word was: "We don't want to be Canadians any more than the Czechs want to be Russians or the Mennonites want to be Catholics.

"We just want to be ourselves and get what's rightfully ours. . . . "

G. Gambill, *Akwesasne Notes.*

A further approach is that tried by Robert Smallboy, a 71-year-old leader from the Ermineskin Band in Hobbema, Alberta. On July 4, 1968 he led a group of 150 men, women and children out of the reserve at Hobbema. They set up camp in the Kootenay Plains, where they have since lived a self-sufficient life. They have lived in tents through winters when the temperature has dropped to 50° below zero or more. The main reason for the move was dissatisfaction with life on the reserve, loss of faith in the Indian Affairs educational system, and concern about the influence of the White Man's ways on the young people. Chief Smallboy has spoken of this attempt to get away from the White Man and to live a separate, independent life, one more in keeping with Indian tradition.

The group is still in existence. In 1969, Robert Smallboy was removed by the people remaining on the reserve from his position as Chief of the Ermineskin Band.

Finally, we were ready to move and we left Hobbema on the 4th of July, 1968. We have been here ever since (Kootenay Plains) and we are enjoying our (Pim-atis-soo-win) livelihood. We have time to think freely and we try to follow the realities of life each day. The youngsters are living in peace, including the young men who are now settling down away from problems.

The only setback we are encountering is (Ki-sinuh-ama-kewin) education, which was promised to us. However, this does not affect our lives too much, because the parents are teaching their youngsters how to live. They are learning how to adapt to the good values in life, and this land that we dwell on is (Ka-na-tan) clean.

Before we made the move, we came here several times to inspect this territory, and now that we are here we are happy, because we feel it is a gift to live with nature.

We are able to develop gocd attitudes and healthy minds by living in a clean and healthy environment. Back where we came from there are many difficulties. The young people are growing up with the social problems. Many live in fear from day to day because of the lack of discipline. The parents are worried constantly, and sometimes there is no sleep because they fear the social activities will harm their youngsters when they leave home, especially at nights.

Here in the mountains, they do not encounter these fears, because there are no problems to contend with. You people out there, think carefully, we are not running into any problems. We are forever thankful to see our youngsters enjoying life. We all live in tents, but this is not a problem because this was our way of life. The Indian lived on land and with nature. Our ancestors who lived this way were strong and healthy. They did not encounter any diseases and every Indian was strong and healthy. The white man has ruined all these good things for our people. So we are now trying our aspirations by living this way, and thus far no one has been sick since we moved here.

We have no desire for anything in Hobbema that we should go back for. Besides the white man is not providing this kind of life for our people, as we have here. There are many curious white men coming to our camp to see how we live. It is true that the (the white man) is afraid of the effects of nature, and certain to crawl in a nice cosy place where there is no draft. He even goes so far that he builds for himself an outhouse in his building. This shows how physically weak he is. Unfortunately, this is how he was gifted, never to live with nature in this world. Everything he eats is artificial. He has to grow what he eats and if he does not produce any food for himself – he is dead.

As soon as nature changes and takes its course in the season to a colder climate the least little draft or wind chill affects him, and at times he gets seriously ill. This is the kind of life that the white man has developed, which means that he, in effect, is not living with nature. He even applies his own way of life on the animals that he has to raise to survive. He feeds them and waters them, because if he didn't they wouldn't survive; because he does not allow them to live with nature. In wintertime he has to make sure that his animals are well fed, and locked up in a warm place. He goes so far that he has to warm the water for the animals to drink so that they can survive.

This is why everyone is so concerned about our survival here in the mountains. They feel that everyone should live like the white man in order to get by in this world, but this is not so. We are different, because this is how the great spirit wants us to live, and we are here to live with nature as people.

Mind you, we have no difficulties to obtain food. We hunt for meat and fish. The people hunt for whatever they wish to consume. If they want to eat fish all they do is go down to the river and get it. And these are some of the other reasons why they will not return to Hobbema.

I would like to add further on my previous comments regarding leadership. As I mentioned earlier, I have been working as a leader for nine years, and prior to that I had observed just how the Indian leaders operated as councillors and chiefs.

Generally, in the past, the elected leaders have had a tendency to work mostly with the farm instructor or the Indian agent as they were referred to in the earlier times. I say this because I have seen it with my own eyes. The old type of leadership has phased out now, but an old chief who had stepped down from his position also told me what I have been repeating.

While the old type of leadership was in operation on the reserve, there were no social problems, and the younger generation would listen to their leaders when they spoke about maintaining good discipline. Incidentally, these old chiefs and councillors did not have the education of the white man. All they knew literally was to sign their names. When others became leaders, this is when the old leadership was replaced with the white-man's philosophy of organization.

Education was imposed on the young people and the councillors. This is when everything bad, including all the social problems began. The elected leaders drank, and they introduced new ideas to the people. Consequently, with all this bad example imposed on them, the younger generation developed many of the white man's social problems.

First Citizen, January, 1970, p. 8.

1. Do you think Chief Smallboy's experiment is a useful example to Canadian Indians in general? What are its strengths? Its weaknesses?
2. Do you think it likely that many groups of Indians will follow this example? Give reasons for your opinions.
3. Summarize the obstacles which may prevent separation from being a realistic objective for the Indians of Canada. Do you consider separation an achievable goal?

Assimilation or Integration?

When the majority of Indians consider what the future holds for them, they see a choice between two alternatives. Either they will be assimilated into Canadian society or they will achieve some form of integration into it. With assimilation they see that they will become Canadians at the cost of the loss of their identity as Indians. Many are not prepared to pay this price. Some believe that Indian values are superior to those of White society, and they see no reason for adopting, or being pressured into adopting, values that they do not admire. They recoil against the idea of becoming whitewashed red men. Some, like Lloyd Caibaiosai, feel that, because of racial differences, assimilation can never be achieved anyway, because the White Man will not agree to it. A good question to ask is: Who is proposing assimilation? It may be that no one is. But past experiences have made the Indians suspicious of the White Men, and many feel that the long-term aim of the White Man is to obliterate them as Indians. As one Indian has said, "Cultural genocide is the nameless fear of the Indian people."

The alternative to assimilation is integration. That is, Indians would fit into Canadian society as an identifiable part of it. They would not be politically and economically separate, nor would they be swallowed up by the larger society. They would be a part of Canadian society on their own terms, responsible for the administration of their own affairs, and retaining those elements of their culture which they wish to keep. In other words, they would be responsible for the major decisions affecting their own lives. Those who believe in integration emphasize the need for the cultivation of a positive Indian identity. Indians should shake off the shackles of dependency. Government funds now used for welfare payments should be used to create Indian industries which would provide Indians with jobs and a sense of personal worth. An education system should be established which would meet the needs of Indians, both children and adults.

In all this, the decisions must be taken by the Indians themselves. The role of the government would be to help with money and expert assistance where required. In this way, they claim, and only in this way, will Indians be able to find themselves, adjust to modern society, and raise themselves to the status of first-class citizens.

It is important to understand these two concepts and how they differ, because they enter into any discussion about the future of Indians in Canada. In 1969, the Trudeau government issued its *White Paper on Indian Affairs*. This document contains a series of important and far-reaching proposals affecting the future of Indians. The proposals are intended as a basis for discussion between the Federal Government and the Indians, and there is no doubt that discussions will go on for a long time before any measure of agreement is reached. In the following section, we will examine the proposals contained in the *White Paper* together with the responses of Indians and others to these proposals.

Before proceeding to look at the actual proposals, let us suppose that you were given the task of drawing up a set of proposals which would shape future policy in Indian affairs. You have already studied the important facts. You know something of the historical background to the problem and the nature of the problem as it exists today.

1. Make a list of the proposals which you think should make up the policy of the Federal Government.

2. Assume you are an Indian spokesman, a council member of the National Indian Brotherhood.
   Make a list of the proposals which you would expect the Federal Government to make which would be acceptable to Indian leaders.

3. Keep these lists for comparison with the proposals in the Government White Paper, and the responses of Indian spokesmen.

5.   The White Paper: Proposals and Responses

Background

The Government has reviewed its programs for Indians and has considered the effects of them on the present situation of the Indian people. The review has drawn on extensive consultations with the Indian people, and on the knowledge and experience of many people both in and out of government.

This review was a response to things said by the Indian people at the consultation meetings which began a year ago and culminated in a meeting in Ottawa in April.

This review has shown that this is the right time to change long-standing policies. The Indian people have shown their determination that present conditions shall not persist.

Opportunities are present today in Canadian society and new directions are open. The Government believes that Indian people must not be shut out of Canadian life and must share equally in these opportunities.

The Government could press on with the policy of fostering further education; could go ahead with physical improvement programs now operating in reserve communities; could press forward in the directions of recent years, and eventually many of the problems would be solved. But progress would be too slow. The change in Canadian society in recent years has been too great and continues too rapidly for this to be the answer. Something more is needed. We can no longer perpetuate the separation of Canadians. Now is the time to change.

This Government believes in equality. It believes that all men and women have equal rights. It is determined that all shall be treated fairly and that no one shall be shut out of Canadian life, and especially that no one shall be shut out because of his race.

This belief is the basis for the Government's determination to open the doors of opportunity to *all* Canadians, to remove the barriers which impede the development of people, of regions and of the country.

Only a policy based on this belief can enable the Indian people to realize their needs and aspirations.

The Indian people are entitled to such a policy. They are entitled to an equality which preserves and enriches Indian identity and distinction; an equality which stresses Indian participation in its creation and which manifests itself in all aspects of Indian life.

The goals of the Indian people cannot be set by others; they must spring from the Indian community itself – but government can create a framework within which all persons and groups can seek their own goals.

The New Policy

True equality presupposes that the Indian people have the right to full and equal participation in the cultural, social, economic and political life of Canada.

The government believes that the framework within which individual

Indians and bands could achieve full participation requires:

1. that the legislative and constitutional bases of discrimination be removed;

2. that there be positive recognition by everyone of the unique contribution of Indian culture to Canadian life;

3. that services come through the same channels and from the same government agencies for all Canadians;

4. that those who are furthest behind be helped most;

5. that lawful obligations be recognized;

6. that control of Indian lands be transferred to the Indian people.

The Government would be prepared to take the following steps to create this framework:

1. Propose to Parliament that the Indian Act be repealed and take such legislative steps as may be necessary to enable Indians to control Indian lands and to acquire title to them.

2. Propose to the governments of the provinces that they take over the same responsibility for Indians that they have for other citizens in their provinces. The take-over would be accompanied by the transfer to the provinces of federal funds normally provided for Indian programs, augmented as may be necessary.

3. Make substantial funds available for Indian economic development as an interim measure.

4. Wind up that part of the Department of Indian Affairs and Northern Development which deals with Indian Affairs. The residual responsibilities of the Federal Government for programs in the field of Indian affairs would be transferred to other appropriate federal departments.

In addition, the Government will appoint a Commissioner to consult with the Indians and to study and recommend acceptable procedures for the adjudication of claims.

The new policy looks to a better future for all Indian people wherever they may be. The measures for implementation are straightforward. They require discussion, consultation and negotiation with the Indian people – individuals, bands and associations – and with provincial governments.

Success will depend upon the co-operation and assistance of the Indians and the provinces. The Government seeks this co-operation and will respond when it is offered.

The Immediate Steps

Some changes could take place quickly. Others would take longer. It is expected that within five years the Department of Indian Affairs and Northern Development would cease to operate in the field of Indian affairs; the new laws would be in effect and existing programs would have been devolved. The Indian lands would require special attention for some time. The process of transferring control to the Indian people would be under continuous review.

Statement of the Government of Canada on Indian Policy, p. 6.

1. After carefully reading the section entitled *Background*, state what reason is given for the presentation of proposals at this time. What

basic idea underlies them? According to this statement, is the purpose
of the proposals assimilation or integration?

2. Note the six principles which make up the framework of the *New
Policy*. We will return to these later.

3. The Federal Government proposes to abolish the Indian Act and to
wind up the Department of Indian Affairs. Under whose jurisdiction
would Indians then fall? Can you think of any Indian objections to
these steps? List probable objections with reasons.

4. Study the cartoon below. If the cartoonist is correct, how did the
Indians respond to the White Paper? Check your answer against the
information in the press reports which follow.

James Reidford, reprinted from *The Globe and Mail*.

Here's how Indian and government spokesmen from across the country
reacted yesterday to yesterday's announcement in Ottawa on Indian affairs.

Ontario

TORONTO – The organizer of the Union of Northwestern Ontario Native Organizations said the federal government's new deal for Canada's Indians means
"we would be going to get it in the rear again."

Harold (Buddy) Sault, an Ojibway spokesman for Indians north of Lake
Superior where many Indians live under poor conditions, said his people feared
a takeover by the provincial government.

Referring to John Yaremko, minister of family and social services. Mr. Sault said: "From what we know of Yaremko, we can't be at all sure we'll be any better off."

Saskatchewan

FOAM LAKE, SASK. – Clarence Estey, minister of Saskatchewan's recently created department of Indians and Métis, said there should be consultation between Indians and governments on Ottawa's plans to hand responsibility for Indian matters over to the provinces.

Mr. Estey, also Saskatchewan's minister of municipal affairs, said cost-sharing arrangements between federal and provincial governments would have to be worked out on a long-term basis.

British Columbia

VICTORIA – "This is going to be a real challenge," said the chairman of British Columbia's Indian advisory board.

Ross H. Modeste, who is also band manager for the Lake Cowichan Indians on Vancouver Island, said the proposal by Mr. Chrétien would mean "we have our work cut out for us."

Mr. Modeste said the phasing out of Indian affairs officials on reserves would place the responsibility for isolated groups in the hands of Indian organizations.

"When the Indian affairs people pull out we've got to be in a position to move in," he said.

"Indian organizations will have to get down to the grassroots level and put development workers into isolated communities to help the residents keep up with society."

Alberta

EDMONTON – Harold Cardinal, Alberta Indian Association president, said he welcomed the announcement that the federal Indian affairs branch will be phased out.

However, he said that prior consultations with Indian leaders referred to by Jean Chrétien, Minister of Indian Affairs and Northern Development, were understood by Alberta Indian leaders to be "preliminary."

"We are disappointed that the federal government has outlined their proposals without adequate consultations," Mr. Cardinal said in an interview.

In a telegram sent to Prime Minister Trudeau and Indian Affairs Minister, Jean Chrétien, the association asked that a "new federal policy be formulated with the full and total involvement" of Indian organizations.

The association said it is appalled that the federal government's policy statement "was written in isolation from the Indian people of Canada without any consideration whatsoever to the issues most sacred to them."

New Brunswick

FREDERICTON – Premier Louis Robichaud of New Brunswick said his government will await full details of an Ottawa proposal to transfer responsibilities for Indian affairs to the provinces before making a decision.

Andrew Nicholas, vice-president of the Union of New Brunswick Indians, said he was "most disturbed" by Mr. Chrétien's proposal.

He said the proposal had not come from Indians in New Brunswick or any other Canadian province, adding that he was "very disappointed" that the minister chose to make the suggestion without first consulting Indian officials.

He viewed the proposal as an "admission of failure" on the part of the federal Indian affairs branch to solve the problems of Indians in Canada.

The Globe and Mail, June, 1969.

WINNIPEG – The Manitoba Indian Brotherhood said Friday the province's Indians reject the federal government's proposals to transfer responsibility for Indian affairs to provincial governments.

Dave Courchene, Brotherhood president, said meetings would begin next week to obtain a province-wide consensus among Indians for a brief opposing the plan.

The new federal policy on Indian affairs, designed to erase the status of Indians as wards of the state, was tabled in the federal House earlier this week.

The policy would put Manitoba Indians in the same position as Métis here, Mr. Courchene said, and undo the work pioneered in this province in self-responsibility for Indians.

"The Métis are completely under provincial jurisdiction today and where the hell are they today?"

The Globe and Mail, June, 1969.

Chief Peter Diome of the Caughnawaga Indian reserve here said yesterday that the transfer of health, welfare and education to the provinces "would be just another step toward destroying our identity."

Chief Diome told The Gazette the federal proposal would slowly assimilate the Indian into Canadian life "making us just other Canadian citizens."

"Partitioning Indians among the provinces would cut the communication links of our people across the country," he said.

"Our ties among all Indians would be severed and we soon would lose all contact."

Chief Diome said the federal government seems to plan making citizens out of the Indian "but we are not citizens of either Canada or the United States.

"As far as transferring the land is concerned, certain individuals would sell their share – just another step in destroying out society.

"The land we now have is community land and should not be handed over to individuals," he said.

"In no time nothing would be left and we won't even have title to the lands.

"Perhaps the federal government can make a stipulation that the land cannot be sold."

Chief Diome said that transfer of education to the provinces, especially Quebec, would be fatal.

"Right now Quebec is the worst place for education.

"The first thing we'd have to learn is French, and we don't want this because English is the working language," the Mohawk chief said.

The Montreal Gazette, June, 1969.

OTTAWA – Reawakened Indian nationalism clashed publicly Thursday with
the Canadian government's newly-declared intention to encourage the Indians
to be citizens just like other Canadians.

"Cultural genocide" and "destruction of a nation of people by legislation,"
charged the National Indian Brotherhood at a news conference called to comment on a new policy announced Wednesday by Indian Affairs Minister Jean
Chrétien.

The essence of the conflict seemed to be that Mr. Chrétien intends the Indians to have the same status as other citizens, while the Indians see themselves
as "more than just citizens of Canada."

The Indian Brotherhood argues that Mr. Chrétien's new policy ignores
previous recognition by the federal government that Indians have aboriginal,
residual and statutory rights that make them more than ordinary Canadians.

Central among these rights is the land question, especially in British Columbia where the Nishga tribal council has launched legal action asking the courts
to declare that the Indians still legally own all of the province.

In Manitoba, Saskatchewan and Alberta, the Indian bands signed treaties
with the white man years ago which set aside land tracts owned jointly by band
members. Some Ontario and Quebec bands also signed treaties and were
assigned reserves.

The Indian brotherhood argues that, as in British Columbia, lands in the
Atlantic provinces really belong to them, that the Indian title was never
extinguished.

The brotherhood took a similar stand about the Yukon and Northwest
Territories. The Indian affairs department takes the stand that the Indians are
entitled to reserves in the territories or to some other settlement of their claims
to be determined by negotiation.

The Globe and Mail, June 27, 1969.

1. Generally speaking, what was the reaction of Indian leaders to the
   White Paper?
2. What do the Indians think the intent of the *White Paper* is –
   assimilation or integration?
3. Specifically, what are the Indian reactions to:
   a) responsibility for Indian affairs being transferred to the provinces.
   b) the Government's intention that Indians should have the same
      status as other Canadians.
   c) the way in which the Government prepared the proposals in the
      White Paper, and the role of the Indians in shaping the proposals.
4. After reading the letter below, summarize the main Indian objections
   to the proposed new policy.

When, when, and, again, when will the whiteman look at me as an Indian and
not as a little brown whiteman?

When, when, and, again, when will the whiteman live up to his promises?

When will he have respect for those things that are sacred to me such as treaty promises?

When, when, and, again, when will the whiteman learn that I am different, that my philosophy of life is different from his?

When will he say, "Integration," and mean it? and stop carrying around in his back pocket "assimilation."

Oh, when will he realize the fact that my way of looking at life, at things, my way of living, my way of doing things is as legitimate as his?

When will he know that imperialist, capitalist, urban, middle class, factory labouring is not the only way to salvation? That this way of living is being seriously questioned, even by his own kind? And he expects me to walk into this burning house?

When, when, and, again, when will he stop dictating my life for me? When will he stop implementing policies unilaterally? When will he ask me what I want?

When will he sincerely believe and practice his Christian beliefs from which he has taught me that not even I own my own life, that the Almighty above owns it . . . if this is so, when and from whom did he get the authority to act unilaterally in matters pertaining to my very existence? When, when, and, again, when will he listen to his own words . . . "you cannot legislate equality"? Precisely what he is trying to do in my case. Friends, your new Indian policy smells of perfume but means death for me. You never asked me if that was what I wanted. I'll tell you now . . . it is not what I want. I sincerely believe that you are directing your policy statement to the wrong person . . . it should have been directed to the whiteman, not to me.

When will you stop trying to get out from under your responsibilities? When will you try to correct past injustices? These you tell me are of the past . . . they are of the past but the scars are now mine because many of them still hurt. You cannot get the correct answer to a long math problem if you err at the beginning . . . to get the right answer, you must start at the beginning.

When, when, and, again, when will you stop kidding yourself that my lot will be improved if I become a whiteman? That I am hindering my own progress by remaining Indian? Friends, you are telling me that out of a clear blue sky you finally got the answer to all these problems that you have made for me . . . the answer being so worthwhile and all-solving that all past experience can be disregarded . . . the answer being "shoving responsibilities on somebody else . . . erasing the Indian from your conscience."

I will consider your policy only, and only when, it is in proportion, to the amount of correction of past injustices.

Your recent actions further confirm that every time I turn my back on you, you try to pull a 'quickie' on me.

I have said what I wanted to say. I do not think you have anymore to tell me. But you now know a little bit of what I want. If your new Indian policy becomes reality, then I guess 'might is right'.

Leroy Little Bear, Blood Reserve.

There was an immediate response also from non-Indians, in Parliament, and through news media. In an emergency debate in the Commons on the Indian reaction to the Government's proposals, Mr. Frank Howard, M.P. for Skeena, B.C. criticized the government's policy on two counts: failure to guarantee Indian rights and failure to consult adequately with the Indians in developing policy. The Indians, he claimed, had been consulted, but not listened to, because the government went into the consultation process with its mind made up.

"There has been almost universal rejection of this policy by the native Indian people in Alberta, Ontario, New Brunswick and parts of Manitoba," he said. "In face of this rejection the minister still goes blindly on his way like a man compelled by a hidden force, unable to see, unwilling to hear."

Mr. Robert Stanfield, leader of the Opposition, attacked the government's concern with which level of government – federal or provincial – would deal with the Indians while neglecting the Indians' chief concern – the preservation of their treaty rights. "The statement of the government very nearly treats as irrelevant the issue of treaty and aboriginal rights which the Indian people consider paramount," he said.

At the same time, a non-Indian student of Indian affairs expressed this opinion on a CBC radio program. His main point is that the government is acting in bad faith. What support does he provide for this point of view?

The Federal Government is headed for direct political conflict with Canada's Indians and their allies. During the last year, the government has gone through the motions of consulting the Indians in a series of short superficial meetings about complex legal matters. The announced purpose of the talks was to find out what lands and powers the Indians wanted, but now Indians Affairs Minister Jean Chrétien has dropped the pretence of trying to fill the Indians' wishes.

He has told them what the government intends to do, whether they like it or not and they don't like it because what the government intends to do is exactly the opposite of what the Indians asked for.

A lot of Indians are angry. They reject Mr. Chrétien's proposal to phase out what is left of special Indian rights, discard the traditional Federal responsibility for Indian affairs, hand over Indian affairs to the provinces and pressure Indians into giving up their tax exemptions.

Mr. Chrétien's white paper did not state the government's intentions as bluntly as I have done. The white paper is a clever public relations piece. It is ornamented with fancy words about Indian discrimination and setting the Indian people free to control their own destiny. It says the Indians must set their own goals and run their own show and by verbal slight-of-hand it hides the fact that the government is brushing aside what the Indians want and ordering them to do what they are told.

It is a white paper for white people, and many editors and reporters have accepted it at face value. They are hailing it as a statesmanlike document. Most Indians take a different view. The polite Indian leaders say it is well-intentioned but wrong headed. They give a diplomatic nod towards the government's good intentions.

The outspoken Indian leaders call it a betrayal and a fraud. They accuse the Trudeau government of lying to them. The Indians gave their answers plainly enough: they wanted a clear-cut and generous restatement of Indian rights. They wanted payment in full for past injustices and a clear guarantee of the special legal position granted them by treaties, law and usage in exchange for three million square miles of land. They wanted other things as well, but above all they wanted their rights: tax exemptions, fish and game rights, and payment for lost lands.

In reply Mr. Chrétien now tells them to forget about their rights. He promises to hand the Indians over to the provinces with a development fund of ten million dollars a year for five years as a parting gift, not enough to even nibble at the edge of the vast Indian poverty, and alienation.

Some political leaders sincerely believe that they know better than the Indians what is good for them and they sincerely believe that special treatment for any group is a bad principal. This is a tricky point. Should we break promises because we no longer find it convenient to keep them?

But the key fact is that the government is not really playing the game of participatory democracy at all. It is playing the game of power and is treating the Indians as a conquered people who must be assimilated, despite the fact that in large areas of the north, Indian people are in overwhelming majority. Power is an old and honoured game, but we should strip it of hypocrisy and double-talk and once it is brought out into the open, the Indians will have the power of all minorities to raise a loud voice in public and give Canada a bad name in the eyes of the non-European world. Rightly or wrongly, a lot of Indian leaders are getting angry enough to make a noise that can be heard a long way off.

They may not be such a pushover in the power game as Mr. Chrétien thinks.

> G. E. Mortimore, on *Preview Commentary* (CBC radio program), July 2, 1969.

Mr. Chrétien replied to these criticisms by emphasizing that the *White Paper* was offered as a basis for discussion "by the Indian people and by all the people of Canada," not as a fixed policy. The government's purpose was not to dump the Indians but to eliminate the paternalistic role of the government over Indian affairs. If his purpose was to gain the confidence of the Indians, he was not successful. Their opposition continued to grow.

Who is right in this matter? Is the *White Paper* in the best interests of the Indians and of the country as a whole? Is it based on fairness and justice? Is it a step in the right direction? If implemented, will it satisfy the aspirations of the Indian people for a better life? Or is it an attempt to rid the Federal government of a difficult and tiresome problem by having its responsibilities shifted to the provincial governments? Does it show a callous disregard for the rights and wishes of the Indian people? Does it mean assimilation and an end to them as Indians?

In order to answer this question, we need to look more closely at the new policy proposed in the *White Paper*. We have already seen that the framework of the new policy consists of six principles. We shall study each of these principles in turn, remembering that in the words of the *White Paper*, "the policy rests upon the fundamental right of Indian people to full and equal participation in the cultural, social, economic and political life of Canada."

1. The Legal Structure

Legislative and constitutional bases of discrimination must be removed.

Canada cannot seek the just society and keep discriminatory legislation on its statute books. The Government believes this to be self-evident. The ultimate aim of removing the specific references to Indians from the constitution may take some time, but it is a goal to be kept constantly in view. In the meantime, barriers created by special legislation can generally be struck down.

Under the authority of Head 24, Section 91 of the British North America Act, the Parliament of Canada has enacted the Indian Act. Various federal-provincial agreements and some other statutes also affect Indian policies.

In the long term, removal of the reference in the constitution would be necessary to end the legal distinction between Indians and other Canadians. In the short term, repeal of the Indian Act and enactment of transitional legislation to ensure the orderly management of Indian land would do much to mitigate the problem.

The ultimate goal could not be achieved quickly, for it requires a change in the economic circumstances of the Indian people and much preliminary adjustment with provincial authorities. Until the Indian people are satisfied that their land holdings are solely within their control, there may have to be some special legislation for Indian lands.

1. It is proposed to abolish the Indian Act. What reason is given for this proposal?

2. Most Indian leaders do not like the Indian Act, but they do not want it repealed until the question of Indian rights is settled. They insist on the prior re-negotiation of the treaties and the settlement of aboriginal claims.
   a) How does this position differ from that taken in the White Paper?
   b) Is this a reasonable position? Explain why you agree or disagree with it.

3. For the purpose of eliminating discrimination, the *White Paper* proposes to remove specific references to Indians from the constitution and to abolish laws of a similar nature.
   The Indians argue that, if discriminatory legislation is to be removed, references to the English-speaking and French-speaking groups in the constitution should be removed, and legislation such as the French language bill should be repealed.
   Do you consider this a logical argument? Are the French-speaking citizens of Canada being discriminated against by the passing of the language bill? What conclusions can you come to about this proposal?

2. The Indian Cultural Heritage

There must be positive recognition by everyone of the unique contribution of Indian culture to Canadian society.

It is important that Canadians recognize and give credit to the Indian contribution. It manifests itself in many ways; yet it goes largely unrecognized and unacknowledged. Without recognition by others it is not easy to be proud.

All of us seek a basis for pride in our own lives, in those of our families and of our ancestors. Man needs such pride to sustain him in the inevitable hour of discouragement, in the moment when he faces obstacles, whenever life seems turned against him. Everyone has such moments. We manifest our pride in many ways, but always it supports and sustains us. The legitimate pride of the Indian people has been crushed too many times by too many of their fellow Canadians.

The principle of equality and all that goes with it demands that all of us recognize each other's cultural heritage as a source of personal strength. . . .

For many years Canadians believed the Indian people had but two choices: they could live in a reserve community, or they could be assimilated and lose their Indian identity. Today Canada has more to offer. There is a third choice – a full role in Canadian society and in the economy while retaining, strengthening and developing an Indian identity which preserves the good things of the past and helps Indian people to prosper and thrive. . . .

The Indian people have often been made to feel that their culture and history are not worthwhile. To lose a sense of worthiness is damaging. Success in life, in adapting to change, and in developing appropriate relations within the community as well as in relation to a wider world, requires a strong sense of personal worth – a real sense of identity.

Rich in folklore, in art forms and in concepts of community life, the Indian cultural heritage can grow and expand further to enrich the general society. . . .

1. Do you agree with the sentiments expressed in this statement?

2. Does the statement that "there must be positive recognition by everyone of the unique contribution of Indian culture to Canadian society" have any real meaning? Can it be brought about?

3. Suggest some ways in which schools could contribute to the realization of this aim.

4. It has been suggested that, until Indians have much more economic power, they will not be treated with respect by the majority of Canadians. Do you think this is true?

5. Outline the steps you consider to be necessary if Indians are to develop the "strong sense of personal worth – a real sense of identity" mentioned in the *White Paper*.

3. Programs and Services

Services must come through the same channels and from the same government agencies for all Canadians.

This is an undeniable part of equality. It has been shown many times that separation of people follows from separate services. There can be no argument about the principle of common services. It is right.

It cannot be accepted now that Indians should be constitutionally excluded from the right to be treated within their province as full and equal citizens, with all the responsibilities and all the privileges that this might entail. It is in the provincial sphere where social remedies are structured and applied, and the Indian people, by and large, have been non-participating members of provincial society.

Canadians receive a wide range of services through provincial and local governments, but the Indian people and their communities are mostly outside that framework. It is no longer acceptable that the Indian people should be outside and apart. The Government believes that services should be available on an equitable basis, except for temporary differentiation based on need. Services ought not to flow from separate agencies established to serve particular groups, especially not to groups that are identified ethnically.

Separate but equal services do not provide truly equal treatment. Treatment has not been equal in the case of Indians and their communities. Many services require a wide range of facilities which cannot be duplicated by separate agencies. Others must be integral to the complex systems of community and regional life and cannot be matched on a small scale.

The Government is therefore convinced that the traditional method of providing separate services to Indians must be ended. All Indians should have access to all programs and services of all levels of government equally with other Canadians.

The Government proposes to negotiate with the provinces and conclude agreements under which Indian people would participate in and be served by the full programs of the provincial and local systems. Equitable financial arrangements would be sought to ensure that services could be provided in full measure commensurate with the needs. The negotiations must seek agreements to end discrimination while ensuring that no harm is inadvertently done to Indian interests. The Government further proposes that federal disbursements for Indian programs in each province be transferred to that province. Subject to negotiations with the provinces, such provisions would as a matter of principle eventually decline, the provinces ultimately assuming the same responsibility for services to Indian residents as they do for services to others.

At the same time, the Government proposes to transfer all remaining federal responsibilities for Indians from the Department of Indian Affairs and Northern Development to other departments, including the Departments of Regional Economic Expansion, Secretary of State, and Manpower and Immigration.

It is important that such transfers take place without disrupting services and that special arrangements not be compromised while they are subject to consultation and negotiation. The Government will pay particular attention to this.

1. As the Department of Indian Affairs is phased out, which level of government will take over the responsibility of providing services to the Indians? What reasons are given for this proposed step?

2. Indian spokesmen have repeatedly claimed that the Federal Government is escaping its responsibilities by dumping the Indians and their

problems on the provincial governments. They fear the change would be harmful to Indian interests.

Why do you think they are fearful? (Consider the conditions of the Métis people of Manitoba or Saskatchewan who already are under provincial jurisdiction.)

3. "Separate but equal services do not provide truly equal treatment." This is accepted as true in the case of services provided for black people in the United States, and black leaders have fought for integration of services (for example, of schools, and public facilities such as restaurants). It is, however, rejected by most Indian leaders. What reasons can you think of which might explain this attitude?

4. Points 1, 2 and 3 of the *White Paper* have been described as a "hollow commitment."
    a) Explain what you think this expression means.
    b) Do you think this is a fair judgment? Support your opinion with facts and arguments.

4. Enriched Services

Those who are furthest behind must be helped most.

There can be little argument that conditions for many Indian people are not satisfactory to them and are not acceptable to others. There can be little question that special services, and especially enriched services, will be needed for some time.

Equality before the law and in programs and services does not necessarily result in equality in social and economic conditions. For that reason, existing programs will be reviewed. The Department of Regional Economic Expansion, the Department of Manpower and Immigration, and other federal departments involved would be prepared to evolve programs that would help break past patterns of deprivation.

Additional funds would be available from a number of different sources. In an atmosphere of greater freedom, those who are able to do so would be expected to help themselves, so more funds would be available to help those who really need it. The transfer of Indian lands to Indian control should enable many individuals and groups to move ahead on their own initiative. This in turn would free funds for further enrichment of programs to help those who are furthest behind. By ending some programs and replacing them with others evolved within the community, a more effective use of funds would be achieved. Administrative savings would result from the elimination of separate agencies as various levels of government bring general programs and resources to bear. By broadening the base of service agencies, this enrichment could be extended to all who need it. By involving more agencies working at different levels, and by providing those agencies with the means to make them more effective, the Government believes that root problems could be attacked, that solutions could be found that hitherto evaded the best efforts and best-directed of programs.

The economic base for many Indians is their reserve land, but the development of reserves has lagged.

Among the many factors that determine economic growth of reserves, their location and size are particularly important. There are a number of industrial areas which could provide substantial employment and income to their owners if they were properly developed. There are other reserves in agricultural areas which could provide a livelihocd for a larger number of family units than is presently the case. The majority of reserves, however, are located in the boreal or wooded regions of Canada, most of them geographically isolated and many having little economic potential. In these areas, low income, unemployment and under-employment are characteristic of Indians and non-Indians alike.

Even where reserves have economic potential, the Indians have been handicapped. Private investors have been reluctant to supply capital for projects on land which cannot be pledged as security. Adequate social and risk capital has not been available from public sources. Most Indians have not had the opportunity to acquire managerial experience, nor have they been offered sufficient technical assistance.

The Government believes that the Indian people should have the opportunity to develop the resources of their reserves so they may contribute to their own well-being and the economy of the nation. To develop Indian reserves to the level of the regions in which they are located will require considerable capital over a period of some years, as well as the provision of managerial and technical advice. Thus the Government believes that all programs and advisory services of the federal and provincial governments should be made readily available to Indians.

In addition, and as an interim measure, the Government proposes to make substantial additional funds available for investment in the economic progress of the Indian people. This would overcome the barriers to early development of Indian lands and resources, help bring Indians into a closer working relationship with the business community, help finance their adjustment to new employment opportunities, and facilitate access to normal financial sources.

Even if the resources of Indian reserves are fully utilized, however, they cannot all properly support their present Indian populations, much less the populations of the future. Many Indians will, as they are now doing, seek employment elsewhere as a means of solving their economic problems. Jobs are vital and the Government intends that the full counselling, occupational training and placement resources of the Department of Manpower and Immigration are used to further employment opportunities for Indians. The government will encourage private employers to provide opportunities for the Indian people.

In many situations, the problems of Indians are similar to those faced by their non-Indian neighbours. Solutions to their problems cannot be found in isolation but must be sought within the context of regional development plans involving all the people. The consequence of an integrated regional approach is that all levels of government – federal, provincial and local – and the people themselves are involved. Helping overcome regional disparities in the economic well-being of Canadians is the main task assigned to the Department of Regional Economic Expansion. The Government believes that the needs of Indian communities should be met within this framework.

1. Where would the funds be found to help those who need help most?
2. What part would the Department of Regional Economic Expansion play in providing opportunities for Indians?

3. What would be the role of the Department of Manpower and Immigration?

4. What is the ultimate purpose of all the proposals in this section?

5. Claims and Treaties

Lawful obligations must be recognized

Many of the Indian people feel that successive governments have not dealt with them as fairly as they should. They believe that lands have been taken from them in an improper manner, or without adequate compensation, that their funds have been improperly administered, that their treaty rights have been breached. Their sense of grievance influences their relations with governments and the community and limits their participation in Canadian life.

Many Indians look upon their treaties as the source of their rights to land, to hunting and fishing privileges, and to other benefits. Some believe the treaties should be interpreted to encompass wider services and privileges, and many believe the treaties have not been honoured. Whether or not this is correct in some or many cases, the fact is the treaties affect only half the Indians of Canada. Most of the Indians of Quebec, British Columbia, and the Yukon are not parties to a treaty.

The terms and effects of the treaties between the Indian people and the Government are widely misunderstood. A plain reading of the words used in the treaties reveals the limited and minimal promises which were included in them. As a result of the treaties, some Indians were given an initial cash payment and were promised land reserved for their exclusive use, annuities, protection of hunting, fishing and trapping privileges subject (in most cases) to regulation, a school or teachers in most instances, and, in one treaty only, a medicine chest. There were some other minor considerations such as the annual provision of twine and ammunition.

The annuities have been paid regularly. The basic promise to set aside reserve land has been kept except in respect of the Indians of the Northwest Territories and a few bands in the northern parts of the Prairie Provinces. These Indians did not choose land when treaties were signed. The government wishes to see these obligations dealt with as soon as possible.

The right to hunt and fish for food is extended unevenly across the country and not always in relation to need. Although game and fish will become less and less important for survival as the pattern of Indian life continues to change, there are those who, at this time, still live in the traditional manner that their forefathers lived in when they entered into treaty with the government. The Government is prepared to allow such persons transitional freer hunting of migratory birds under the Migratory Birds Convention Act and Regulations.

The significance of the treaties in meeting the economic, educational, health and welfare needs of the Indian people has always been limited and will continue to decline. The services that have been provided go far beyond what could have been foreseen by those who signed the treaties.

The Government and the Indian people must reach a common understanding of the future role of the treaties. Some provisions will be found to have been discharged; others will have continuing importance. Many of the provisions and practices of another century may be considered irrelevant in the light of a rapidly changing society, and still others may be ended by mutual agreement. Finally, once Indian lands are securely within Indian control, the anomaly of treaties between groups within society and the government of that society will require that these treaties be reviewed to see how they can be equitably ended.

Other grievances have been asserted in more general terms. It is possible that some of these can be verified by appropriate research and may be susceptible to specific remedies. Others relate to aboriginal claims to land. These are so general and undefined that it is not realistic to think of them as specific claims capable of remedy except through a policy and program that will end injustice to Indians as members of the Canadian community. This is the policy that the Government is proposing for discussion.

At the recent consultation meeting in Ottawa representatives of the Indians, chosen at each of the earlier regional meetings, expressed concern about the extent of their knowledge of Indian rights and treaties. They indicated a desire to undertake further research to establish their rights with greater precision, elected a National Committee on Indian Rights and Treaties for this purpose and sought government financial support for research.

The Government had intended to introduce legislation to establish an Indian Claims Commission to hear and determine Indian claims. Consideration of the questions raised at the consultations and the review of Indian policy have raised serious doubts as to whether a Claims Commission as proposed to Parliament in 1965 is the right way to deal with the grievances of Indians put forward as claims.

The Government has concluded that further study and research are required by both the Indians and the Government. It will appoint a Commissioner who, in consultation with representatives of the Indians, will inquire into and report upon how claims arising in respect of the performance of the terms of treaties and agreements formally entered into by representatives of the Indians and the Crown, and the administration of moneys and lands pursuant to schemes established by legislation for the benefit of Indians may be adjudicated.

The Commissioner will also classify the claims that in his judgment ought to be referred to the courts or any special quasi-judicial body that may be recommended.

It is expected that the Commissioner's inquiry will go on concurrently with that of the National Indian Committee on Indian Rights and Treaties and the Commissioner will be authorized to recommend appropriate support to the Committee so that it may conduct research on the Indians' behalf and assist the Commissioner in his inquiry.

1. One critic of the Government's proposals has claimed that under the heading, "Lawful obligations must be recognized," the *White Paper* affirms that the Government has only minor obligations. How far, in your opinion, is this true?

2. This section plays down the importance of the treaties. The promises, it claims, were "minimal and limited." Indian leaders, however, are claiming that a plain reading of the words used in the treaties does not reflect the spirit in which they were signed. They are insisting that the

treaties be re-negotiated to bring them into line with Indian needs in the 1970's. Which interpretation do you agree with? Which seems more just?

3. The *White Paper* here proposes the ending of the treaties. If the Indians insist that they be retained and re-negotiated, what choices are open to the government? List the policies the government might adopt and evaluate each one.

4. The Indians of Quebec, British Columbia, the Yukon, and most of the Northwest Territories have never entered into treaties with the government or otherwise surrendered title to their land. What is the attitude towards their aboriginal claims expressed in the *White Paper*? Do you agree with this point of view, or do you think such claims should be recognized and compensation paid?

5. The appointment of a Commissioner to deal with matters relating to claims and treaties has been criticised by Indian spokesmen. They want the legal right to present their claims directly to a court or other judicial body. In what way are the rights of the Indians limited by the powers of the Commissioner? Do the Indians have legal equality with other Canadians?

6. Indian Lands

Control of Indian lands should be transferred to the Indian people.

Frustration is as great a handicap as a sense of grievance. True co-operation and participation can come only when the Indian people are controlling the land which makes up the reserves.

The reserve system has provided the Indian people with lands that generally have been protected against alienation without their consent. Widely scattered across Canada, the reserves total nearly 6,000,000 acres and are divided into about 2,200 parcels of varying sizes. Under the existing system, title to reserve lands is held either by the Crown in right of Canada or the Crown in right of one of the provinces. Administrative control and legislative authority are, however, vested exclusively in the Government and the Parliament of Canada. It is a trust. As long as this trust exists, the Government, as a trustee, must supervise the business connected with the land.

The result of Crown ownership and the Indian Act has been to tie the Indian people to a land system that lacks flexibility and inhibits development. If an Indian band wishes to gain income by leasing its land, it has to do so through a cumbersome system involving the Government as trustee. It cannot mortgage reserve land to finance development on its own initiative. Indian people do not have control of their lands except as the Government allows, and this is no longer acceptable to them. The Indians have made this clear at the consultation meetings. They now want real control, and this Government believes that they should have it. The Government recognizes that full and true equality calls for Indian control and ownership of reserve land.

Between the present system and the full holding of title in fee simple lie a number of intermediate states. The first step is to change the system under which ministerial decision is required for all that is done with Indian land. This is where the delays, the frustrations and the obstructions lie. The Indians must control their land.

This can be done in many ways. The Government believes that each band must make its own decision as to the way it wants to take control of its land and the manner in which it intends to manage it. It will take some years to complete the process of devolution.

The Government believes that full ownership implies many things. It carries with it the free choice of use, of retention or of disposition. In our society it also carries with it an obligation to pay for certain services. The Government recognizes that it may not be acceptable to put all lands into the provincial systems immediately and make them subject to taxes. When the Indian people see that the only way they can own and fully control land is to accept taxation the way other Canadians do, they will make that decision.

Alternative methods for the control of their lands will be made available to Indian individuals and bands. Whatever methods of land control are chosen by the Indian people, the present system under which the Government must execute all leases, supervise and control procedures and surrenders, and generally act as trustee, must be brought to an end. But the Indian land heritage should be protected. Land should be alienated from them only by consent of the Indian people themselves. Under a proposed Indian Lands Act full management would be in the hands of the bands and, if the bands wish, they or individuals would be able to take title to their land without restrictions.

As long as the Crown controls the land for the benefit of bands who use and occupy it, it is responsible for determining who may, as a member of a band, share in the assets of band land. The qualifications for band membership which it has imposed are part of the legislation – the Indian Act – governing the administration of reserve lands. Under the present Act, the Government applies and interprets these qualifications. When bands take title to their lands, they will be able to define and apply these qualifications themselves.

The Government is prepared to transfer to the Indian people the reserve lands, full control over them and, subject to the proposed Indian Lands Act, the right to determine who shares in ownership. The Government proposes to seek agreements with the bands and, where necessary, with the governments of the provinces. Discussions will be initiated with the Indian people and the provinces to this end.

1. How are reserve lands at present controlled?
2. What are the disadvantages of this system of control?
3. The government proposes to transfer ownership and control of reserve lands to the Indians. Eventually these lands would be subject to taxation.
   Read the following statement. What Indian objection does it reflect?
   "I am much concerned that where Indians have potentially valuable land that they are not able to develop, outside interests will put pressure on the government to secure it. For instance tax assessment could be put so high Indians couldn't pay the taxes. Then once the developer secured the property, what would stop the government from reducing the assessment?"
   Ernest Benedict, Cornwall Island, Ontario.
4. Some Indian leaders are opposed to the idea of the taxation of Indian lands. The government, they say, could never repay the Indians for all the land and resources which were taken from them. To tax the

land left to the Indians is both illegal and immoral. Do you think their lands should be taxed or not?

Questions for Discussion

The White Paper

1. Which parts of the *White Paper* are definitely unacceptable to the Indians? Why are these parts unacceptable?
2. The *White Paper* argues in favour of integration. Indian and non-Indian critics say that it spells assimilation, if adopted and implemented. What do you think it means for the Indians?
3. The *White Paper* was put forward to promote discussion and to lead to action, with the eventual aim of raising the quality of life of the Indians. Clearly the Indians are suspicious of much of it. Which parts of the *White Paper* will be useful as a basis of discussion, negotiation, and action?
4. Suppose you were on the board of the National Indian Brotherhood. In the board's discussions what would be your stand on these important issues?
   a) The future of the treaties.
   b) Aboriginal claims.
   c) The abolition of the Indian Act.
   d) The education of Indians.
   e) The proposed taxation of Indian lands.
   f) Separatism, assimilation, or integration?
5. Suppose you were asked to advise Mr. Chrétien and the government about the next step to take in Indian Affairs. Present a brief analysis of the situation as you now see it, together with your recommendations.

6.   Steps to Progress

In view of the Indian responses to the *White Paper* it is highly unlikely that the proposals it contains will be accepted by the Indians. There are too many points on which they have doubts or to which they are outright opposed. Too many Indians regard the *White Paper* as part of a plot to solve the problem by assimilating them into Canadian society. Nevertheless, events are on the move. Indians are now more aware of their disadvantages than ever before, and they are set on improving their conditions. The *White Paper* may not be accepted, but it sets the stage for further discussion of Indian grievances. It is essential that plans of action emerge out of these discussions which will satisfy the Indians that they are being fairly dealt with and give them hope for the future.

It seems obvious that the government will have to come up with new proposals more acceptable to the Indians. For their part, the Indians will have to work at defining ever more clearly what they wish to achieve, and how they wish to achieve it. They must hammer out policies on the important issues that affect them – economic development, leadership, education, relationships with local, provincial and federal governments, and so on – so that they can present the Federal Government with clear and specific counter-proposals.

Treaties or No Treaties?

Central to the bargaining which will come is the question of the treaties and aboriginal claims. The *White Paper* suggests that the treaties have outlived their usefulness and should be phased out as soon as practicable. The Indians take a contrary view which was expressed in December, 1968, by the Manitoba Indian Brotherhood:

From reading these treaties it is apparent that:

1. The officials representing the Government full well knew the value of the land requested to be ceded to the Crown;

2. . . . they were aware that the Indian was not able to communicate with them;

3. . . . the Indian had no counsel;

4. . . . the Indian was impressed by the pomp and ceremony and the authority of the officials;

5. . . . they [the officials] were dealing with uneducated people;

6. . . . the respect and ceremony with which the officials were dealing with the Indians lulled the Indians into a passive mood;

7. . . . a father image was being advanced by the authorities;

8. . . . the Indians, although it is alleged were explained the terms of the Treaties, really did not know or understand fully the meaning and implications;

9. . . . the alleged consideration that was being advanced by the Government to the Indians in exchange for the ceded land was not totally appreciated by the Indians, nor could they understand the concept of binding their heirs and executors, administrators and assigns to these documents;

10. . . . forever and a day it will be obvious to all who read the said Treaties and the history of their making, that the officials of Her Majesty the Queen committed a legal fraud in a very sophisticated manner upon unsophisticated, unsuspecting, illiterate, uninformed natives.

The terms of the treaties must be extended and interpreted in light of present social and economic standards. To renegotiate the treaties does not necessarily mean to rewrite the treaties, nor does it mean to repudiate the treaties.

Quoted in: Cardinal, *op. cit.*, pp. 36-37.

The federal government and the Indians seem to be at an impasse on this crucial point. One side or the other is going to have to make concessions. In the discussions that will follow, the position taken in the *Hawthorn Report* may become of more than passing importance. This report, made to the federal government in 1966–67, is the most far-reaching inquiry into the conditions of the contemporary Indians of Canada. The position it takes on the matter of Indian rights is as follows:

It seems to us that there is a category of rights which can be called charter rights which derive from history and long respect. They relate ultimately to the fact that the Indians were here first; that a series of bargains were made by the ancestors of the present generation of Indians and Whites by which the latter were allowed to develop peacefully the northern half of a richly endowed domain, in compensation for which the original possessors, however their title may be classed by anthropologists or lawyers, were accorded a special status, partially contained in the treaties, and partially sanctioned by long usage in the Indian Act. In retrospect it is clear that the privileged position to which Indians are entitled was historically used as a justification for depriving them of services of a quality and quantity equal to those received by non-Indians. By any standard of measurement a privilege was turned into a millstone.

At the present time a postwar version of egalitarianism is responsible for a very desirable attempt to see that Indians are brought within the framework of all normal public programs which are not inherently incompatible with their unique status. The position we strongly hold is that Indians are citizens plus; that in addition to the normal rights and duties of citizenship they also possess certain rights simply by virtue of being Indians. This position is supported by the rather vaguely worded recommendation of the 1959–61 Joint Committee which stated the Committee's belief "that the advancement of the Indians towards full acceptance of the responsibilities and obligations of citizenship must be without prejudice to the retention of the cultural, historical and other economic benefits which they have inherited.

H. B. Hawthorne, ed., *A Survey of the Contemporary Indians of Canada*, Part I (Ottawa: Indian Affairs Branch 1967), p. 396.

1. The *Hawthorn Report* takes the position that the Indians are "citizens plus." On what grounds is this position taken? What does it imply for the treatment of Indians by the Federal Government?
2. Which position does the "citizens plus" idea tend to support, that taken in the *White Paper* or that taken by Indian spokesmen?
3. What is your position? Do you support the "citizens plus" position or not? Give your reasons.
4. Check your newspapers for news of developments in this crucial area.
5. Write to your Member of Parliament, stating your views, and asking him for a statement of his position in this matter.

Education – What Kind?

Another important area in which action will have to be taken is education. Though it is not directly referred to in the *White Paper,* it is of deep concern to the Indians. The great majority of them believe that education will somehow help to solve their problems. Yet they are troubled because experience clearly shows that education has failed to do for them what they had hoped for. It has not provided their children with the skills which would enable them to compete with Whites on an even footing. Often it had created a barrier between the children and their parents. And as statistics show, Indian children have been frustrated and eventually defeated by their school experience.

Many adult Indians remember their own school experiences with feelings of bitterness and resentment. Some of the failings of the schools are here discussed by Indians in the CBC radio program, *The Way of the Indian.* What seem to be the principal faults mentioned?

PETER YELLOWHORN.   In the Treaty of 1877, when the treaty was signed, it was stated in there that the government would pay for our education. And that treaty stated that as long as the sun shines and the rivers flow that treaty will hold, but I don't know who's broken it now. See, if they had educated us good from the start like that, these guys that are seventy years old now, they would have a good education right now.

ANNOUNCER.   That was Peter Yellowhorn, at Brocket in Alberta, and here's his brother Tom again:

TOM YELLOWHORN.   I was raised at the residential school. Just two grades in seven years, and when I came out of that school I can't figure out numbers, I don't know nothing about mathematics, what I should say, and how to write letters. I can't write letters, but all I could do is write my own name.

ANNOUNCER.   There were a good many complaints about Indian schools a generation ago, and they're still not popular. Children were taken from their parents' homes often quite young, and kept in boarding school till they reached their middle teens. Some managed to get home for the summer holidays, others didn't. In most schools they were forbidden to speak their own language, and had to work, study, play and pray in English. At some of these schools, determined efforts were made to render the situation self-supporting by raising vegetables for the kitchens. The work in the fields was done by the Indian children themselves, and the Indians complained that more time was spent in this way and at prayers than over their school work. The results of this kind of teaching were often unfortunate. When the children left school and went back home to their reserves they couldn't share in the life of their own people. In many cases they had forgotten much of their own language, and many of them were repelled by the squalid living conditions of their parents. They were outcasts, unsuited either to life on the reserve or to striking out on their own. And the little schooling they did manage to pick up was not, as a rule, enough to enable them to get and hold more than a labouring job. Listen to George Clutesy, a Nootka on Vancouver Island:

GEORGE CLUTESY.   We sent our children to the school and they looked after the children from beginning to end. They clothed them and fed them and in the meantime we were more less cut off entirely from our children. And the result was that, when they did grow up and when we got to see them again, we had absolutely no control over our children, and they had absolutely no, or very little, respect for their parents. I say that because that was how I felt in my period at school. I am pretty sure that most pupils would have the same feeling – I was somehow made to be ashamed of my own father and my parents, and to forget everything that concerned my past or the teachings of my own people. In fact, we were not permitted to speak in our own language at all, any time during our stay in that school.

GERALD TAILFEATHERS.   I never went to a mixed school. I went to the Anglican boarding school. And this is kind of a bad thing to say, but we tried to get into the town school and we were refused. The system I never did like, and I don't think I ever will. We had good teachers there, but it was just the idea of being confined and being away from our parents. I didn't like it there. We stayed there, at least I did, for about a year. And I vowed that I'd run away. You know, I just didn't want to stay there. With the set-up now they depend on too many things. They're just sort of helpless, even the parents. They send their children to the schools and forget about them and the children expect everything to be done for them. I mean, it's reflecting right here on the reserve; they won't stand on their own feet.

ANNOUNCER.   That's how Gerald Tailfeathers, a Blood, feels. And these feelings die hard. Many youngsters feel the same way even now. Like Percy Yellowhorse, a Blackfoot in Alberta:

PERCY YELLOWHORSE.   Some of them don't like the way the Indian schools are being run, and as soon as they are sixteen they just leave. And I think there's only been about one or two that has gone right through school, and only one of them is making a living on it, but the rest on the reserve aren't doing nothing. I don't like the way them boarding schools are being run. In some of them you have to do what the supervisor says to do, and that some of the kids don't like.

ANNOUNCER.   Bad teachers. Too much gardening and not enough learning. No family life. Too much restriction. Regimentation that's foreign to the Indian character. Suppression of everything that was Indian. All these complaints and more were levelled at the residential schools. In far too many cases they were well founded. And yet, how many youngsters today find no fault with their schools? No doubt many of the features of residential school life which the Indian hated were unavoidable under the existing circumstances. The churches were accused of simply wanting to extend their influence – using the Indians as soul fodder, one woman called it. Yet few Indians would have learned even to read and write if the churches hadn't opened mission schools. And today there are three kinds of school the Indian child can attend: day school on the reserve, residential school, or the local non-Indian school – and education is compulsory as with non-Indian children. (There are still groups of nomads who don't live in any fixed area and it's difficult to enforce the regulation when the children can't be found.) But for the majority living on the reserves or in the cities school facilities are as good as they could wish. Some reserves have their own schools run by their own school boards, and government supervised.

The Way of the Indian, pp. 45-46.

> From the point of view of the Indian Affairs Branch, which is responsible for Indian education, the problems appear somewhat different but nevertheless complex and difficult.

Today every Indian child on a reserve or in an Indian community can receive the education he desires and from which he is capable of profiting, and the federal government will pay the total costs – if necessary – right through university. Not all Indian parents, however, appreciate the new opportunities. Where schools are aloof from communities, where school committees do not exist and where parents themselves lack education, the importance of learning in the lives of children sometimes is little appreciated.

Then, too, many Indian parents place more emphasis on parental training than on school instruction. They resent the fact also that their children return with non-Indian ways, unfamiliar with the traditional pursuits of hunting and fishing, that they are sometimes scornful of their parents' viewpoints and of Indian culture.

Association of Indians with non-Indians is a voluntary process. It cannot be forced. It cannot be hurried. There are bound to be setbacks and frictions – for instance, when Indian children, trained in the non-Indian world, return to homes traditionally Indian in outlook.

To be successful and lasting, the process must be at a pace, and in a manner, acceptable to Indians and non-Indians alike. Desire and need on both sides are prerequisites; isolation and wide gulfs in economic circumstances are gaps to be bridged. One cannot force people to associate with one another, if they are averse to such contacts. The most that one can do is to persuade and to encourage such association. . . .

The Indian population of a little more than 204,000 as of January 1, 1964, is scattered throughout the country; bands are at widely different stages of development. Some live in remote settlements, some in urban areas.

There is a multiplicity of dialects. In British Columbia alone, eleven different Indian dialects are spoken. Many Indians do not know either the French or English languages.

A number of children leave remote settlements at an early age and are educated in central institutions – with the emotional upheaval such changes entail.

A new way of life must be taught. Some pupils have never before seen water flowing out of taps, experienced central heating of buildings, or encountered electric lighting. Planes are familiar to many but not cars, trains or bicycles.

A new philosophy is encountered. To the non-Indian, time waits for no man; to the Indian, time is related traditionally more to the demands of the changing seasons than to a daily timetable.

It has often been said that the Canadian Indians are a neglected race. There were grounds for such accusations in the past – but not now so far as education is concerned. The education budget is increasing every year. For many older Indians, unfortunately, the assistance comes too late.

Many of the problems which Indian children still face arise out of their background. One major hurdle is that the lessons are taught in what is to nearly all of them a foreign language.

How fast would any non-Indian child progress if he had to learn his lessons in Cree or Ojibway? If the teacher used the word "netam" would a non-Indian recognize in that word, "my dog", or if he were asked in Kwakiutl, "masis, uksukw dakwa?" would he understand that she had said: "What are you doing?"

Then, there is the problem of figures. The Blackfoot Indians, for instance, have no numerals.

Texts also incorporate symbols and a way of life foreign to Indians from isolated areas. Indian pupils are familiar with hunting equipment but not with vacuum cleaners; they know about caribou but are unfamiliar with escalators. They do not understand the subtleties of children's stories or the reasoning about real estate or interest rates.

Conditions in many Indian homes make it difficult for pupils to do their homework. This is especially true when whole families live in one or two-room dwellings, equipped with only a limited amount of furniture, and a student's ear is assailed by a cacophony of crying children, blaring radio programs and adult conversation.

Such conditions are not unknown in non-Indian homes. They make it difficult for children to concentrate on their studies. The result is that often pupils are absent from school rather than face the consequences of neglected homework.

Low standards of living and limited education of parents often result in children leaving school at an early age. Uncertainty about job opportunities – even with education – also makes a student feel that there is little reason for him to continue studying.

It has been no easy task, therefore, to provide facilities satisfactory to all Indian families – and to the educationists.

> *The Indian in Transition* (Ottawa: Department of Indian Affairs and Northern Development, 1964), pp. 5-8.

> Clearly, education is going to become of greater importance to the Indians. Therefore ways will have to be found of making education more productive. The drop-out rate must be decreased. What is done in the schools will have to be made more meaningful to the children, so that their learning difficulties can be overcome, and more acceptable to the parents who, too often, are suspicious of the influences schooling has on their children. There are some clues as to what might be done in this description of a remote reserve school in northern Ontario.

I had been driven in by the cold, and sat down at one of the desks pushed back against the wall, for there was a clinic in progress. I looked around: it was like any other one-roomed schoolhouse on a reserve, with cut-out pictures from magazines pinned on the wall, a brightly coloured alphabetic mural, a cylindrical wood stove. On the blackboard three straggling lines of variously crippled letters told a sorry story: "Albert Duck is a noisey little boy; Happle Meekis must learn to bave himself; Semolia must learn to work Faster." On the wall beside my desk was a large simple poster depicting an eighteen-inch red toothbrush and a nice fat and tidy tube of toothpaste with a curl of pink paste issuing from it. Large black letters proclaimed WE MUST BRUSH OUR TEETH AFTER EVERY MEAL. I asked the nineteen-year-old schoolteacher what hopes he had of such a dictum being carried out in this very poor community, where the average family would consider anything other than food, equipment or clothes a scandalous outlay of money. He had no hopes at all, he admitted, but he was so appalled at the state of the children's teeth that he had instituted toothbrush drill at the school. He opened a cupboard and there was a row of some twenty labelled toothbrushes hanging from nails, and a large tin of tooth powder. He had bought the toothbrushes himself, but was finding the upkeep of tubes of paste for twenty enthusiastic little brushers twice a day too much for his budget, until fortunately he had come across a recipe for powder in an old book on cookery and household hints.

He was very fond of the children, and they obviously liked him in turn, but sometimes, he said, he despaired of leaving any imprint, any improvement, having been defeated only too often by the passive resistance put up by the parents, and his knowledge that, from the moment the children stepped back over the threshold of their homes, they were frequently adjured to forget the rules, golden or otherwise, that were taught in the white man's school. He knew too that if he pushed too far, perhaps about work, or truancy, it only made things more difficult for the child caught in the conflict of authority. He had two exceptionally intelligent pupils whom he had tried to persuade the parents to send out to residential school, where they would receive an education enabling them to be trained for a responsible position in life. Reasoning with them that it is this generation that must start taking on the responsibilities of their own people in their internal affairs, he quoted the changes that were taking place "outside." But in a land far removed from the medium of mass communication, "outside" could be outer space for all it meant to the parents. The answer of one father had been to remove his twelve-year-old son forthwith from school and take him on the trapline, and a flat "no" came from the parents of the other, a girl – she was needed at home, even if she did have three other sisters.

He despaired too of the educational materials he had to work with, the standard reading books for white children. They contained little of any recognisable import to these children. I looked inside one and there was "Father" skipping, his briefcase on the ground, and Mother standing by with a plate of buns – presumably as a reward: "Jump, Father, jump!" exhorted his children, one of them, inexplicably, standing on its head. It was small wonder that the parents dug their heels in if their children were going to be exposed to such curious and unseemly goings on "outside," said the teacher bitterly. And why did the entire population have to be represented by this insipid, unreal family who never apparently went anywhere beyond some regional suburbia except on a Visit to the Zoo, the Circus, or Uncle John's Farm? Why not here, or to an Eskimo settlement for at least an enlightening start? The history books he showed me contained little of Indians except their ultimate defeat and submission (and one could not help getting the impression that those who resisted the invasion of their territory had done so in a very ungentlemanly way; first they "rose" and then they "massacred," whereas the invaders, having failed to "quell" these uncouth risers, thereafter merely "subdued" them). There were many and lengthy accounts of the first great explorers and voyageurs – every man jack of whom, as the young teacher pointed out, would have perished without the endurance and skill of those anonymous people who not only guided them but taught them how to survive, without the courtesy, help, and hospitality from the many unmentioned tribes encountered on the way.

Burnford, *op. cit.*, pp. 230-234.

1. Children's learning experiences should relate to the world that they know. How do the children's reading books fail to do this? What kinds of topics in the reading books would be more suitable, in your opinion?

2. It has been said repeatedly that education should help young Indian children to develop a feeling of pride in their race and a worthy sense of identity. Do the social studies materials mentioned here contribute to this end? What would you suggest in their place?

3. The parents mentioned were suspicious of what was taught in "the White Man's school." As a result they did things that were perhaps not in the best interests of their children. What do you think might be done to secure the co-operation of parents and generally develop more positive attitudes towards education? (Consider such things as: the employment of Indian teachers; increased participation of the parents in the organization and running of schools; modification of attendance regulations to fit in with the way of life of the people of an area.)

Too often in the past, the dissatisfaction of the Indians have not been heard beyond the local area. Now they are being stated more clearly and more loudly, both by Indians themselves and by interested people who wish to improve Indian education. "Moreover, not only are dissatisfactions being aired but constructive suggestions for change are being put forward. An example of this trend is the statement made by Mr. Walter Currie to the House of Commons Standing Committee on Indian Affairs and Northern Development in May, 1969. Mr. Currie, at the time, was President of the Indian-Eskimo Association of Canada, and Assistant Superintendent of Supervision in the Ontario Department of Education. He is himself an Indian.

His job with the province is to review and make recommendations on education in the isolated communities of Northern Ontario, and this brings him into contact with many parents and children. In his address to the Members of Parliament comprising the committee, he presented a clear statement of the main issues as seen by the Indians.

It misses the boat because it does not make education relevant to the child, to his community, to his environment, or to the future which lies ahead of him. Until education does this for Indian children, our Indian people are going to persist in the economic system in which they find themselves struggling.

One of the simple things wrong about it, and one of the most obvious ones relative to co-education for Indian people, is the fact that it does not involve Indian parents. It is true that we have school committees, but if you examine the records you will find that school committees have been in existence for 15 years. Fifteen years ago they began to have school committees whereby parents were asked to participate in one way or another in education. Examine a school committee and you will find out what kind of authority and responsibility they have. They cut the grass, paint the fence and clean out the toilets, but they are not involved in education. They are not responsible for the education given to their children. And that to me, is a democratic right in any community.

Let us be positive. I have here the notes that I kept as Chairman of the Workshop on Education at the National Conference of the Indian-Eskimo Association last September in Toronto. These are the points that the Indian people there raised – the things that they said they wanted to see happen and felt needed to happen if education was going to mean anything to their children and to the Indian people of this country.

The most vital thing they felt, was that the Indians must be recognized as a people who do exist, who have existed and who are diversified in language, in culture and in where they live. This has not been so in the past. The very name "Indian" says so. Until the systems that serve Indian people recognize the fact that we are different – Ojibway, Cree, Blackfoot, Chilcotin, and so forth – until this is recognized by the educational system then problems are going to continue to exist. After all, what is good for a reserve in Southern Ontario is not necessarily good for a reserve in Northern Ontario, or in the mountains of B.C.

The next point they were most unhappy about, and about which they felt a great deal needed to be done, was the kind of teachers who go to teach in Indian communities. In the past, they have not been the best teachers, and for obvious reasons. You do not get the best teachers unless you can compete economically with dollar bills for the best in the community.

Gentlemen, this applies in any community. In North York, where I was, we always give at least one-week's orientation course to new teachers coming in. At one time it was two weeks, but it has now been cut back to only one. Obviously, teachers going into an Indian community should be aware that, for one thing, they are going to be in the midst of a culture conflict. They are bringing into the community a culture which in many cases has no relativity to the community in which they are going to teach. The teacher must be prepared to understand, and must be made aware of the fact, that he or she must change. It is the teacher who must change an elementary system, not the child. It is the teacher who must serve the child and the community; it is not for the community and the child to serve the teacher.

Let me come to the next point. For the past 15 or 20 years the Department of Indian Affairs and Education has been espousing and exercising a system called integration. The Indian parents at this meeting – and you can find this anywhere across the country – were quite unhappy with integration, *per se,* as it now stands, because in their estimation integration is only a one-way street. As one of the fellows from out West said, "The integration system is making Indian children into brown-skinned white men."

A true integration system should be one which presents to the Indian child something that is Indian. There is nothing in the integrated school system that says, "You are an Indian. This is what it means to be an Indian. And this is what it can mean to be an Indian." Everything there is foreign, it is non-Indian. There is no Indian language, no Indian culture, no Indian music and no Indian art. There is nothing in there that says "Indian."

This creates conflict in the mind of a child. It must, because indirectly it says to him, "What you are and from where you come is wrong. This is the right way." Until we brighten up and improve this in systems the Indian child is going to continue to suffer.

The Indian people felt that integration must, and should, become a two-way street in at least the educational program if not in physical movement of children. There must be many communities, especially in the West, where the children off the reserve could go to school on the reserve. Why must Indian children participate in an integrated school system? Why is it better? The only thing I can think of that makes it better is a better school building. It is a better equipped school system. There are better trained teachers. If these are the reasons, then why cannot those same things be offered in a reserve community? The Indian child in a reserve community should receive an equivalent education plus.

The fourth point they were very concerned about was the education of non-Indians about Indians; the education of Indians about Indians, and the education of Indians about non-Indians. They felt this needed to be done in the classroom most extensively. They felt this had to be done most extensively by media, the press at the back of this room. Television and radio had not done, and do not do, a good job of presenting to the Canadian public what an Indian is, what an Indian was, and what an Indian could be.

It almost seems as though history began in 1492 when Columbus arrived and nothing happened before then and nothing has happened since then involving Indian people. There is nothing, unfortunately, in our school systems today which says, "It is good to be an Indian and we, the people of Canada, are proud of those people who were here when the first white man arrived." This is a shame in a country like this.

Indian people need to be made aware of the non-Indian in Canada because I think in many cases, I do not think, I know in many cases, Indian people do not understand white people, just as white people do not understand Indians. There is a difference in culture and this must be made clear, it must be explained, and it must be understood.

The fifth point they raised, was the use of the Indian language, which ever it might be in that community, in the teaching of children; Cree or Ojibwa or whatever the community might be. They did not ask that this be a total involvement; they asked that it be a partial involvement. Not 15 minutes a day as we teach French in Ontario in grade 6, but a fair percentage of the day must have teaching of those children in their native language.

In Southern Ontario, let us go to Walpole Island, my mother's reserve. Let me introduce you to 400 children, who go to school right now and there is not one of them who speaks Ojibwa. Come with me into the North, a place called Gogama. There are 21 children who go to school in Gogama or rather there are 21 Indian children who go to school in Gogama and there are 33 schoolchildren altogether. Those 21 children come from Mattagami and not one of those children speak Ojibwa. Their parents do, but they do not.

Gentlemen, the only thing the Indian has left to him that is really Indian, aside from the colour of his skin, is his language. We have destroyed his culture you notice I say we, I am a teacher. We have destroyed his religion. We have through overpopulation, pollution, and so forth destroyed his means of survival. The only thing we have left him is his language and the colour of his skin. And, by God, we are damn well getting rid of his language in our school systems right now.

At one time, as you know, the word went out to the teachers that children were to be forbidden to speak their native language in school and on school property or in the residence. Fortunately this has changed, this order has been revoked but the damage has been done.

The last point in this group of points they raised was the existence or the need for schools in the smallest community instead of shipping children outside. Why should a six-year-old child have to go 100, 200 or 300 miles to school? Why should there not be a teacher and a school in that community? The parents were very, very definite about this point.

They will buy integration at a certain grade level, but they do not want it at such an early level. They do not want their children taken away from them.

As a matter of fact, I can introduce you to reserve communities in Northern Ontario that have forbidden their children be to taken outside grade 9. They have finished grade 8, but they will not let their children go out. I sat in their houses and talked to them last winter, and when I asked about this they said, "We do not like what happens to our children out there. Who are the people who will look after our children, are they good people? We do not like what happens to our children. When they come home they do not talk to us anymore, we cannot communicate." You and I have the problem with children who stay at home. We say we cannot communicate with our children. What about when your children have been away for ten months?

The next major point they raised was the involvement of Indian parents in education as it relates to their children. Unfortunately there has not been any of this and, I think, you would recognize the fact being fathers, that only as you are involved in education and only as you are concerned, are your children involved and concerned. You must set an example for children to get an education. When you are involved you set a fine example, you talk about it, you are concerned about it. Too many of our Indian parents have no reasons nor ideas why their children go to school nor what school is going to do for them nor what it is supposed to do for them. They can tell you all the negative things that it does for them. Yet these parents says, "We want our children to get an education." But, they do not know what they mean when they say it in too many cases.

There is another major point they raised and maybe this is the real key to it, I do not know. If we build a beautiful school, beautifully equipped with electric lights, hot and cold running water, flush toilets, you name it, and we provide an excellently trained teacher to that community, but the children go home every night to over-crowding, to poverty, to a welfare community, to a negative community, then the education is a waste of time, money and energies. We cannot do one thing only. If we are going to build a home for Indian children, we have to build all four walls and put a roof on it and lay a floor. We just cannot do one wall and say, "There, this is what we have done."

The Indian parent must provide for his child an environment which makes sense. At present, the school and the environment of the home are in conflict. If these things were done, and this is what the Indian people are saying, Crees, Ojibwas, Delawares, Six Nations People, if these things are done, then education will change. Fundamentally, along with that, they are also saying that education must provide the means for Indian people to regain pride in being an Indian. It has not been doing this, but it must. Until this is done, the Indian people are going to be walking around in confusion.

Gentlemen, you represent an opportunity to Indian people. This House of Commons represents an opportunity. What will you do with it?

> House of Commons Standing Committee on Indian Affairs and Northern Development, May 28-29, 1969.

1. Why are statements such as this by men of the calibre of Mr. Currie important for the cause of Indian educational reform?

2. Integration of Indian children in schools with White children is increasing. In what ways can it be harmful to Indian children? Why can it be particularly harmful to young children?

3. If integrated schooling is to be fair to Indian children what conditions must exist?

4. Do you think the concept of integration in education is a good one? If so, at what level should integration begin? What purposes should it serve?

5. Mr. Currie emphasizes the need to have Indian children learn their native language. Why is this considered important? Do you agree that it should be done? Give your reasons.

6. What is the important relationship referred to by Mr. Currie, which exists between the success of education and the children's home conditions? What are the implications of this for the economic development of Indian communities?

> For questions 2, 3, and 4 above, the following viewpoint of integration may be useful in providing additional ideas. To Harold Cardinal, the question of Indian education is of fundamental importance. Education is intimately related to two things which are essential if the Indians are to make progress – a strong Indian identity and economic development. Here he puts forward his ideas on the kind of education which is needed to enable Indians to achieve these objectives.

Almost equally important is the area of education. Here too, both sides must move forward into new concepts. The institution of education is largely a cultural phenomenon. Since the introduction of formal white education to the Indians of Canada, their own original educational processes have either been shunted completely aside or discouraged. The only purpose in educating the Indian has been to create little brown white men, not what it should have been, to help develop the human being or to equip him for life in a new environment.

A new look must be given, then, to the fundamental purpose of educating the Indian. It is not enough for the government to promise it will change the content of history books more truly to tell the Indian story. In comparison to the real purpose of education, this is an almost frivolous approach. Of course we would like the falsehoods deleted and Indians characterized more truthfully in what the youth of Canada is taught, but Indians are much more interested in and must approach education with completely new ideas. Indian leaders must be given the opportunity to see and study the educational processes of different peoples in different countries. Only in this way can they help to develop a new conceptual framework related to education and to the solving of their own social problems.

I believe that different forms of education are both possible and available. The majority of our people do not have the opportunity to benefit from existing provincial institutions of education, especially those at the postsecondary level. Few of our people have sufficient academic background to make proper use of the technological schools, trade schools, colleges or universities. Even if they did, there would still be a need for some new form of education or institution that would help them develop a living, dynamic culture. For education to mean anything to our people a new kind of institution or process to bridge the gap between where we stand now and the available postsecondary institutions must be created. This means some form of temporary but special mass educational process. Indian initiative, channelled through our own organizations, must develop such institutions to enable our people to benefit from programmes now offered by existing education systems.

These new institutions must be prepared to help Indians develop their sense of identity. The function of such institutions will lie in the areas of social rebuilding, psychological renewal and cultural renaissance. Indian organizations must operate these schools, for only they qualify for the task of identifying teachers and administrators with the resources to meet the cultural needs of Indians.

The white person must come to realize that the Indian cannot be a good Canadian unless he is first a responsible and a good Indian. Few Indians can discover a sense of purpose and direction from the white society. They must find such a sense of identity within themselves as human beings and as Indians before they can begin to work creatively with others. The government must understand this, because it is in this area that Canadian society can form a successful partnership with the Indian, in working together to find ways and means through which the educational process will develop human beings with purpose and direction.

The Indian communities themselves carry the responsibility for solving the social problems faced by Indians. Social development is irrevocably intertwined with leadership development, educational progress and economic advance. To tackle these problems the Indian communities will need extensive resources, both human and economic. The federal government's proposal to transfer all services to provincial governments does not solve anything. This changes nothing; it leaves the Indian in the same bogged-down bureaucratic predicament. Attempts to solve his social problems will still be initiated by people from the outside who know little and understand less of the Indian. It is true that the provincial governments can play a useful role in providing support services to Indian communities, but first there must be created, within the communities, structures that attack the problems at their source. Ideally, most of the services within a community should be provided by the community itself. Before this can happen, huge sums of money must be provided, aimed at community problems. No outside bureaucracy, whether in Ottawa or in a provincial capital, is flexible enough either to meet the problems head-on, or better yet, attack the causes. Before the local communities can take over such responsibility, skilled, highly trained leadership at the local level must be found. Once again, that premises educational institutions geared to the needs of the Indian and controlled by the Indian.

> Cardinal, *op. cit.*, pp. 166-168.

1. According to Cardinal, what has been the sole purpose of Indian education in the past? Why has it largely failed?

2. What does he think the purposes ought to be?

3. How does he propose to "bridge the gap between where we stand now and the available post-secondary institutions"?

4. Why does he think it essential for Indians to have control over their own education?

5. Why does he think that the *White Paper* proposals on education are ineffective?

6. Cardinal believes that, if the Indians are to make progress, changes must come from inside Indian communities. How can education help make possible this kind of change?

7. Do you agree with Cardinal's analysis of the problem? Do you think that his proposals for the future of Indian education are sound?

Economic Development: Which Way?

Closely related to the question of education is the problem of improving the economic status of Indians. Education must help foster the growth of a sense of Indian identity and a positive self-image. But these things cannot be achieved unless the Indians can break the barriers of unemployment, poverty and dependency that have nurtured a welfare psychology in too many of them. Regular work breeds self-confidence and a sense of personal worth in addition to providing an income that means a reasonable share of this world's goods.

There is no argument about the urgent need to improve the

economic status of Indians or about its importance in any plan to improve their position in Canadian society. There is, however, considerable disagreement as to how it should be brought about. The Federal Government in its *White Paper* has made proposals which are unacceptable to the Indians. The following newspaper article sums up the main points of disagreement:

VANCOUVER – When Indian Affairs Minister Jean Chrétien realsed his policy statement on Indian rights, it was angrily booted back to Ottawa with a ferocity unequalled in the history of white-Indian relations in British Columbia.

Moderates and militants among the province's 46,000 Indians combined to condemn what one Indian leader termed "the worst piece of legislative garbage ever to come from the Crown."

At first glance, the paper, tabled in the Commons in late June seemed to fit in nicely with Prime Minister Pierre Elliot Trudeau's master plan for the Just Society.

Mr. Chrétien proposed repealing the hated Indian Act, abolition of the Indian affairs department within five years, surrendering jurisdiction to the privinces and a program of massive economic aid in the interim.

In other words, Indians would have exactly the same status as whites. Generally, the Indians of this province agree with abolition of the Indian Act and Mr. Chrétien's economic proposals.

But they feel he is going too far when he suggests destruction of the Indian affairs department and handing over the responsibility for the native population to the provinces.

The Indians say Mr. Chrétien has not considered their stake in reserve lands – 844,000 acres of real estate worth between $70,000,000 and $100,000,000.

The reserves constitute the only tangible asset the Indians held collectively and the last repository for a shattered heritage they are attempting to rebuild.

They want safeguards built into the future for the 1,621 reserves, less than half of which have Indians living on them. They want guarantees that the reserves will not become targets for land speculators.

And they want assurances that their hereditary hunting and fishing rights won't be trampled by provincial authorities.

The government, say the Indians, has to stop looking at their problems through white eyes, and it has to stop trying to turn Indians into white men.

"The average Indian is not prepared to stand the ferociousness of the land grabbers," says George Calveley, manager of the Kamloops band, which has 32,000 acres worth $20,000,000.

"If the land goes, there won't be an Indian left in Canada 20 years from now. It is his last refuge."

Chief Philip Paul of Vancouver Island's Tsartlip band, by no means a militant, accused the federal government of "trying to improve Canada's international image by asking the Indian people to commit cultural suicide."

These men contend white society is trying to destroy the reserve system at a point in history when, for the first time the Indians are acquiring the educational and fiscal tools to make it work for them.

"This policy is a real farce," said Chief Paul. "This kind of superimposition is the hallmark of colonialism and the Indian people in general loathe it."

A jurisdictional surrender to the provinces now would "breed political expediency for greedy politicians," said Guy Williams, president of the Native Brotherhood of B.C.

In addition to virtually unanimous condemnation from the B.C. Indian community, Mr. Chrétien's policy statement also flies in the face of the Hawthorn Report, viewed by many as the most comprehensive study of contemporary Indians in North America.

The study, headed by Prof. H. B. Hawthorn of the University of B.C., has been in the hands of the Indian affairs department for two years but few of its 91 recommendations have been implemented.

The report urged expansion of the department to handle a huge off-reserve migration, rather than abolition of it altogether and noted that the provinces and municipalities would be largely unable to help.

Mass migration that Prof. Hawthorn foresaw is materializing now. Today, 11,500 B.C. Indians live off the reserves – 4,000 more than did five years ago.

The exodus of young people is another reason why Indian leaders feel the reserves have to be preserved and strengthened economically if the race is to survive.

One of the hard economic realities is that only 36 per cent of the B.C. Indians fall into the wage-earning bracket, from 20 to 60 years of age, compared with 51 per cent of the white population.

Even if Indians were the highest-paid workers in the province instead of the lowest, they would be hard-pressed financially to provide adequately for the needs of their young.

The median age for Indians is 16. Three-quarters of the population is under 32 and the birth rate is 2½ times as high as that of the white population.

These are among a myriad of contradictions built into Indian society. Indians feel they can overcome these contradictions through proper industrial and agricultural utilization of reserve lands.

From white society they ask access to education, financial assistance but not handouts, and most of all, compassion and understanding. If these are not forthcoming, many of them say the only alternative is militancy and confrontation.

Dennis Bell in the *Vancouver Province*, August, 1969.

In the *White Paper*, the Federal Government proposes to phase out the Indian Affairs Branch within five years, to transfer responsibility for Indian affairs to the provincial governments and to transfer control of Indian lands to the Indian people. The Federal Government would assist Indian economic development on the principle that "those who are furthest behind must be helped most." As an interim measure, the government would make available "substantial additional funds" to encourage economic progress. The sum of fifty million dollars has been mentioned in this regard.

As you can see from the newspaper article, the Indians

object strongly to a number of these proposals. They do not want to be transferred to the jurisdiction of the provinces. They have reservations about the proposal to transfer control of Indian lands to individual bands. They want safeguards against the possible disappearance of the reserves which they regard as their only protection against assimilation. They do not want government departments to be in charge of planning. They consider it essential for Indians to take on the responsibility of decision-making in the development of their resources. In order to end paternalism and foster the growth of Indian autonomy, Indians must take on these responsibilities. They are doubtful of the ability of government-controlled schemes to achieve changes beneficial to the Indians, and they point to past government performance to back up their belief. Indian leaders are arguing that, instead of control being in the hands of government officials, it should be in the hands of a body controlled by Indians. This argument is stated forcefully by Harold Cardinal:

Within the next five years the Department of Indian Affairs is to be abolished. That is the one welcome aspect of the new government policy, but from a practical point of view, some interim body will have to be created. The duties and responsibilities of the department will be passed on to other federal agencies, and from past Indian experience, we know that all government departments have a tendency to pass the buck from one to another. To meet this prospect, the National Indian Brotherhood can play the role of a human resources authority, coordinating the services offered to the Indian by the many federal departments. This role would save the Indian many headaches and aid him in all his dealings with the federal government. At the same time the brotherhood would be in a position to help the various government agencies establish priorities in relation to the needs of the Indians of Canada.

Because of its political structure, the Indian people are assured of continuing control over the activities of the National Indian Brotherhood. This enables the Indians of Canada to participate in the democratic process and assures them an active role in the broad workings of government. In practical terms, this may be the closest the Indians of Canada can come to achieving Prime Minister Trudeau's concept of participatory democracy. . . .

The Indian peoples of Canada are just beginning to be aware of the broad implications of economic development. Any progress to be made must be bolstered by basic sound economic programmes. For the first time the Indian peoples are beginning to realize that this means more than isolated, make-do farming, fishing, trapping or lumbering. Huge sums of money are needed to enable Indian groups to take advantage of economic development opportunities on our own reserves.

An economic development corporation, funded by both national and provincial levels of government, should be founded in each province. Qualified Indians must have control of such fund resources to enable them to finance the necessary programmes at the community level. Such development corporation funds would initiate research into the economic potential of every reserve, then get the necessary development programmes underway.

To handle properly matters like these, Indians must have the resources to hire the best brains in the country as consultants. Voluntary workers are not trained for such work. Indians will gain from the psychological advantage of knowing that such hired consultants are their employees, that they do not come as civil servants who in the process enslave the Indian.

> Cardinal, *op. cit.*, pp. 163, 169.

1. What organization does Cardinal propose as a central co-ordinating body? On what grounds does he propose it?
2. Why is he opposed to control by federal agencies?
3. What would be the function of the provincial development corporations? Who would control them? Do you think this is a sound proposal?
4. The money for development would have to come mainly from the Federal Government. The figure suggested by the government is fifty million dollars. Chief Walter Dieter, president of the National Indian Brotherhood, described this amount as "chickenfeed." One project alone in the Qu'Appelle area of Manitoba would require thirty million dollars. The cost for successful development would run into hundreds of millions. Do you think that the government should provide this amount? Give your reasons.

An alternative set of proposals is provided by the *Hawthorn Report.* It is interesting to note that although this in-depth study of Indian affairs in Canada was available to the government officials who drew up the *White Paper,* its recommendations were largely ignored. Here are some excerpts from the *Report* which illustrate the position its authors take. As you read them, compare the position taken in the *Hawthorn Report* with that in the *White Paper.*

The trend of the analysis offered in this Report and a basic and general goal of its recommendations is to find courses of action which will be profitable for the Indian and to improve his position to choose and decide among them.

This is not advocacy that he acquire those values of the major society he does not hold or wish to acquire. Because the issue is a burning one, and at certain junctures in the analysis it is a complex one, it is worth reiterating clearly and simply that the research group do not think that the Indian should be required to assimilate, neither in order to receive what he now needs nor at any future time. The possibility that many Indians should reject some values or institutions held dear by the Canadian majority is comprehended in the goal of the economic and political recommendations made in this Report. Ordinary respect for what values and institutions, languages, religions and modes of thought, persist in their own small societies, which were once fully viable and to varying extents are so today, calls for maintenance of this principle. Almost certainly some Indians will choose not to accept what we regard as the benefits of our society and will choose instead what they regard as the benefits of theirs.

But no choice by Indians, neither to accept nor to reject Canadian values and opportunities, can have a sequel of purposeful action and successful result unless they have certain capacities to sustain it. The attractions and pressures of the major society, the changes in natural resources and the whole new social ambience now render completely helpless the person who lacks the shields and weapons of adequate schooling, rewarding employment, good health and fit housing; and the capital equipment, training and knowledge adequate for the enterprises he undertakes.

These prerequisities for proper choice and decision must be supplied in sufficient amount for them to be at all effective. Indeed inadequate aid may be worse than none at all because it will almost certainly drain off hope and courage.

> Hawthorne, *op. cit.*, Vol. I, p. 6.

1. Does the *Report* advocate that the Indians become Canadians like any one else? What is its position with regard to assimilation?
2. What argument does the *Report* put forward in support of adequate aid to the Indians in terms of education, social services, and economic development?
3. Is the position taken in the *Report* more similar to that of the *White Paper* or to that taken by Cardinal.

As to the way in which changes will be administered, the *Hawthorn Report* is not in favour of the phasing out of the Indian Affairs Branch as recommended in the *White Paper*.

We made the study of the functions and operations of the Branch one of our central concerns, and the balance of our argument is that we cannot agree with this approach and this conclusion. The facts and their significance appear to us to lead a very different result. For quite a long time the special needs of the Indians and the special status they should maintain will require the sponsorship and backing of the Indian Affairs Branch. It is true that other people with needs and claims that may be partly similar could benefit from the sort of sponsorship advocated for Indians but that is another issue and at first glance it would appear that no other group in Canada has the same entitlement to consideration. (This study did not include the Eskimo; however, in general their socio-economic situation is similar to that of many Indians, and it might not be far wrong to include them in the more general statements we make about the Indians.)

Our discussion of the continuing responsibilities of the Branch takes up the matter of assistance with the management of resources. This assistance may in the future be less often of a direct sort, for it is as impossible for the Indian Affairs Branch staff to control all the needed financial and other skills as it is for Indians to do so. More often effective assistance will consist of aiding the Indians to recognize when help is needed, and aiding them to seek it from the best quarters. Another responsibility may be assisting Indians to seek and obtain the benefits offered by the provinces to all provincial citizens.

Other new responsibilities are pointed out that are likely to call for assumption by the Branch. At least one of these new responsibilities can be foreseen. In the not so distant future some agency, the Indian Affairs Branch or perhaps the Citizenship Branch, will need to get set for a vast cityward movement of Indians that is now in its beginning phases. At the present rate of growth of Indian population, a critical phase of this movement could be reached in ten years' time and if the reserves continue to hold their present numbers. Problems of housing, placement, recreation and training will be intensified and in many ways will be special to Indians. The problem facing the Branch will be to aid in filling the needs that cannot be met by existing municipal and provincial agencies. Present experience, in Canada and elsewhere, indicates that no other government agency is likely to be ready for a large movement of this nature. Perhaps the role of the Branch will be to be prepared with blueprints drawn from experience elsewhere, in the United States for example; to keep close watch on the situation and initiate action in time; to point out at once the growing needs of these new people in the city, needs that existing agencies are likely to be slower to recognize and respond to.

Ibid., pp. 12-13.

1. Why does the *Report* recommend continuation of the Indian Affairs Branch? In what ways can it help in Indian development and in solving emerging problems?

2. What suggestions does the *Report* make as to the respective roles of Indians and the Indian Affairs Branch as far as assistance is concerned? How does this position compare with the Indian position as outlined by Cardinal?

The following recommendations of the *Hawthorn Report*, selected from a total of ninety-one, convey a good idea of the *Report's* approach to Indian affairs, and in particular to economic development.

General

1. Integration or assimilation are not objectives which anyone else can properly hold for the Indian. The effort of the Indian Affairs Branch should be concentrated on a series of specific middle range objectives, such as increasing the educational attainments of the Indian people, increasing their real income, and adding to their life expectancy.

2. The economic development of Indians should be based on a comprehensive program on many fronts besides the purely economic.

3. The main emphasis on economic development should be on education, vocational training and techniques of mobility to enable Indians to take employment in wage and salaried jobs. Development of locally available resources should be viewed as playing a secondary role for those who do not choose to seek outside employment.

4. Special facilities will be needed to ease the process of social adjustment as the tempo of off-reserve movement increases. Where possible these should be provided by agencies other than the Indian Affairs Branch. However, if other agencies prove inadequate, either due to incapacity or unwilling-

ness, the Indian Affairs Branch must step in itself regardless of whether the situations requiring special attention are on or off the reserve.

5. As long as Indians are deficient in the capacity for self-defence in a society of large and powerful private and public organizations they must be given supplemental consideration by government.

6. The Indian Affairs Branch should act as a national conscience to see that social and economic equality is achieved between Indians and Whites. This role includes the persistent advocacy of Indian needs, the persistent exposure of shortcomings in the governmental treatment that Indians receive, and persistent removal of ethnic tensions between Indians and Whites.

7. Indians should be regarded as 'citizens plus'; in addition to the normal rights and duties of citizenship, Indians possess certain additional rights as charter members of the Canadian community.

8. The Indian Affairs Branch has a special responsibility to see that the 'plus' aspects of Indian citizenship are respected, and that governments and the Canadian people are educated in the acceptance of their existence.

9. An autonomous public body, to be known as the Indian Progress Agency, should be established. Its main function would be the preparation of an objective annual progress report on the Indian people.

Economic Development

11. Larger expenditures than hitherto will have to be made on reserves in order to bring their standards of housing and other facilities and services closer to White norms.

12. A working blueprint for a viable economic development program for Indians will require a more detailed cross-country survey to provide an inventory in terms of job aptitudes and capabilities, potential income-yielding resources, job opportunities locally available, and numbers in each community requiring special training and migration to other areas. Such a survey should be carried out jointly by the Indian Affairs Branch and the new Department of Manpower, with the aid of various experts in industry and resources.

13. An adequate program for economic development of Indians will require public expenditures on their behalf in the hundreds of millions of dollars per annum over the foreseeable future. This will entail a much larger budget and staff for the Indian Affairs Branch, as well as more assistance from other government agencies at all levels.

14. The Indian Affairs Branch should be given every support in its announced objective of providing Indians with maximum educational and training opportunities and services. Inseparable from education and training, job placement should play a major role in a viable economic development program for Indians.

15. Because of problems facing Indians in urban life and industrial or business employment, the Indian Affairs Branch should possess a staff of specially trained placement officers with supporting facilities, services, and personnel to fit in with the larger labour market, training and placement program developed by the Department of Manpower.

16. Wide differences in degree of economic development among Indian bands and in the types of problems they face in different regions and localities, should be reflected in a highly flexible and variegated overall program with different priorities for different cases.

17. People in semi-isolated bands across the Northern wooded belt face special problems of development that require special types of programs, and should receive maximum support in moving away to obtain employment in areas or urban centres offering adequate job opportunities.

18. For those who do not choose to leave their reserves, training programs should be devised with travelling teams of instructors to train reserve residents in skills and functions that would enable them to cope better with their actual environment.

19. Inseparable from such training, adequate provision of efficient up-to-date equipment on a liberal rental or purchase basis will be needed to enable Indians in isolated areas to exploit more effectively the resources and job opportunities available to them.

26. Employment of Indians in low-paid farm labour with substandard working conditions should be discouraged.

27. The main emphasis for economic development of the more depressed and underdeveloped reserves located within, or close to, urban or industrial centres offering many potential job opportunities should focus on expanded social work programs for rehabilitation of disorganized households, intensive training programs for potential workers, and counselling work among women and mothers to assist them in the complexities of urban living.

28. Community development should be directed as much to Whites as to Indians, in view of the many barriers which the former put in the paths of the participation of the latter.

29. Among relatively high-income bands whose members specialize in high paid seasonal manual labour, younger workers or students should be encouraged to train for a wider diversity of jobs. The present pattern of specialization renders such communities vulnerable to serious economic reversals, in the form of unemployment arising from technological changes or cyclical downturns.

30. For bands occupying reserve land strategically situated for industrial or commercial development of various kinds, adequate capital and technical aid should be provided to band members deemed capable of developing and operating business establishments of their own.

31. Where Indian-owned and operated businesses are not feasible, and where it would be more economical to lease land to outside concerns, every effort

should be exerted to assure that band members are given prior opportunity and training for new jobs that the tenant firms make available.

Ibid., pp. 13-15.

1. How do these recommendations protect the Indians as they attempt to bridge the gap between their present status and one of economic equality with the rest of the population?
2. What would be the function of the proposed Indian Progress Agency? How would it contribute to Indian progress?
3. The sum of money mentioned in the *White Paper* to be set aside to help the Indians has been given as fifty million dollars. In view of the above recommendations of the *Hawthorn Report*, and in particular of recommendation 13, do you consider this adequate?
4. Does the *Hawthorn Report* make provision for the different circumstances of Indians, for example, in the potentially more prosperous reserves and in the poor and remote reserves?
5. Do the recommendations of the *Report*, in your opinion, provide Indians with the choice of integration or assimilation? Give examples to support your answer.
6. What are the principal differences between the position taken in the *Hawthorn Report* and that taken in the *White Paper*? What reasons seem to you to explain why the *Hawthorn Report* had so little influence on the authors of the *White Paper*?
7. What are the main differences between the position taken in the *Hawthorn Report* and the position taken by Harold Cardinal?
8. Action in the future will proceed along one of the lines suggested by the *White Paper*, the *Hawthorn Report* and Harold Cardinal? Which would you support? Give your reasons.
9. Consult your newspaper and other sources of information for signs of the way events are moving. Look in particular for government pronouncements, and by politicians, Indian Affairs officials, and Indian leaders.

7.   The Problem is Urgent

Experience in other countries has shown quite clearly that when the aspirations of underprivileged groups are continually ignored civil disobedience and violence result. Rational discussion gives way to sloganeering and the use of force. In an atmosphere of fear and suspicion, freedoms are threatened in the attempt to maintain order. Such a course is disastrous for a democratic society if it is not checked in time. The time for action is now. Already Indian spokesmen are giving warnings of the consequences of continued frustration.

I have outlined some of what must happen if the Indian is to realize his potential and take part in today's world. We have seen what frustration, deprivation and misery can lead to in the United States and throughout the world. The young generation that is even now flexing its muscles does not have the patience that older leaders have shown. If the present leadership is unable to come to terms with the non-Indian society, unable to win respect for Indian rights and dignity, then the younger generation will have no reason to believe that the existing democratic political system has much meaning for them. They will not believe that the present system can work to change our situation. They will organize and organize well. But, driven by frustration and hostility, they will organize not to create a better society but to destroy your society, which they feel is destroying our people. This is the choice before the Indian; this is the fork in the road that the government and non-Indian society must recognize.

Controlling our choice of a path – the realization of the full potential of the Indian people, or despair, hostility and destruction – is our belief that the Indian must be an Indian. He cannot realize his potential as a brown white man. Only by being an Indian, by being simply what he is, can he ever be at peace with himself or open to others.

The present course of the federal government drives the Indian daily closer and closer to the second alternative . . . despair, hostility, destruction.

> Cardinal, *op. cit.*, pp. 170-171.

> And already there are signs of what may happen unless a well-planned and determined attempt is made to deal with Indian grievances.

Hopefully, ethnic tensions between Indians and Whites may not assume major proportions, and indeed should not, given concerted efforts now. There are, however, certain long run tendencies which could precipitate 'racial' troubles of a serious nature. By the year 2,000 the Indian population probably will have reached half a million. This is a far cry from the demographic considerations which prevailed into this century and which allowed the comfortable belief that Indian problems were only transitory and would pass away as Indian proved incapable of resisting the aggressive contact of a technologically superior civilization. It must also be noted that this much larger Indian population will not be hidden away in the enclaves of the reserves. Many will be living, at acceptable and unacceptable standards, in the towns and cities of Canada.

There are already a number of frontier communities, mainly northern, which possess the ingredients for ethnic strife. These northern communities are typically possessed of characteristics which include a low tax basis, a difficulty of tax collection, an influx of Indians squatting on taxable lands but unwilling or unable to pay taxes themselves, and a poorly developed civic sense among the residents. These are the communities in which problems of shack towns, unemployment, and general social disorganization are likely to be especially pronounced, and where local capacities for their solution are least developed. An alternative type of frontier area, the boom town, is more hopeful in its economic prospects, but it too, as Indians flock in from the surrounding reserves, is likely to need outside help in seeking a peaceful accommodation between the sometimes competing interests of poorly trained Indians, White workers, and powerful private employers.

Should the move from the reserves in these and other circumstances prove unsuccessful in providing Indians with satisfactory living standards in terms of prevailing community conceptions of what is appropriate, the possibilities are little less than frightening. Recent marches of aggrieved Indians in Thompson (Manitoba), Kenora (Ontario), the march of the Hay Lake Indians to the provincial capital in Alberta, and the tensions described by Shimpo in his study of ethnic relations in and around Kamsack, Saskatchewan, are reminders of what may ensue more frequently and on a larger scale if adequate funds, personnel, and understanding are not applied now. Only the short range perspective of a generation which has given up responsibility for the future can explain the uneconomic postponement of action now when, relative to the conditions which may prevail, ten, twenty, and thirty years from the present, the problem is manageable.

Hawthorn, *op. cit.*, p. 170.

Two years after the *Hawthorn Report* appeared, an organization came into existence which underlined the need for action. The *Native Alliance for Red Power* (NARP) put out its first newsletter in June, 1968. The tone of the newsletter is angry and impatient. Its language and the ideas expressed reflect the influence of the Black Power movement in the United States, but the concern is with the conditions of Canadian Indians. The membership of NARP is quite small, but its numbers will grow unless conditions improve. Its recruits will come mainly from the young people. Already, from a beginning in Vancouver, B.C., several chapters have been established across Canada. Here is a statement from the first newsletter defining NARP and outlining its program:

What is NARP?

This is the first issue of NARP NEWSLETTER. It is published by the Native Alliance for Red Power (NARP for short). We came together as a group 6 months ago; since that time, we have held meetings, gone on demonstrations, and started this newsletter. Our purpose is to promote and build the ideals which we support – and they are RED POWER – Indian Power.

Since we formed NARP we have, as we fully expected, been attacked by some established Native groups, and, of course, by the whiteman. We have been called hippies, young punks, trouble makers, disrupters, and many many other names. We wish to say at this time that we are not interested in spending our time attacking other Native organizations. However, we wish to present an alternative to their ideas, and that alternative is RED POWER.

How many times have you heard a whiteman say, "those stupid Indians – they just don't want to become a part of our society, they ain't got enough brains, or enough desire to make it in our world." NARP's answer to this is:

"You're right, whitey. We don't want to become a part of your society." Let's take a closer look at this great white society.

Remember how it started here in North America? By systematically destroying our ancestors, they committed every form of cruelty known to mankind: robbery, rape, mass murder of men, women and children. They infected us with their diseases, made treaties and then broke them at their will, yes, they used every treacherous trick they could think of to destroy our very existence. That's how this great society was founded, over the murdered bodies of our ancestors. And what about their society today? What are its high ideals and values like? Look around you, brothers. What do you see? A society that is full of ugliness, where the greatest thing a man can do is accumulate as much wealth and status as he can, by any means he can. There are great gaps between the rich and the poor, some people have so much money they can never spend it while others have nothing. They spend millions of dollars building rockets and missiles to go to the moon when thousands of people need money to buy food and clothes here on earth. Some have gigantic houses with 3 or 4 bathrooms and several cars while others live in rotten old shacks without any plumbing at all. Wheat is rotting in granaries because they say it can't be sold at a big enough profit, 25,000 pigs were butchered and buried recently because prices for pork were falling – all this is happening in the great white society while one third of the world starves to death.

White society is a great war machine: they take their armies across the sea and steal and plunder the countries of other people. They drop napalm bombs on defenceless poor people, send in their preachers and teachers to destroy their culture. Big companies suck the natural resources from them and leave them starving.

They do all this in the name of freedom and democracy. These are the values of white society, and when they say "you Indians don't fit into it" we say you're god damn right, whitey, and we don't want any part of it. You can have your world and your values and your society, in the words of the great Native folksinger Buffy St. Marie "you can choke on your blue white and scarlet hypocrisy!"

RED POWER is not only a movement like NARP. We don't claim to be spokesmen for anybody. We feel we are part of a growing resentment among Native people. Like others, we are quickly becoming disillusioned by the whiteman's world.

June, 1968.

NARP Eight Point Program

1. We will not be free until we are able to determine our destiny. Therefore, we want power to determine the destiny of our reservations and communities. Gaining power in our reservations and communities, and power over our lives will entail the abolishment of the "Indian Act," and the destruction of the colonial office (Indian Affairs Branch).

2. This racist government has robbed, cheated and brutalized us, and is responsible for the deaths of untold numbers of our people. We feel under no

obligation to support this government in the form of taxation. Therefore, we want an end to the collection of money from us in the form of taxes.

3. The history of Canada was written by the oppressors, the invaders of this land. Their lies are perpetrated in the educational system of today. By failing to expose the true history of this decadent Canadian society, the schools facilitate our continued oppression. Therefore, we want an education that teaches us our true history and exposes the racist values of this society.

4. In this country, Indian and Métis represent 3 per cent of the population, yet we constitute approximately 60 per cent of the inmates in prisons and jails. Therefore, we want an immediate end to the unjust arrests and harassment of our people by the racist police.

5. When brought before the courts of this country, the redman cannot hope to get a fair hearing from white judges, jurors and court officials. Therefore, we want natives to be tried by a jury of people chosen from native communities or people of their racial heritage. Also, we want freedom for those of our brothers and sisters now being unjustly held in the prisons of this country.

6. The treaties pertaining to fishing, hunting, trapping and property rights and special privileges have been broken by this government. In some cases, our people did not engage in treaties with the government and have not been compensated for their loss of land. Therefore, for those of our people who have not made treaties, we want fair compensation. Also, we want the government to honour the statutes, as laid down in these treaties, as being supreme and not to be infringed upon by any legislation whatsoever.

7. The large industrial companies and corporations that have raped the natural resources of this country are responsible, along with their government, for the extermination of the resources upon which we depend for food, clothing and shelter. Therefore, we want an immediate end to this exploitation and compensation from these thieves. We want the government to give foreign aid to the areas comprising the Indian Nation, so that we can start desperately needed programs concerning housing, agricultural and industrial co-operatives. We want to develop our remaining resources in the interests of the redman, not in the interests of the white corporate-élite.

8. The white power structure has used every possible method to destroy our spirit, and the will to resist. They have divided us into status and non-status, American and Canadian, Métis and Indian. We are fully aware of their "divide and rule," tactic, and its effect on our people.

RED POWER IS THE SPIRIT TO RESIST

RED POWER IS PRIDE IN WHAT WE ARE

RED POWER IS LOVE FOR OUR PEOPLE

RED POWER IS OUR COMING TOGETHER TO FIGHT FOR LIBERATION

RED POWER IS NOW!

June, 1968.

Questions for Discussion

1. "We are not going out of Ottawa with answers but with questions. We must, for the love of God, find a means of consultation with the Indians that is honest, open, complete, sincere and constructive. We must ensure that the choices dictated by their values are made available to them. The best thing the government could do is get the hell out of the way."

   The Honourable Robert K. Andras, Minister without Portfolio, October, 1968.

   This statement was made by the Minister as he began a series of consultations with Indian leaders across the country. To what extent do you think the intention in this statement was reflected in the government *White Paper* on Indian policy?

2. Would you support the *White Paper*, in whole, in part, or not at all? Support your answer with relevant facts and arguments.

3. Give an outline of the Indian affairs policy you would recommend. Make it in the form of a number of recommendations. Briefly justify each recommendation.

4. Predict the consequences of a government attempt to carry out the proposals in the *White Paper*.

Acknowledgements

This page constitutes an extension of the copyright page. For permission to reprint copyright material, grateful acknowledgement is made to the following:

THE ANGLICAN CHURCH OF CANADA, Toronto, for use of material from *Beyond Traplines*, by C. Hendry.

THE CANADIAN BROADCASTING CORPORATION, Toronto, for extracts from *The Way of the Indian*. Reproduced by permission of The Canadian Broadcasting Corporation.

THE CANADIAN CHURCHMAN, Toronto, for the use of various articles.

THE CHAMPLAIN SOCIETY, Toronto, for extracts from *John McLean's Notes of a Twenty-five Years Service in the Hudson's Bay Territory*, edited by W. S. Wallace; and for the extract from *David Thompson's Narrative, 1784-1812*, edited by R. Glover.

CLARKE, IRWIN AND COMANY LIMITED, Toronto, for the extract from *Canadian Portraits: Famous Indians* by Ethel Brant Monture. Copyright 1960 by Clarke, Irwin & Co. Ltd. Used by permission of Clarke, Irwin and Co. Ltd.

THE DEPARTMENT OF AGRICULTURE AND IMMIGRATION, Manitoba, for extracts from *A Study of the Population of Indian Ancestry in Manitoba,* by Jean H. Legassé.

WILSON DUFF, for extracts and illustrations from his book *The Indian History of British Columbia*, Vol. 1.

THE FIRST CITIZEN, Vancouver, for the use of various extracts.

GERRY GAMBILL, for the extracts from *Akwesasne Notes.*

THE GLOBE AND MAIL, Toronto, for the use of various articles, and the cartoon by James Reidford.

HARPER AND ROW PUBLISHERS INC., New York, for the extract from *The New Indians* by Stan Steiner. Copyright © 1968 by Stan Steiner. Reprinted by permission of Harper & Row Publishers Inc.

M. G. HURTIG LIMITED, PUBLISHERS, Edmonton, for the use of the cover copy of, and extracts from *The Unjust Society: The Tragedy of Canada's Indians,* by Harold Cardinal. By permission of M. G. Hurtig Ltd.

INFORMATION CANADA, Ottawa, for the use of the following: *A Survey of the Contemporary Indians of Canada,* Part 1, edited by H. B. Hawthorne.

Canada Year Book, 1968.

The Indians of Canada, by D. Jenness.

Indian Treaties and Surrenders from 1680-1890, Vol. 1.

Indian Days on the Western Prairies, by Marius Barbeau.

Indian Affairs 1875-1879.

Indians and the Law.

Statement of the Government of Canada on Indian Policy.

The Indian in Transition.

KING FEATURES SYNDICATE, New York, for use of the *Redeye* cartoon.

THE MACMILLAN COMPANY OF CANADA LIMITED, Toronto, for extracts from the *Journal of Duncan M'Gillivray,* edited by A. S. Morton (1929); and for extracts from *The Letters and Journals of Simon Fraser 1806-1808,* edited by W. Kaye Lamb. By permission of The Macmillan Company of Canada Ltd.

THE MANITOBA INDIAN BROTHERHOOD, Manitoba, for the extract from their submission to the Brandon Conference on Human Rights.

MCCLELLAND AND STEWART LIMITED, Toronto, for extracts from *The Jesuit Relations and Allied Documents,* edited by S. R. Mealing; extracts from *Coppermine Journey* by Farley Mowat; extracts from *Raven's Cry* by Christie Harris; and extracts from *Without Reserve* by Sheila Burnford. Reprinted by permission of the Canadian Publishers, McClelland and Stewart Ltd.

THE MONTREAL GAZETTE, Montreal, for use of material.

THE MONTREAL STAR, Montreal, for use of material.

G. E. MORTIMORE, for his remarks made on the CBC program *Preview Commentary.* Copyright © 1969 by G. E. Mortimore.

THE NATIVE ALLIANCE FOR RED POWER, Vancouver, for extracts from *NARP Newsletter.*

CLARENCE OPPENHEIM, for his poem *Loss for Progress.*

UNIVERSITY OF TORONTO PRESS, Toronto, for the extracts from *The Conflict of European and Eastern Algonkian Cultures,* by A. G. Bailey. By Permission of the University of Toronto Press.

THE VANCOUVER PROVINCE, Vancouver, for use of various articles.

THE VANCOUVER SUN, Vancouver, for use of various articles.